Constitution and Erosion of a Monetary Economy:
Problems of India's Development since Independence

CONSTITUTION AND EROSION OF A MONETARY ECONOMY

Problems of India's Development since Independence

WALTRAUD SCHELKLE

FRANK CASS • LONDON
Published in association with the
German Development Institute, Berlin

First published in 1994 in Great Britain by
FRANK CASS & CO. LTD.
Newbury House, 900 Eastern Avenue,
Ilford, Essex IG2 7HH, England

and in the United States of America by
FRANK CASS
c/o International Specialized Book Services, Inc.
5804 N.E. Hassalo Street
Portland, Oregon 97213-3644

British Library Cataloguing in Publication Data

Schelkle, Waltraud
    Constitution and Erosion of a Monetary
    Economy: Problems of India's Development
    Since Independence. – (GDI Book Series);
    Vol. 3)
I. Title   II. Series
332.4954

ISBN 0-7146-4138-3

Library of Congress Cataloguing-in-Publication Data

Schelkle, Waltraud.
    Constitution and erosion of a monetary economy : problems of
India's development since independence / Waltraud Schelkle.
        p.   cm. – (GDI book series ; 3)
    "Published in association with the German Development Institute,
Berlin."
    Includes bibliographical references.
    ISBN 0-7146-4138-3 (pbk.) : £23.00
    1. India–Economic conditions–1947–   2. India–Economic
policy–1947–   3. Monetary policy–India–History.   4. Finance–
–India–History.   I. Title   II. Series.
HC435.2.S294   1994
338.954–dc20   94-17159
                                                                CIP

Printed in Great Britain by
Watkiss Studios Ltd, Biggleswade, Beds.

Contents

Abbreviations

EPW	Economic and Political Weekly
FCNR	Foreign currency non-resident accounts
GNP	Gross national product
ICICI	Industrial Credit and Investment Corporation of India
IDBI	Industrial Development Bank of India
IFCI	Industrial Finance Corporation of India
IMF	International Monetary Fund
iR	Indian rupees
IRCI	Industrial Reconstruction Corporation of India
LDC	Less developed country
LTO	Long-term operation
MRTP	Monopolies and Restrictive Trade Practices Act
NABARD	National Bank for Agricultural and Rural Development
NHB	National Housing Bank
RBI	Reserve Bank of India
SFC	State Finance Corporation

Summary

Ever since Shaw and McKinnon published their path-breaking works on financial development in 1973, there has been extensive research on the effects of monetary and financial policies on the economic growth of developing countries. Focussing on misguided policies and microeconomic distortions, the ensuing literature failed to analyze monetary development as a more far-reaching process of setting up a coherent macroeconomy. And it downplayed the difficulties of newly independent countries to do so in a world of established currency areas.

Neo-structuralist critics rightly pointed to the monetarist bias in financial liberalization programs, which proved to have disastrous consequences for the respective countries' stability and development prospects. But the neo-structuralists failed to provide a theoretical alternative based on monetary economics.

This book puts forward a new paradigm of monetary development theory along Keynesian lines. It proceeds from the hypothesis that development under monetary conditions requires a growing measure of social cohesion through debtor-creditor-relationships mediated by the domestic currency. The ensuing obstacles to development and the remaining options for development policy are explored in general terms in Part I. In Part II, specific problems confronting India in its development toward a monetary economy are interpreted on the basis of these explorations.

Development of a monetary economy presupposes its constitution in the sense that the national currency must establish itself both against other currencies and against tangible assets as the medium in which asset formation takes place. External and internal constitution is a prerequisite for monetary income to be generated and national productive capacities increased - development in the traditional, narrower sense of the term.

A stylized historical comparison highlights that the constitution of a currency area has as a rule been distinctly more difficult for today's developing countries than it was for today's industrialized countries in the second half of the nineteenth century. A hierarchy of free-currency areas that has become more complex and attempts at modernization which, though well-meant, appear to have been decisive for the evolution of persistently weak currencies. I.e., the currency weakness emerging from the problems involved in constitution - namely a low propensity to hold domestic financial claims - has become a persistent obstacle to development in most LDCs.

This is linked indirectly to another problem of development under monetary conditions. The low volume of financial claims held voluntarily - together with market conditions typical for developing countries such as uncertainty on repayment of outstanding claims - is responsible for an inherently stagnative tendency in income generation. At the same time the problem of inflation is virulent. It makes itself felt in the growing frequency of such triggering factors as rises in agricultural prices and an economic policy stemming from constraints on political legitimacy that seeks to counter stagnation through fiscal and monetary measures. Together, they may sustain a process of general price rises, i.e. inflation, bearing the danger of an erosion of the monetary economy concerned. Emerging monetary economies thus face the dilemma of stagnation and erosion. The more disruptive threat is that of erosion, since it endangers the very constitution of the national economy.

Their weak position within the hierarchy of currency areas gives rise to a situation in which the capacity of emerging monetary economies to combat inflation through monetary policy is manifestly curtailed. Consequently, the economic policy of such countries often attempts to counter the dilemma of stagnation and erosion by repressing inflation. The failure of these attempts, however, becomes evident in the fact that stagnation is accompanied by diminishing capacity for monetary control.

The emergence of nation states is closely linked to development under monetary conditions. Nation states are constituted economically as sovereign currency areas and become the originators and guarantors of the modern monetary constitution. Neither of these functions can be performed by individual economic actors. At the same time, one condition for a monetary economy to proceed is that individual claims to wealth be safeguarded. This norm, which, for reasons that can be explained on theoretical grounds, generally implies underemployment, gives rise to a specific problem of legitimacy. Regimes of a monetary economy can be distinguished in terms of how precarious for government the conflict is between employment interests and claims to the protection of wealth. A regime that might be called commercial is able to take the norm of safeguarding wealth interests as a maxim governing economic policy. In contrast, a redistributive regime is confronted with irreconcilable demands posed by the norm on the one hand and by legitimacy on the other. In such situations, governments have attempted to find a solution via the centralization and subsequent redistribution of financial resources. For systematic reasons, the fundamental weakness of a redistributive regime is probably its inherent difficulty to maintain an intertemporal budgetary equilibrium without resorting to central-bank credits.

Finally, *conclusions for development policy* must also be drawn from the fact that monetary economies develop as national economies. This statement implies a priority of domestic economic development, although this is measured in terms of the capability to compete in world markets. Macroeconomically, the ensuing necessity of a selective integration into the world market is to be seen above all in the fact that it can contribute to overcoming currency weakness. This criterion is decisive for rejecting a neoclassical strategy of export-oriented devaluation. Like a post-Keynesian strategy of resource transfer, it consolidates a state of currency weakness. Macropolicy is able to support integration into the world market by creating a constellation of undervaluation, although the structural effects relevant to the development of dynamic comparative advantages are beyond its reach. There are also limits to the effectiveness of macropolicy aiming directly at developing the domestic market. If it is not to risk adverse reactions, macropolicy must attempt to improve expectations with regard to the certainty of repayments of outstanding claims, but cannot do so by influencing directly the two market variables of credit volume and investment volume.

That, in the end, also biases propositions on financial-sector development with which the theory and policy of monetary development began. In a monetary economy in which decisions concerning wealth dominate resource allocation, a supply-side strategy that aims chiefly at expanding the credit facilities and services offered by banks cannot be sustained. Greater financial depth is not the precondition for the development of a monetary economy, but its outcome. It reflects heightened confidence in the repayment of money advanced, i.e. in the credit status of borrowers. Therefore, financial-sector development has rather to provide for macroeconomic preconditions that allow producers to recover their debts. This conclusion points again to the supportive role of an undervaluation strategy. The analysis also suggests that conventional development policy to further agriculture and industry might be more helpful to foster financial development than measures focusing exclusively on financial institution building.

Part II of this study attempts to gain new insights into India's development problems by examining them in the light of the concepts previously elaborated. Phenomena that have been discussed at length in the relevant literature on India, such as stagnant income generation and far-reaching sectoral-policy intervention, are subjected to a systematic interpretation, in that they are elements of what amounts to a system of repressed inflation.

The various stages in India's development make it possible to study the phase of constitution *in concreto* (1947-55). For subsequent phases, the dilemma can be demonstrated which is inherent in the fact that rudimentary monetary economies tend to stagnate, while, conversely, forced income generation (1956-66) culminates in the erosion of the monetary economy concerned (1967-80). The *system of eco-*

nomic policy emerging over these decades may be called the *redistributive regime of a monetary economy*. The relevant literature on the subject has generally interpreted the most recent attempts at reform (1981-90) as a step-by-step replacement of this regime with a more commercial approach. This decade would then appear as the outcome of a process in which those responsible for economic policy had finally glimpsed the light.

An examination of *three problem areas in India's development*, namely agriculture, industry, and banking, leads to rather different conclusions: Neither was the liberalization policy due to mere voluntarism and greater insight nor did it represent a radical break with the past. It can, rather, be interpreted as a theoretically understandable response to India's inability, at the end of the 1960s, to combat inflation with monetary means and its subsequent failure in attempting to repress inflation.

The various arguments advanced to explain stagnating income generation since the mid-1960s need not be disputed. This study, however, attempts to identify stagnation as a intrinsic problem of development. A temporary decline in government investment, an agricultural sector stagnating in spite of the Green Revolution, a distinct rise in agricultural and industrial regulation, and the nationalization of the banking system can be seen as consistently related if they are interpreted as elements of a system designed to repress inflation.

The idea behind this approach to combatting inflation was the notion that combatting inflation serves the end of restoring a disturbed equilibrium between the flow of goods and the stock of money. But this notion of inflation makes sense only in a barter economy where money is only a means of transaction. Intervention in resource allocation and pricing resulted in stagnation becoming a persistent phenomenon. This, or even the collapse of investment activity, might just as well have been the outcome of a monetary approach to combatting inflation. Rather, what happened was that the government came to the brink of a debt trap and the monetary control capacity of the Indian central bank was nearly lost. Under these circumstances, a policy of liberalization could not fail to lead to a lingering erosion of India's monetary economy.

One consequence of this development that has largely been overlooked was a dichotomization of India's financial system. The Reserve Bank of India initially took on some functions of a development bank in order to create the institutional conditions in the banking sector required for this approach to combatting inflation. In its role as a central bank, however, it saw itself compelled to cut the banks off from refinance so as to compensate for the persistent monetization of government deficits. It has largely transferred this refinancing function to the national agricultural development bank, and the national industrial development bank is now for the most part serving, as it were, as the government's banking facility. The two development banks can now be controlled only via their annual budgets.

In view of the accumulated potential for crisis, it is hard to believe that conventional adjustment policies along IMF lines will succeed in stabilizing the Indian economy without strangulating income generation. Even if the conditions for an effective monetary policy were given, which would require above all clearing bank balance sheets of bad debts, the domestic public debt is so high that any increase in interest rates represents a step towards the debt trap. There have been signs indicating that flight out of the rupee was imminent. Three economic policy considerations therefore suggest that a currency reform should have been undertaken right at the beginning of the reform process: the relief it would have entailed for the national budget, a reduction of producer debt, and savers' acceptance of the national currency, since then under threat. A *reconstitution of India's monetary economy* could have created much more favorable conditions for credible macroeconomic stabilization and for reform of the economic policy regime. Although the Indian government then in office refrained from so drastic a step - understandably given a fragile legitimatory basis -, it is worthwhile to keep in mind the case for currency reforms at the start of stabilization and reform programs: that mone-

tary development requires not only macroeconomic stability but also
accumulation, and that both in turn require a credible currency.

Part I   Theory of Development under Conditions of a Monetary Economy

1   Money in Development Theory

For the majority of today's states, development means or has meant developing under the conditions of a monetary economy. In other theoretical contexts, these are referred to as market-economy or capitalist conditions. The choice of concepts is of course fraught with consequences. It will condition the decisions made concerning both choice and treatment of the development subject and they, in turn, will determine which problems are identified as relevant. This link between development theory and economic categorization will be examined systematically in the first part of this study. Part Two will then attempt to show how new insights into various problems of India's development already discussed in the literature can be gained if they are regarded as problems associated with development under the conditions of a monetary economy.

Both parts are based on the conviction that there is need for a theoretical alternative to previous approaches dealing with monetary aspects of development. This alternative is guided from the outset by a cognitive interest in "monetary economies" as opposed to barter economies using money as a medium for transactions. Its central argument is that money and credit are not neutral to the extent that disposition over wealth determines resource allocation - and do so above and beyond the short-term effects ascribed to them by traditional theory. This has already been accomplished for established monetary economies by an interpretation of Keynes' work as a monetary theory of production and employment.[1] The attempt made here to analyze development under monetary conditions proceeds from these investigations on "Monetary Economy, Keynes, and the Others" (Riese 1983).

The first chapter begins by defining the concepts essential to an understanding of the subject and briefly explaining the methodological approach adopted. This is followed by a cursory description of the most important works on the theory of monetary or financial development. It will become apparent that these studies and the view advanced here differ significantly in the way they define the functions of money and in the relative importance attached to them. With reference to historical and sociological research on money, it is, however, argued that the role and functions of money cannot be assessed simply in narrow terms of economic paradigms.

1.1 Definitions and Methodology

The subject of "development under the conditions of a monetary economy" clearly includes two concepts that require explanation: "development" and "monetary economy". The former is a problematical concept in that it has always represented the liberal philosophy of history within the sphere of economic theory. Since the 18th century, its use had teleological (Sen 1988, p. 10) connotations as if as all development leads to a well-defined and desirable goal, i.e. a developed national economy. The general consensus that development is invariably bound up with specific historical and socioeconomic constellations has not prevented this teleological background from gaining methodological currency. In its models, the dominant school of development economics abstracts both from the dimension of historical time and from the historical dimensions of its subject matter. Its core is a microeconomic situation of decision-making which puts its subjects in a historically and socially indeterminate setting.

This indeterminacy, however, would seem to prevent an understanding of essential aspects of development under monetary conditions. A brief hypothetical suggestion must suffice at this stage: development under monetary conditions in essence implies growing socioeconomic integration as a result of an ever closer network of relationships between debtors and creditors. Its standard situations can therefore not be constituted atemporally; its intertemporal character is conditioned by the character of debt contracts. Nor can the basic model of such an economy be reduced to a tale imagined along the lines of Robinson Crusoe, i.e. the struggle between man and nature, since in its very essence it consists of social relations. After all, the process of development is not constituted by the sum total of individual actions: what fundamentally defines the actions open to concrete individuals is an anonymous macroeconomic context.

These three features of a monetary economy, i.e. its intemporal, fundamentally social and macroeconomic character, indicate the difficulties posed by the development of such an economy. It is not at all self-evident that individual production and reproduction requires contracts to be concluded over given periods of time, personal social relations to be replaced with anonymous debtor-creditor relationships, or persons to submit to equally anonymous constraints instead of direct personal domination. This, however, is the socially extremely demanding process that is implied by the formation of a monetary economy. These propositions also entail that the theory of monetary development presented here is not based on an affirmative or teleologically tinged concept of development. On the contrary, a constantly recurrent motive of this study will be that a formally successful development of a monetary economy - i.e. above all one acceptable to the society concerned - is an unlikely event. This is due both to the factors already mentioned, which are likely to be significant in particular for emerging monetary economies, and to the hierarchy of interests and needs in an established monetary economy.

But rejection of a teleological concept of development at the same time means not applying external critical standards. The methodological approach followed here is moderately functionalist in that it rules out lines of argument based on welfare economics and the ends-means thinking underlying it. It is derived from a theory of monetary development what functions, of money in particular but also of actors and institutions, have to be performed if such development is to occur at all, and if it is to be sustained.

The distinction between "occur" and "sustain" points to two aspects of development, which can be distinguished at least analytically. On the one hand, development requires the constitution of a monetary economy and, on the other, a specific way of income generation to proceed, i.e. accumulation. The constitution of a monetary economy stands for the national currency to be accepted in its various functions, which entails, as visible phenomena, the emergence of a specific rationality as the basis for action and the rise of an interdependent market system. To a certain extent, accumulation presupposes constitution and signifies rising income generation on the basis of financial debtor-creditor relationships.[2]

Accordingly, a distinction can be made between two sets of difficulties and obstacles affecting the development process. The first complex, summarily designated as the "problem of constitution", outlines the requirements arising from the need for a national currency to achieve, in a world of established monetary economies, a status so credible that it will become the basis of domestic debtor-creditor relationships. The problem of constitution is thus also due to the fact that for every nation development has had to take the course of late development, or, euphemistically: of modernization, ever since the British Empire emerged as the first hegemonic industrial power.

The second set is summarized under the heading of "dilemma": It designates the contradictory situation that rudimentary monetary economies tend to stagnate, while on the other hand forced income generation can easily lead to erosion of the monetary economy concerned. To strip these two scenarios of their ominous character, reference is made to the external circumstances and the economic rationale of action that foster this dilemma, the aim being to reveal them as the outcome of reactions and interactions that can be countered with economic policy.

In this brief summary of the main problems with which monetary development is fraught, it should have become obvious that the intention here is not to constantly to blame faulty development policy for lack of development. This means on the one hand identifying the objective difficulties to which economic policy may not have an answer appropriate in every respect. On the other hand, it requires that even dysfunctional interventions be examined to determine whether they are not in fact reactions to predicaments that are not accessible to harmonious resolution. This is intended not as an excuse but as a rejection of hasty apportionments of blame.

Historical evaluations, especially when they describe the problems surrounding the constitution of monetary economies, are meant to illustrate the systematic side of the matter or to make it perceptible as such. As long as it has not been shown how the deformations, identifiable today only as consequences, have emerged, it is all too easy to attribute them entirely to erroneous policy. This, however, would be to point to deficiencies of behavior rather than to explain deficiencies of development. Here again, by determining the functions of government policy, it can be shown that intervention may be appropriate, though quite possibly inconsistent with the liberal philosophy, and that it may provoke counterreactions that frustrate precisely the achievement of the objectives pursued. The assessment of national economic policy thus also attempts to develop an immanent critique, to identify inconsistencies between intention and effect rather than to contrast this policy with social welfare functions or to point to standards of microeconomic efficiency.

The approach can be summarized as follows: the debate on the question of how money should be considered in development economics will of course be conducted at a theoretical level. Of prime importance here is the idea that empirical evidence cannot simply be contrasted with theory. Thus while no economic theory denies the existence of money, its influence on structural change, production, and employment cannot be observed directly. There is no such thing as perception that is not prestructured by theory, nor are there systems of scientific propositions that have not stylized the object under observation, if only through their line of vision, their choice of concepts, and the context in which they place their subject matter. They thus, to one extent or another, become resistant to direct refutation by confronting them with observations. For substantive and methodological reasons, it is therefore impossible to make partial adjustments to the above-mentioned approaches in order to providing them with a supposedly more realistic character.

This also means that the study does not resort to theory as an abstract counterpart to empirical research. The empirical sources have been specified: historical recourse and a case study of India's development. Quantitative analysis in the econometric sense, on the other hand, has been eschewed. For one thing, interest here focuses on long-term development processes, which, by definition, is bound to mean that structural breaks will occur. It is thus impossible to regard the basic framework as a given parameter as required in regression analyses. For another, this omission follows from what has been said about the theoretical nature of all experience. Identifying correlations, meaningful though it may sometimes be as a means of providing material for interpretation, is no substitute for determining links between effects.[3] In this sense the methodological approach followed in this study might be called heuristic. An attempt is made to interpret the material and the phenomena discerned by at the same time reflecting on the theoretical context in which they are regarded as relevant.

1.2 Money and the Monetary Economy in Different Schools of Development Theory

Development economics did not begin to consider monetary issues systematically until the 1970s. This extension of its horizon was heralded by the construction of models in monetary growth theory (Tobin 1965) and in empirical studies of long-term monetization processes (Goldsmith 1969). The present focus on "money, interest, and banking in economic development"[4] is due above all else to the works of McKinnon (1973) and Shaw (1973). They introduced into development economics findings that had emerged from the debates on monetary theory in the 1960s. Their position might be described, perhaps somewhat oversubtly, as "developmental monetarism" (FitzGerald/Vos 1989, p. 21). Characteristically, the spiritus rector of monetarism, Milton Friedman, also published two lectures entitled "Money and Economic Development" in 1973.

The Monetarist Approach

How Shaw and McKinnon define the object of a theory of monetary development says a great deal about the stand taken against the structuralism then dominant. According to them, the issue is the "lagging economy" (Shaw) or the "fragmented economy" (McKinnon) that is suffering from *financial repression* as a result of persistent government intervention.[5] Financial repression is described as a consequence of structuralist development strategies, since the latter were based on distrust of market forces and pessimistic assumptions as to the elasticities of supply and demand. They maintain that rigidities and market imperfections should be seen not so much as the cause but as the result of government intervention.

Following two decades of development policy and planning, there was every justification in asking how apparently unalterable structural deficits had occurred and addressing them as an outcome rather than a pre-existing situation. Yet this advance in the approach to the matter was partly reversed by the superficial explanation given by Shaw and McKinnon for what initially motivated such intervention. It was attributed to an almost pathological propensity to intervene,[6] to mistakes, distrust, post-colonial impatience, bureaucratic class interest, or shortsightedness (Shaw 1973, pp. 14f.). Seen from the angle of economics and social theory, however, these sociopsychological explanations seem hardly any more satisfactory than the reference to structural factors that only government can eliminate.

What form, then, does a *typical developing economy* or, more precisely, an *emerging monetary economy* take according to Shaw and McKinnon? Although both see the developing country as financially repressed, they differ widely in their approach and thus in their characterization as well. Shaw derives his "debt-intermediation view" from a theoretical analysis of the neoclassical and Keynesian theory of monetary growth, whereas McKinnon seeks to paint as realistic a picture as possible. Consequently, they differ in their ideas on who the relevant actors are and, closely associated with this, how the liberalization of a financial market actually occurs.

According to Shaw (1973, Chapter 3), a developing monetary economy essentially consists of three sectors: a savings and an investment sector, with a financial sector mediating between them. Money becomes purely inside money when the division into a private and a public sector is abandoned.[7] This levelling enables him to agree with the popular view that money is a debt of the issuing authorities. In view of Shaw's broad definition of money, which includes cash and deposits, these bodies comprise both the monetary authorities and commercial banks. At the same time, however, he rejects the conventional view that money is outside money and thus an asset of private individuals for which the state ultimately stands as debtor. The alternative presented here will retain the concept of inside money, but regards government as an independent actor.

If money is seen as an intersectoral debt and not as a claim held by private individuals against the state, the situation for debtors should deteriorate as financial markets are liberalized, since in a financially repressed monetary economy liberalization leads to a real increase in interest rates. However, Shaw infers from empirical data on the high returns that enterprises, i.e. the prototypic debtors, realize in developing countries that they are rationed by a lack of savings, not by prices: "There is no shortage of investment opportunities: there is a shortage of savings for their finance, especially for the best ones among them" (Shaw 1973, p. 81). Higher interest rates would therefore help to reduce the imbalance in that rising deposits with the banks would enable them to finance a larger volume of investment.

McKinnon takes another route to arrive at a similar conclusion. For him it is not so much differentiation into specific sectors that is characteristic but the amalgamation of different functions in the most important actor of a fragmented monetary economy, the traditional productive household (McKinnon 1973, p. 10). The traditional productive household combines the functions of saver, investor, worker, and entrepreneur. As long as this type of economic subject predominates, financial and nonfinancial assets do not compete with one another and are not mutually exclusive, but complement one another. This complementarity, it should be noted, is related less to the economy as a whole than to the individual productive household. Financial assets thus include hoarding, i.e. cash holdings.

Now, if the real interest rate rises as repression abates, these productive households accumulate more internal funds with which they can finance a larger volume of investment in the future (McKinnon 1973, p. 38 and pp. 57ff.). Money is thus always been a form of income and, even when hoarded, subsumed under the category of savings. In the present study, this is, for reasons relating to the concept of money and the theory of income, not considered very convincing. A rise in interest rates does not, in this case, have so unequivocally favorable an effect on the average productive household as McKinnon would have it.

Their *concept of economic development* can now be explained. They proceed from the idea that the emerging monetary economy is characterized above all by financial repression, which gives rise to the crucial barrier to growth, a low level of savings, in that savings depend on interest rates. In Shaw's case (1973, p. 9) economic development appears as a movement of the "lagging economy" towards the financially deepened economy, which is characterized by absolute and relative growth in the formation of financial assets (Goldsmith 1969). Such a process of financial deepening begins with a monetary reform, which - as already indicated - is intended to lead to a higher volume of savings, increased financial intermediation, and more efficient investment.[8] This causality, with the liberalization of financial markets resulting in savings, investment, and growth, is also expressed by the World Bank (1989, p. 48) when it states: "Efficient financial systems contribute to the growth of countries, partly by mobilizing additional financial resources, partly by steering such resources to the best uses."

McKinnon does not see the financial system as quite so central to economic development. For him it consists in the integration of the fragmented economy as reflected in the approximation of social rates of return on private investments. This would make for a socially and individually efficient allocation of consumption over time. In particular, the internal return on deferred consumption would also rise for productive households dependent on self-financing (McKinnon 1973, p. 9 and p. 13), which would increase their investment activity. With the growth process thus launched, even the phenomenon of "reverse causation" may occur: as individuals would want to maintain a certain ratio of income flows to assets, rising incomes, due initially to higher savings, would themselves encourage increased saving. The result would be a *circulus virtuosis* (ibid., pp. 123ff.).

Seen from the angle of financial deepening or financial integration, economic development consequently appears as a one-way movement of rising income and asset formation. Although structural factors or development-related market imperfections may delay this process, only financial repression by government may cause genuine setbacks. Despite their different approaches, the two formulations of a developing monetary economy arrive at this conclusion on the basis of their *shared view of monetary theory*: this view rests on barter and welfare economics. Shaw (1973, p. 53) expresses concisely the dominant theory in defining the role of money:

> "'Money' yields private and social services because it is the one good for which all others exchange, and its use permits escape from search-and-bargain processes that are more costly in factor services. As a means of payment, in reserve for expenditure, it may dominate other abodes of purchasing power."

The function of money as a store of value proves to be a function of intertemporal exchange. The social and individual efficiency gains arising from the use of a universal transaction medium are thus extended from atemporal to intertemporal economics. The welfare-increasing effects of the use of money essentially depend on this primacy of the exchange function, an issue that will be described at greater length - and criticized - later in this study.

If money is unable to fully perform its function as a store of value or medium of exchange, the *imperative of economic policy* becomes that markets, led by the financial markets, must be liberalized. But this much-discussed, because politically sensitive, conclusion drawn from the monetarist approach has now given way to a more cautious and modified assessment of liberalization measures. For one thing, the deregulation of financial markets is no longer recommended as the first step in overall liberalization (McKinnon 1973, p. 8; idem 1988, pp. 388 and 398). Instead, it is thought that the first step should be macroeconomic stabilization. For a time this may even require increased regulation, or at least regulation via indirect monetary-policy instruments (Leite/Sundarajan 1990, pp. 735 and 746). This means, on the other hand, that deregulation is no longer raised to the status of a program for its own sake. The experience of Latin American countries with radical liberalization measures indicates that high interest rates and the absence of supervision lead to endemic collapses of banks and enterprises.

This sequence of macroeconomic stabilization and opening up of financial markets now agreed upon was already heralded by McKinnon (1973, Chapter 11, especially pp. 160f.). In distinct contrast to his own two-gap approach,[9] he considered massive foreign aid to assist the opening-up process to be counterproductive. It is thought to sustain a tendency toward overvaluation and thus to make reorientation in foreign trade in particularly difficult or even impossible. However, he regards macroeconomic destabilization due to capital imports not as such but rather as the outcome of an antithesis between partial liberalization encouraged by such aid and complete liberalization that would appropriately follow the deliberate eschewal of aid.

Accordingly, liberalization was also recommended because it encourages the shift from the previously dominant, "inefficient" forms of investment to financial savings. The holding of assets in tangible wealth and foreign currencies was thus not perceived as a sign of a macroeconomically unstable situation. If it had been interpreted as flight from the currency, the simple recommendation to liberalize would surely have had to be qualified. As it was, however, it was treated as the retention of purchasing power. This being disadvantageous in terms of welfare economics, the conversion of purchasing power through liberalization promised major efficiency gains (Shaw 1973, p. 9; McKinnon 1973, pp. 63 and 162).

Shaw's and McKinnon's original approaches imply that liberalization should have priority over (discretionary) monetary policy. Anti-inflationary measures are instrumentally related to liberalization, since the latter becomes far more difficult when price rises are high and fluctuative (McKinnon 1973, p. 79). That little importance was attached to inflation on its own is even more apparent in Friedman (1973, p. 41), who can hardly be suspected of playing down the inflation problem. In his opinion, there is no correlation between inflation and development, because cases can be found for every possible combination, i.e. for development with and without inflation, for inflation with and without development. Surprisingly for a monetarist, Friedman concedes the possibility of inflationary development in Israel, Japan in the 1960s, and Taiwan. In the present study, this connection is addressed under the heading "Dilemma".

The development monetarism represented by Shaw, McKinnon, and Friedman tends towards a welfare-economic approach to inflation. With their poorly developed financial systems and the pressure to sustain growth, developing countries should not be recommended to pursue a policy of stabilization geared to the short-term ("fine tuning"). A long-term monetary policy, however, is reduced to selecting the "desirable" inflation rate and the best means of achieving this rate (Friedman 1973, p. 40). Shaw (1973, p. 65) and McKinnon (1973, p. 61) similarly assume that monetary authorities are capable of determining this optimum rate of inflation. Only the peculiarities of emerging monetary economies prompt them to advocate general price stability. This, they argue, will at least ensure that the holding of money will not be depreciated even if positive real interest rates cannot be carried through politically via deflation. Moreover, in a situation of optimum monetization, the state' seigniorage, i.e. its gain from operating the money press, is minimal (McKinnon 1973, pp. 116ff.).

It is most obvious that this line of reasoning, namely relating externally set ends to their appropriate means, is of welfare economic origin. Anti-inflationary measures become the means of increasing welfare and of preserving a free market order. It is almost impossible to imagine a view more different from the argument for the need of antiinflationary measures advanced below (see chapter 2): they are considered indispensable on functional grounds, the monetary economy concerned otherwise being threatened with dissolution, although their effects can in no way be seen as increasing welfare.

Closely related to the question of a rationale for monetary policy and the significance of antiinflationary measures, is the question of the currency regime suitable for an emerging monetary economy. It is remarkable that each of the aforementioned founding fathers of development monetarism should advocate a different exchange-rate arrangement. Friedman (1973, pp. 44 and 59) recommends as the first best solution tying the currency firmly to the stable currency of a large country, a fixed-rate system without a central bank. He argues that doing without a central bank will ensure a minimum of intervention and thus the greatest possible stability. The system of flexible exchange rates he favours for developed economies is in this case only the second best solution, because in developing countries government economic policy tends more to intervene and would thus be in a position to do so.

McKinnon (1973, pp. 166ff.) seeks to achieve precisely this with his appeal for "gliding parities". This system is intended to prevent a sudden collapse of the exchange rate due to the policy of lowering external barriers, while ensuring controlled and continuous devaluation.

Shaw (1973, pp. 183ff. and 221ff.) calls for completely flexible exchange rates, because these would enable a small economy to outdo the rest of the world in price stability and to avoid the "import of inflation" associated with fixed exchange rates. He explicitly considers how the "lagging economy" can or should be related to other currency areas through foreign exchange market links. Friedman's proposal is, in Shaw's terms, tantamount to a colonial currency regime. But this, he argues, is not feasible because it requires an unacceptable sacrifice of sovereignty. McKinnon's recommendation, on the other hand, comes close to what Shaw would call a regime of disequilibrium. It is characterized by a high level of intervention by the monetary authorities and so corresponds to the systems which he believes most developing countries have already adopted. - The approach advocated here will follow Shaw as regards his foreign exchange market perspective. Despite, or rather precisely because of this, it does not follow that exchange rates should be as flexible as possible.

The Structuralist Approach

Toward the end of the 1970s, structuralism was forced to accept the monetarist challenge. Within a decade, it, formerly the orthodox approach to development economics, was displaced by the "new orthodoxy" (FitzGerald/Vos 1989, pp. 1ff.). The challenge was accepted theoretically and empirically, in that the structuralists self-critically identified their own eclecticism and the need for a more systematic approach (idem) and conceded their helplessness in the face of the stabilization problem to which a solution was urgently needed, particularly in Latin America (Jansen 1989, p. 71). This prompted theoretical reformulation and rigorous modelling. Nonetheless, "monetarily enlightened" structuralists too point primarily to empirical findings in substantiating their fundamental propositions. This may explain why this approach cannot be identified with a limited number of seminal works. It is made up of a wide range of papers that seek to describe the situation in Latin American, African and Asian countries as accurately as possible and emphasize different aspects accordingly. A number of essential features and common elements can nonetheless be identified.[10]

The *prototype of a developing economy*, as structuralism still conceives it, is made up of highly disparate actors, who can be distinguished by their institutional affiliation, their productive and technological capacities and the class to which they belong. The macroeconomy cannot, then, be derived from a simple aggregation of microeconomic decisions taken by homogeneous economic agents with analogous objective functions. Instead, the various entities act as a social group, institution or political organization in markets characterized by unequally distributed market power, adjustment lags, imperfect information, etc. The structuralist macroeconomy is always a whole divided into sectors which are not traced back to individual entities (FitzGerald/Vos 1989, pp. 22 and 39ff.). That, in principle, is how the present approach can be described, even if the disaggregation criteria differ in various respects and less importance is attached to phenomena of market failure. The assumptions of perfect markets in traditional methodology are also accepted here, as conditions that hinder ad hoc explanations, since they prevent refuge from being sought in reference to particular features. Cognitive interest can be focused on problems that cannot be eliminated, however perfect the market, and stem from the monetary mediation of decentralized decisions in the widest sense of the term.

In an economy of this kind the relevant actors are, firstly, the wage-earning households which, though already forming part of the modern sector, contribute little to the formation of financial assets because of their low income level. The traditional sector, secondly, is made up of the productive households which McKinnon also takes into account, but which here have no active significance in terms of development strategy. The other actors are the enterprises, from which foreign enterprises are sometimes separated, and the state complex, comprising government, publicly owned enterprises and the dependent central bank (ibid., pp. 47ff.; Jansen 1989, pp. 62f.).

This breakdown is crucial if the state is to be taken into account and the process of income generation described. On regulatory and structural policy grounds, the state appears as an actor in the economy who must not be overlooked.[11]

Income generation is presented classically, i.e. it results from the decision taken by enterprises or productive households to defer consumption and to reinvest their surpluses. Seen from the angle of this study, the variant in which the households' deferral of consumption is replaced with retained profits cannot be regarded entirely as an analytical advance. It still describes income generation in a barter economy, but not in a monetary economy.

According to this approach, dualism of formal and informal financial sectors, which obtains in the financial sector, is an important structural feature of an emerging monetary economy. Although informal financial markets are also mentioned by Shaw, they do not gain any theoretical relevance (Shaw 1973, p. 183; Fry 1988, p. 105). They embody one inefficiently used resource among others, lying completely or partly fallow as a result of financial repression. In structuralist writings, on the other hand, such markets represent the financial complement of the traditional mode of production (Jansen 1989, p. 63; Taylor 1979, p. 131). They will not therefore necessarily lose importance with liberalization, but will wane appreciably once these production methods change.

The reference to "changes in modes of production" raises the question of the *concept of economic development* which underlies this approach. This continues to mean structural change in a comprehensive sense. But the monetarist turn becomes noticeable in as much as greater importance is attached to macroeconomic stability and balanced sectoral change. Money and credit are introduced no longer as passive media but as "vehicles" of economic policy to be used to advance structural change (FitzGerald/Vos 1989, pp. 28f.). This also marks the difference from the monetarist-liberal position: structural change is not seen primarily as the outcome of the market process but as a requirement for the functioning of markets which must ultimately be created by the state. The explanatory context is thus reversed. Although this study is able to endorse such a concept of economic development, money and credit nonetheless have a completely different status. Their importance for the development process is that they act as "conditioners" rather than instruments of economic policy.

The process of monetization that accompanies structural change has repercussions on the relative development of the economy's sectors. In all likelihood, the formation of nonfinancial assets will be concentrated in the business sector, which will probably become a persistent net debtor to the economy, while the productive households become net savers. Financial intermediaries usually exacerbate this trend in that they prefer large, formal creditors protected by the state.

On the other hand, the process of monetization also creates instability. The more the economy divides into a saving and an investing sector, the more likely it is that macroeconomic imbalances, i.e. discrepancies between planned savings and planned investments, will occur (Jansen 1989, p. 59). This takes up the conclusion drawn in the Keynesian theory that money serves not only, and not even primarily, to overcome uncertainty, but instead gives rise to specific uncertainties or instabilities. Financial intermediation encourages an increase in the occurrence of macroeconomic imbalances, since investments may then exceed planned savings by the amount of credit financing. "Advance financing" is subsequently consolidated by forced saving in the form of rising prices. This mechanism, which entails, after all, a break with the idea that (voluntary) saving is needed if there is to be investment in a monetary economy, will be discussed later. The category of a supposed deferral of consumption will, however, then give way to the category of windfall profits.

Structuralism thus provides a systematic argument for the view that instability may be inherent in the market of monetary economies and that what is needed in the development process to counter it is *macropolicy*. Its main purpose is seen as the elimination of the ex-ante imbalance between savings and investment that appears to arise by and large independently of monetary conditions. Consequently, the greatest importance in striking a macroeconomic balance is attached not to the control of the money supply but to fiscal demand management (e.g. Jansen 1989, p. 78; Taylor 1983, pp. 192f.).

One of the major objectives of this balance is distribution, which means that stabilization is also intended to seek a desirable sharing of adjustment burdens between earned and unearned income.[12] The inclusion of this distribution objective among the tasks of a stabilization policy makes it possible to speak of the welfare economics of stabilization within the triangle formed by "*economic structure, accumulation balances, and income distribution*" (FitzGerald/Vos 1989, p. 17). In contrast, an attempt is made here to show that coordinating objectives in this way is virtually impossible in a monetary economy and that the problem of macrostabilization, which cannot be solved by welfare economics, is due to the very fact that it is hardly capable of controlling distribution effects or, in certain circumstances, ought not consider them if it is to succeed.

The ends-means nature of the postulated stabilization policy becomes even clearer when the structuralist treatment of the inflation problem is considered. Here again, the argument - following on from Kalecki - concerns functional income distribution and the class conflict resulting from it. Any "demand-pull inflation" arising from demand for capital goods that exceeds voluntary deferral of consumption leads to a shift in income distribution to the advantage of government and the business sector. Undesirable though the associated decline in mass purchasing power may be for reasons of accumulation, this shift in favor of income recipients with a higher propensity to save is desirable for reasons of stability (Taylor 1979, pp. 135ff.). Where "cost-push inflation" follows (real) increases in wages, workers or trade unions shift distribution to their own advantage. This reversal of the demand-pull situation may be desirable on accumulation grounds, but it is undesirable on stability grounds. In the case of both cost-push and demand-pull inflation, economic policy finds itself in a situation that can be described as typically post-Keynesian: it must undertake a "trade-off", i.e. seek to achieve an optimal combination of objectives with instruments that work in opposite directions.

Aside from introducing administrative price and wage controls (Taylor 1979, p. 140), a restrictive policy of combatting inflation will attempt to limit demand for credit. The structuralist theory relies in this context primarily on higher interest rates and directives to the banks to reduce their lending. It sees this focus on credit restriction, intended as an explicitly opposite position to the monetarist emphasis on the control of aggregate money supply, as a more realistic option for poor and less integrated monetary economies.

This is due, on the one hand, to the weak position of the central bank in such countries. The money supply is not, de facto or de jure, controlled by the central bank, but by the government demand for money and by the inflows of foreign exchange from abroad, which reflect the balance-of-payments position.[13] The money supply is thus said to be determined "endogenously" by the budget deficit and the current-account deficit, not exogenously by the central bank (Taylor 1979, p. 27). This view of the "endogenous nature of the money supply" comes surprisingly close to Shaw's concept of inside money. The weakness of an actor in a monetary economy, the central bank in one case, the government sector in the other, is made into a theoretical strength: why it is that a supposedly omnipotent central bank, the state note-issuing monopoly, is not inconsistent with the norms of a liberal economy remains an unsolved riddle of the conventional theory of money. It would be more in keeping with these norms that the private sector ultimately determines the quantity of the medium on which its transactions are based. The endogenous nature of the money supply is the formal expression of this problem of harmonizing the theory of money and the economic system. Simply eliminating the difference between the private and public sectors does not solve this riddle: it merely avoids it, since just as it cannot be disputed empirically that the money-issuing authority in many developing countries has become a passive printer of money, this is unsatisfactory as a theory of the money supply. This situation should be - and is in this study - exposed as a dysfunctional institutional form of the financial structure.

On the other hand, little importance is attached to the control of the money supply because such countries have an informal financial system to which the central bank does not have access. This system has, it is claimed, a high liquidity potential, especially as it itself produces "money in the broad sense" i.e. money substitutes in the form of bills of exchange, etc. (Taylor 1979, pp. 129ff.). Yet here again the question is whether this is not to call the problem a theoretical solution. With the reference to the existence of liquidity potential that leaves the control of the money supply powerless, the very factor that necessitates stabilization becomes a factor which prevents such stabilization from succeeding. From this it then follows that preference should be given to credit, wage and price controls. This assessment ultimately depends on whether the money supply is conceived as reacting passively to demand for money or whether - as in this study - it is assigned an actively limiting role.

Combatting inflation by merely restricting credit is an extremely insecure business. This is blamed both on the dualism in the financial sector and on the way in which price levels are determined in a heterogeneously structured monetary economy. The higher interest rate in the formal sector will, after all, result in credits being made available in the informal sector or in the demand for credit moving to the informal sector. Enterprises will also try to pass on higher interest costs in their prices. The average enterprise in the formal sector can do this because of its oligopolistic market position, which enables it to add a fixed mark-up to costs (Jansen 1989, pp. 74f.; Taylor 1979, p. 132). Where such oligopolistic pricing occurs, the attempts to pursue a restrictive macropolicy will typically end in stagflation, i.e. the coincidence of stagnant income generation due to falling demand and price increases due to the cost-push inflation triggered by the entrepreneurial sector and fed by the informal financial sector.

These adverse affects of a rise in interest rates also mean that any liberalization of the financial market that leads to higher real interest rates would not in any way have the effects attributed to it by the monetarists. While they infer that higher interest rates lead to stability of the overall price level and to growth as a result of efficiency gains, it follows from the argument just advanced that stagflation is the most likely outcome given the structural parameters of a developing economy. The two schools of thought thus identify diametrically opposed effects (Fry 1988, p. 107).

This discussion will be continued below. At this stage it suffices to say that a theory of price level determination will be forwarded which derives the price level as a macroeconomic expression of the mark-ups calculated by enterprises. This "mark-up pricing" is not, however, based on the assumption of imperfect competition, but follows from a different theory of the money supply process and the interaction of markets in a monetary economy. - Finally, the alternative presented here also shows that financial repression is unlikely to have the intended effects on economic policy and should therefore be abandoned. However, there is some indication that the phenomena feared by the structuralists do occur.

The conflicting propositions of the two schools as regards the effects of liberalization measures can be attributed to *the theoretical monetary perspective*. It was pointed out above that money and credit have a stabilizing effect in the monetarist approach because the preservation of purchasing power this makes possible ensures the interpersonal, spatial and temporal balance of transactions.[14] Expressed in formal terms, the disposition over assets permits the disposition over flows of goods to be stabilized.

The structuralist approach too singles out money and credit as reflecting flows of goods, but because of the various imperfections that must realistically be assumed they are themselves unstable or destabilizing. The inferred money and credit transactions may increase real economic instability if speculative investments, risk aversion on the part of banks and investors, etc. exacerbate the uncertainties and deficiencies that already exist.[15] Again expressed in formal terms, this means that money and credit flows are perceived as real economic income flows, faithfully reflecting or even increasing their imbalances.

Symptomatic of this explanatory context is the theoretical approach that consists in modelling the real economic sector and discussing the relevant problems before a monetary sector is added to complete the picture (Taylor 1983, Chapter 5; FitzGerald 1989, pp. 85 and 101ff.). Considerable importance is attached to the flow-of-funds analysis, which depicts intersectoral financial flows as changes in stocks over time. Asset transactions are thus primarily seen as duals of real transactions. Although this does not rule out structuralist portfolio models (Jansen 1989, pp. 74ff.), their basic units are not as a rule individual economic agents but sectors. According to structuralism, income rationales dominate asset rationales in microeconomic choices.[16]

In countries where incomes are low, this appears only too plausible. Yet it is precisely here that a distinction can be made between formulating a theory which, like the structuralist approach, is intended to be as realistic as possible and formulating a theory which, as is the aim here, seeks to be empirically meaningful. The formal, supposedly unrealistic-abstract version captures assets as a variable differing from income variables with respect to the time dimension. This formal version may very well open up an access to typical development problems: firstly, this temporal nature of monetary relationships determines the obstacles that stand in the way of the emergence of a monetary economy in the physical sense and its progress in the sense of self-sustaining income generation. Secondly, it can be argued that income generation in a monetary economy always presupposes wealth formation because it is based on creditor-debtor relationships, claims as positive net assets, and liabilities as negative net assets. A possible explanation for the political-economic change in numerous developing countries is that claims to wealth in a socially and legally relevant sense have arisen in the course of four or more decades of government economic policy. These portfolio interests have become increasingly apparent, either in the form of the notorious flight from the national currency or in the form of demands that the economy be privatized. The Latin American continent, the main source of the structuralists' empirical conclusions, is an excellent example of these portfolio interests appearing rhetorically and factually to be increasingly gaining ground on employment, i.e. income, interests. In development economics itself this change has been made through the substitution of market euphoria for planning euphoria. The actors implicitly regarded as relevant are therefore no longer the underemployed households earning subsistence wages but the households that own assets and threaten capital flight.

The wealth perspective even of an infant monetary economy therefore is able to illuminate the problems of development, and especially of development policy. Gaining a perspective of this kind requires above all to define the function of money differently from the monetarist and structuralist approaches, for both of which the exchange function, inter- or atemporal, takes the forefront.

1.3   The Role of Money in Monetary-Keynesian Theory

The above-mentioned writings on the theory of monetary development can be arranged in a time sequence that shows the genesis of financial systems in developing countries to be a tale of continuous corruption (World Bank 1989, Chapters 3-5). With the constitution of a national monetary economy, a country that had become independent also had to ask itself how it should relate to other currency areas. Friedman (1973) complained that in this constituent act most countries failed to impose sufficient self-commitment on the Leviathan by establishing an appropriate monetary structure. Consequently, according to Shaw (1973), fiscal action and political interventionism had prevented the process of financial consolidation from developing unhindered. He and McKinnon (1973) maintain that instead a state of financial repression emerged characterized by a dichotomous structure of the financial system. Although they agree on this finding, Shaw's and McKinnon's approaches and the neostructuralist school differ over what needs to be done to overcome this dichotomous structure.

The leading contributions to the literature appear to have reached consensus on this tale of corruption (Fischer 1982, McKinnon 1988, World Bank 1989). There can be little doubt in their conclusion that numerous countries have been guilty of excessive budget financing with central bank credits and that extensive regulation encourages a dual-economy structure in the financial sector since it provokes evasive reactions. However, this consensus with respect to a "history of financial decline" is to be criticized in that its analytical foundations prevent it from appropriately registering the difficulties encountered in the development of a monetary economy. In the case of the monetarist school, this inadequacy appears to be due, ultimately, to the historical teleology of liberal enlightenment. On this view, the evolution of a global market economy would be inevitable if it were not constantly opposed by governments not confined to preserving external and internal legal security.

The criticism of this conception forms the background to the comments below, but for the moment it is based on arguments derived from economic theory. This pivots on the definition of the functions of money. It will become clear that the conceptual foundations, the formal question of what is understood by exchange, payment and value-storing media, are crucial for the interpretation both of the constitution problem and of the dilemma of development under monetary conditions. The position of the state, conditioned by the historical context, should also be evident at this level.

In Fry's work (1988), which can be described as a compendium of monetary development theory, the functions of money are listed as follows: *"Money's primary function is to act as a medium of exchange. It also serves as a unit of account, a store of value, and a standard of deferred or future payments."* (Ibid., p. 238).

This weighting of the functions of money can be traced back to the beginnings of the science of economics: money is first and foremost a medium of exchange, its other functions, i.e. as the unit of account, as a store of value, and as a medium of deferred payments, taking second place. In what follows, it will be argued that money's function as a medium of exchange is derived - in theory and in the history of money - from its importance as a "medium of deferred payment" (Riese 1989, p. 1). If money performs a value-storing function, the argument continues, it does indicate a monetary economy in its infancy. Money's function as the unit of account is not explicitly discussed since this property is a derivative of the acceptance of money as a medium of exchange and payment.

Its *function as a medium of exchange* forges the macroeconomic link between the money sphere and the commodity or real sphere, which is expressed in the quantity equation as $M \cdot v = P \cdot T$. The revolving fund of the media of exchange, i.e. the product of the quantity of the medium of exchange, M, and the rate of circulation, v, is identical to the turnover of goods over time, i.e. the transaction quantity, T, valued at the prices summed up in the index, P.[17]

In contrast to the traditional interpretation, whereby M stands for "money" and money for medium of exchange, a narrower definition of money is used here. Money means only central-bank money, i.e. reserves with the central bank and cash. The media of exchange designated as M in the quantity equation therefore include not only cash but also deposits or a confirmed credit line, such as bills of exchange. The difference between the two types of media of exchange, cash issued by monetary authorities and the media of exchange created by banks, is that money cancels a contract, whereas media of exchange created by banks can do no more than transfer the debt relationship resulting from a purchase. This simply means that, when used as a medium of exchange, money at the same time serves as a medium of payment.

The difference between money in the sense used here and other transaction media is evident from the fact that, while no interest is paid on money held, it is in principle paid on claims against deposits or bills of exchange (Riese 1989, p. 18). In the literature, including the above-mentioned writings by Friedman, Shaw and McKinnon, the absence of interest on money held is usually interpreted as seigniorage of the mint or, to put it in modern terminology, the privilege of the note-issuing monopolist. This view cannot but presuppose that the money-issuing authority in the financial systems obtaining since the Peel Bank Act (1844) must be seen in economically meaningful terms as having a debt to those who hold money. It disregards the specific character of modern financial systems where the issue of money by a state central bank is separated from the provision of credit by the banking system that is based on the money supply (Lutz 1962).

If the central bank is regarded as a debtor, the privilege derives from the difference between the state's, i.e. central bank's, interest-free debt and the rate of price increases by which money held is depreciated. This view therefore also means that the privilege prevents the charging of explicit positive interest on the money supply, whereas interest is implicitly charged at the rate of deflation or inflation (Shaw 1973, p. 66). The idea that money in circulation is equivalent to a state or central bank debt on which no interest is charged only because of the state's monopoly and the theorem that interest is a commodity market phenomenon therefore belong together. It will be shown later that a different definition of the function of money as a medium of payment, which also qualifies the importance of money as a medium of exchange, is bound to refute both the interpretation of money as the issuer's debt (Shaw 1973, p. 53) and the interpretation of interest as a phenomenon of commodity markets.

The link expressed in the quantity equation between the stock of media of exchange and the turnover of goods during a given period implies that there is no market in which the supply of and demand for media of exchange find expression and a balance is struck between them (Riese 1989, p. 26). The demand for or supply of media of exchange is balanced by the supply of or demand for goods and services, which is bound to trigger corresponding price and quantity effects in the market system. This is the essence of Keynes's "Fundamental Proposition of the Theory of Money", although it should be remembered that he uses a wide definition of money that includes media of exchange:

> "Thus incomes and such prices necessarily change until the aggregate of the amounts of money which individuals choose to hold at the new levels of incomes and prices thus brought about has come to equality with the amount of money created by the banking system. This, indeed, is the fundamental proposition of monetary theory." (Keynes 1936, pp. 84f.)

Keynes's "fundamental proposition" thus forges the link suggested by the quantity theory between money supply and price level (Riese 1989, p. 29), but his monetary theory of interest, known as the liquidity preference theory, prevents the money supply, or the media of exchange based on it, from being neutral with regard to processes in the real economy. The most advanced version of the quantity theory, Friedman's, was able to postulate the longer-term neutrality of money, or of media of exchange, by integrating the real balance effect of the older theory. The holding of real balances, which is apportioned in accordance with the intertemporal allocation of consumption and therefore abides by the time preference theory of interest, here triggers a proportional adjustment of prices to the exogenously created money supply.[18] In contrast, the monetary definition of interest permits the formulation of a Keynesian income theory in which the quantity of media of exchange is created endogenously from the interaction between the central bank, commercial banks, and enterprises. Credit and investment decisions set in motion income generation processes which increase employment and raise price levels, without it being possible to say in advance what weight either effect will carry.

The function of money as a medium of exchange is associated with a specific instability. While the use of media of exchange by goods-market suppliers conforms to the goal of profit-making, where the aim is to turn an asset to account, it is geared on the demand side to consumption and thus to the acquisition of flows of goods in line with preferences commensurate with income. This discrepancy is a fundamental source of uncertainty for investment in a monetary economy, since the media of exchange advanced for production purposes need by no means return to the producers in the form of demand for goods. This is at best true of the entrepreneurial sector as a whole, which is why it is not necessarily true, as Keynes maintained (1936, pp. 25f.), that Say's theorem, according to which any supply creates its own demand, must be rejected in the case of a monetary economy.

Keynes made uncertainty for the individual enterprise the basis of his income and employment theory and used it to contradict the full-employment postulate of neoclassical economics. Although there is a division of labour between households and enterprises in neoclassical economics, they have an economic rationale in common. In the market for loanable funds, the savings volume and the investment volume, the demand for and the supply of nonconsumption as it were, are harmonized, producing a situation that is complementary to the balance of the demand for and supply of goods. As will be discussed later, these different conclusions drawn from the function of money as a medium of exchange are ultimately due to the fact that Keynesian thinking on the part of producers is not geared to the efficient utilization of a given stock of resources. Instead, it is geared to the formation of resources and also to maintaining so large a surplus of them that a balance is struck in the interest on money advances invested in production. The next chapter will revert to this thinking on the part of producers that has recourse to the function of money as a medium of exchange, when the difficulty encountered in the development of a money economy, described in this study as a "dilemma", is discussed.

Media of exchange refer to money's *function as a medium of deferred payment* in as much as their usability ultimately depends on the "medium for deferred payment". Media of exchange, as was said, are in principle interest-bearing since they require of the producer of such a medium to assume the status of a creditor and forgo absolute solvency. Money as a medium of exchange, on the other hand, is not interest-bearing because it is a medium of payment. As such it has the ability to break the credit chains arising from its use as a medium of exchange and to redeem debts once and for all.

Anyone selling a good and receiving in exchange a deposit balance acquires a cash claim against the bank concerned. Anyone accepting a cash payment, on the other hand, has no further claim. Nor can such a claim be made against the central bank. The latter issues money only against debt instruments - normally against debt instruments from abroad (foreign exchange), the state, and banks entitled to access to the central bank - and accepts redemption only in the medium it has issued. It thus assumes the position of a creditor.

For the reasons given it is economically irrelevant that the money supply appears on the liability side of the central bank's balance sheet and so represents a debt for accountancy purposes. In a monetary economy with a state central bank, this liability is an obligation of society to itself. This debt that society owes to itself has historical roots. The "financial revolution" in England in the late 17th century resulted in the court's private debt becoming a public debt, requiring parliamentary blessing, to the Bank of England, the first modern central bank. Money was put into circulation through the monetization of the state deficit and thus assumed the status of a public debt in that the elected legislature authorized it as a liability of the commonwealth to itself (Dickson 1967, pp. 9-14; Rothermund 1978, Chapter 12).

This historical process, during which money became established as a public good, is in principle repeated in any currency reform in which a society becomes indebted, as it were, in a new currency.

It might, of course, be objected to this interpretation that in modern monetary systems the central bank has, or had, to comply with certain legal reserve regulations or redemption obligations. It might therefore be reasonable to say that central bank money in fact embodies a claim to a reserve medium such as gold or foreign exchange. In answer to this objection, it can be said that legal reserve regulations and redemption obligations are normally intended to ensure confidence in money in circulation. The monetary authorities indicate in this way that they will not increase the money supply without restriction, that the provision of the medium of payment of full value is linked to certain requirements, such as an increase in gold reserves. Such arrangements do not therefore form the basis of the central bank's debtor status, but must be seen as analogous to statutory precautions against a boundless increase in central-bank credit to government.[19]

The central bank's position as a creditor also means that interest must be paid on the payment medium it issues. Like any private agent in the same position, it claims interest in the form of the discount or lombard rate. This signifies rejection of the above-mentioned thesis that it refuses the payment of interest because of its monopoly position even though it is a debtor. If money is seen as a government debt, there is no economic justification, only a theory of political conspiracy to explain modern central banks and the payment medium they issue.

This insistence on the payment of interest is one of the requirements to be met if a central bank is to enter into commitments on the economy's behalf and so, in particular, to pursue a restrictive monetary policy (Lüken-Klassen/Betz 1990, p. 314). It is never enough for it to be refunded the quantity of payment medium expended: it always claims some of the income earned with it.[20]

The central bank's claim to interest is borne by the private sector because, being a public good, this guarantees absolute liquidity: in present-day currency systems no one has the legal means to prevent monetary commitments of any kind from being redeemed with the unrestricted statutory payment medium, the national currency. Money did not acquire this property until the civil nation state was constituted. Although historically this may not have been the cause, the institution of money as a public good can be attributed subsequently to the emergence of the capitalist economic system: a form of social constitution based on contracts rather than status needs a medium that ensures a system of law and order in the sense of the definitive performance of contracts. No one, least of all the debtor, can be excluded from using money in order to be, for example, subjected to permanent dominance. The collective obligation that money embodies is equivalent to the possibility of individuals constantly freeing themselves from obligations.

The property of money that consists in its representing a public good in the currency systems of nation states does, however, create a specific acceptance problem: when in doubt, potential creditors avoid entering into a legal relationship whose medium of performance does not promise to return to them their former - and even, as a rule, a higher degree of - power of disposal. This marks the limits to a legalistic line of argument: although the function of a payment medium through which money becomes a public good requires constitutional safeguards, it is a function that cannot be performed unless accepted by the private sector. What is more, constitutional safeguards may, paradoxically, even obstruct the development of debtor-creditor relationships since the creditors do not want to find themselves in a situation in which they are forced to allow the law to be used against them. This aspect of a "State Theory of Money" (Knapp 1918) is crucial not only to the constitution problem connected with emerging monetary economies but also to the restrained nature of income generation in typical developing economies.

For the absolute solvency that an accepted money guarantees, Keynes (1936, p. 194 and Chapter 17) coined the term "liquidity premium". Creditors must do without this non-pecuniary return on money they hold if they abandon their power of disposal over money in exchange for a claim to pecuniary interest. The liquidity premium thus forms the basis of the monetary interest theory of Keynesian economics just as the rate of time preference in neoclassical economics provides a non-monetary theory of interest.[21]

The commercial banking system has a decisive role to play in the determination of the supply of payment media, but one which is not easy to define: in their relationship with the central bank the commercial banks act in what is for modern monetary economies a typical two-tier system in which they are demanders of money on the one hand and suppliers of money to other economic actors on the other. For every credit contract that entails production of media of exchange, typically an enterprise being granted a credit line for salary payments, may require the provision of payment media when, for example, recipients of salaries withdraw cash. The banks' liquidity preference thus controls the money supply (Riese 1989, p. 9, ref. 23). In order to enter into a credit claim, they are forced to give up the power to dispose freely over money, and thus to make use of reserves and refinance contingents with the central bank or flows stemming from customer deposits. Their liquidity preference therefore specifies the interest floor, since they are forced to direct what is in terms of individual economic units an unsafe claim against their debtors and a safe claim against themselves. The liquidity premium thus specifies the lower limit at which potential creditors, banks in this case, forgo the granting of credit to protect their liquidity.

It follows from the above that a monetary economy is an economy based on liabilities. Money is put in circulation only on the basis of credit relationships. While the essential aspects of neoclassical economics can be dealt with in terms of a Robinson Crusoe model, in that this view concerns the struggle between man and nature, monetary-Keynesian economics is constituted on the basis of a certain type of social relations, viz. debtor-creditor relationships. In non-European civilizations this may well be offensive and form a sociocultural barrier to the expansion of monetary relationships. The emergence of an economy based on liabilities is therefore a phenomenon whose legitimacy is fraught with presuppositions, an aspect which forms part of the constitution problem considered only in passing here.

A liability-based economy, i.e. one implying the use of the "medium for deferred payment," also means that economic relations extend over time. Barter transactions in a spot market represent a special case and not the basic model encountered in textbook economics. Under the conditions typical of developing countries, the necessarily intertemporal nature of monetary relationships can entail a demand that is too high to be fulfilled.[22] Uncertainty in being able to assess the creditworthiness of a borrower or the recognizably high risk of default may then prevent creditors from forgoing their liquidity long enough for products to be manufactured and turned to account or from taking the risk of losing assets at all. The same reasoning, coupled with the threat of severe sanctions such as debtor enslavement, may cause potential debtors to act with restraint.

The reference to the danger of losses of assets also raises the question of money's *value-storing function* cited by Fry. Riese (1989, p. 14) rightly argues that as a form of value storage money on which no interest is paid is not consistent with the logic of market behavior. It is in contradiction to the postulate of economic rationality to forgo interest income or the rise in the value of other assets and instead to hold money, whose price as a unit of account is equal to one.

To this methodological critique of money's value-storing function can be added a reference to the property of money of representing a public good in developed financial systems. This implies a separation of the functions of money and assets: money guarantees legally incontestable liquidity and thus a nonpecuniary return, whereas value-storing media do not enjoy universal, state-guaranteed acceptance and are therefore held for the sake of their pecuniary return. It thus follows that money actually held to store value can be considered relevant only empirically, as Riese (ibid.) critically notes. If, however, the storage of value through the hoarding of money is interpreted as the expression of rudimentary acceptance, theoretically highly relevant insights can emerge: firstly, into the genesis of the function of money, and secondly, with regard to the difference between an economy that uses money and a monetary economy.

In economies that are only partially integrated, it is typically observed that money is used in sectors hardly permeated by monetization, but very largely to honor non-economic commitments. As a general rule, money is hoarded so as to accumulate a stock of a payment medium for a large expenditure in the future. Notorious examples of this are commitments to provide children of marriageable age with the necessary dowry or to organize family gatherings on the occasion of birthdays and funerals. Money is used, as it were, asymmetrically as a value-storing, or payment-medium by the debtor to meet his obligations, since the creditor side is represented by non-monetary social demands.[23]

The value-storing function thus appears to be a preliminary form of the payment-medium function in an economy that uses money, but is not yet a monetary economy. Money is typically spent in an economy of this kind not in the expectation that it will produce a return, as is the case when it is invested, but to redeem a debt incurred non-economically.

The *primacy of the payment-medium function* assumed in this interpretation may be based on sociohistorical findings (Laum 1924, pp. 29 and 158; Polanyi 1979, pp. 317ff.): in primitive economies specific types of money are allocated to the different functions of payment, exchange, value storage and compensation. The type of money used for payment, i.e. to meet a social obligation by handing over certain quantifiable objects, cannot necessarily be used to purchase, to acquire a good. At the same time, the later use of money in exchange is derived from its use to fulfill an obligation:

"Once money has been introduced in a society as a medium of exchange, payment becomes the general custom. With the introduction of markets as the physical place of exchange, a new form of obligation takes the fore as the substrate of transactions. (...) At one time a man had to pay taxes, rent, fines or blood-money. Now he pays for the goods he acquires. (...) The idea of payment having an independent origin recedes into the background, and the millennia in which payment was made on the basis not of economic transactions but of religious, social or political obligations sink into oblivion." (Polanyi 1979, p. 325; author's translation)

Unlike a money-using economy, a monetary economy has no special types of money, but just one payment medium to which exchange and value-storing media are referred. The standardization of money was accompanied by the centralization of political power. Eventually the standard money was developed into money as a public good. This process, as has already been implied, was very closely associated with the emergence of the modern constitutional and nation state.

2   Development under Conditions of a Monetary Economy

2.1   The Problem of Constitution

At the beginning of the last chapter reference was made to the link between the formation of nation states and the emergence of a monetary economy in the sense used here. This link must be qualified historically, since the context of national and monetary integration for today's industrialized countries differed entirely from that of today's developing countries. The different *conditions of constitution* will be outlined here schematically to permit a comparison with the problems faced by the countries that gained political independence after the Second World War, including those of Latin America.

The crucial difference is seen in a hierarchy of currency areas changed in comparison with the 19th century, which rendered the outward constitution of these monetary economies even more difficult. The chapter concludes with a discussion of the - in this way handicapped - inward constitution of monetary economies, the aim being to show that separate consideration of an external and internal aspect of the problem of constitution represents an analytical abstraction. This does, however, make it possible to accentuate certain assumed complex interrelationships which would go unheeded if it were simply stated that all aspects were interlinked.

An important condition for the constitution of monetary economies is touched upon by consideration of the factors that stimulate national and monetary integration, since various pressures acting toward the development of monetary relations are created in this way. In economic terms, the modern European state emerges as a mercantilistic tax-based state.[24] During the religious struggles of the 15th and 16th centuries, military spending had become exorbitant, the burden on the population due to marauding armies and confiscations growing intolerable. The beginnings of the early modern state, which superseded the medieval empire, may be dated with the establishment of standing armies and the development of permanent administrative bureaucracies. Standing armies supplanted the case-by-case involvement of privately organized warrior-entrepreneurs, and permanent administration made private tax collectors superfluous (Stürmer 1986). This "inward and outward expansion of the 'state' - i.e. bureaucratically and militarily" (von Müller 1986, p. 110) entailed rapidly mounting financial requirements. Aside from the collection of indirect taxes, it was above all promotion of trade and industry that was intended to ensure government revenues by increasing the tax base or directly providing revenues from state manufactories.

While the leading European countries succeeded in developing a system of taxation, administration, and military affairs, the system of money supply remained medieval in structure until the 19th century. Only in England, as already mentioned, did a relevant "financial revolution" occur prior to the industrial revolution (Rothermund 1978, p. 145; Kindleberger 1984, Chapter 9). Parliamentary control of government, the national debt, and especially of the ensuing increase in the money supply, afforded private individuals better protection than beforehand against arbitrary fluctuations in the supply of the medium in which their economic transactions were effected - and had to be effected if the state was to collect taxes. The outside money that emerged from a private debtor-creditor relationship between the court and the rest of the economy became inside money, society's debt to itself.

The stabilization of state finances - and thus of government as a whole - which the financial revolution helped to bring about, and the emergence of a fiscal system and a private capital market presumably put England at a considerable advantage in competition with other European nations. It was of course to emerge successfully from this process as the first industrial nation. For its competitors, development thereafter assumed the aspect of a Second World seeking to catch up with a hegemonic industrial and financial power. In the second half of the 19th century, these countries laid the foundations for a modern financial system, consisting in the institutionalization of a state-controlled central bank, a two-tier system of money supply commensurate with it, and support for long-term industrial finance (Gerschenkron 1962, pp. 14f.). With the exception of a number of Latin American countries, today's Third World was still in a state of colonial dependence, and hence more an instrument of than an actor in these ventures in late development.

The motives driving the integration of those countries that gained their independence after the Second World War differed accordingly. Unlike the old nations of Europe, they emerged as modernization states. The driving force was not instrumental interest in revenues to finance external power politics and internal pacification: instead, consciously achieved modernization was to establish an identity that was, for lack of time, unable to evolve historically and dictated by the objective political constellations given when the postwar frontiers were proclaimed by the infant nations.

Expansion was thus almost entirely "inward expansion": modernization was seen as a social and economic task to be tackled by a rapidly growing bureaucracy.[25] In some countries much of the corresponding rise in expenditures for development and administration was financed via resource transfers, a good part of which stemmed from the North. This was an element of the Pax Americana now in place. In the Truman Declaration of 1949, the new hegemonic power had delivered its political declaration of intent to accelerate the modernization of the underdeveloped countries and to integrate them into the world market. This declaration marked the beginning of development policy as a means of shaping relations between nations and of cultivating development theory as a separate branch of various scientific disciplines (Hemmer 1990, pp. 506f.)

Support in the form of foreign aid seemed all the more necessary as, economically, modernization was primarily taken to mean industrialization. The large-scale accumulation of non-monetary assets associated with it presupposes sophisticated financial arrangements. This scale of accumulation calls for a more distinct separation of those involved in the formation of monetary and non-monetary assets than is usual, for instance, in trade and manufacturing. And the resulting financial relationships must be sustained in the long term because investment in industry does not on the average pay off as quickly as, say, investment in trade. Development cooperation with external donors thus seemed to be an opportune substitute for the financial revolution, enabling such nations to proceed straight away with an industrial revolution of their own.

What made constitution for late developers in the postwar period essentially different seems to have been a different kind of relations between the newly independent countries and the rest of the world: the term modernization implies that they were compelled to find a modus vivendi with a world already made up of established national economies. They were bound to see their priority task in shaking off dependencies rather than in achieving advantages in economic and political competition with comparable countries. For them, development meant subsequent development as a Third World vis-à-vis a Second and First World, each of which displayed within itself a whole array of stronger and weaker economies.

In these circumstances, technological progress became the guiding light of the development process, the liberal idea of integration into the world market appearing far less attractive. After all, this would have meant competing with countries whose productive capacities, especially as regards levels of training and infrastructure, were superior in every respect and which were competing among themselves for leading positions in what was now a complex hierarchy.

The option of delinking and self-reliance, seemingly borne of necessity, proved deceptive, however. The inherent inconsistency of an import substitution strategy based on technological progress is apparent from the fact that it relied on massive imports of technology and capital goods and so unwillingly entailed integration into the world market.

And yet, it was not only this implication that made delinking an inconsistent strategic reaction to given conditions of constitution: the establishment of a currency area is in itself incompatible with it. The *outward constitution of a monetary economy*, formally accomplished with the proclamation of a national currency, implies in fact defending that currency against others. If a national currency is to become established, claims on and liabilities in that currency must be contracted. In the case of the newly independent countries, this meant persuading domestic investors to retain those of their nominal assets payable in the currency of the colonial government even when they were now payable in the new currency. Some countries issued a kind of insurance policy to this end by tying their currencies firmly to those of their former colonial masters. The price paid for this confidence premium, of course, was that domestic production became subject to the conditions governing the profitability of production in the former colonial country and any changes it might undergo. This was hardly compatible with the development ambitions nurtured by the infant nation states, since it entailed a renouncement of economic policy sovereignty that was regarded as one of the very causes of the colonial legacy of backwardness.

To put it in conventional economic jargon, outward constitution implies that the supply of a new currency is bound to come up against demand that can be satisfied by turning to other currencies. This fundamental aspect of the constitution problem requires theoretically the assumption of the existence of a foreign-exchange market. This stands in contrast to conventional theory as outlined in the next paragraph. However rudimentary a foreign-exchange market may be, it will, in economic terms, emerge as soon as there is a supply of or demand for a domestic currency competing with another currency. It should be added straight away that the constitution of a monetary economy will then find visible expression in a clear-cut criterion, i.e. the ability to stabilize a freely determined exchange rate.

In this foreign-exchange market perspective, a development theory of external trade focuses on the supply of and demand for a domestic currency and the convertibility of its exchange rate. The traditional view, on the other hand, is that the balance on current account and the degree of openness of an economy, meaning the relative weight carried by foreign-trade linkages, are raised to the level of criteria crucial in developing economies. The foreign-exchange market is either completely disregarded or considered merely as a residue of the domestic money market. Accordingly, the distinction made between the open economy model and the closed economy model is achieved by introducing or omitting a balance-of-payments equation. There is no market in which the demand for and supply of foreign exchange coincide: supply and demand are, rather, the outcome of current- and capital-account balances. These balances themselves are determined by real transactions or by national central banks.[26] Neither approach accords a significant role to decisions involving holding claims payable in national currency, which determine a country's capital-account balance or, indirectly via exchange-rate effects, affect its current-account balance. This, however, would provide the only justification for a truly monetary theory of foreign trade, and it would take into account not only the experience of the industrialized countries, but also that of developing countries afflicted by capital flight (Lüken-Klassen/Betz 1989, pp. 220 and 236ff.).

The problem of constitution, in terms of which every currency is defined in relation to others, finds its expression in a price determined in the foreign-exchange market, i.e. in an exchange rate. If this is the price set in the assets market of an economy, i.e. the market in which investments in foreign currency are traded in relation to investments in domestic currency, the level of this price results from the decisions of market traders to hold stocks of this currency. A decision of this kind is guided by the pecuniary return on the claim held in the currency concerned, but also by confidence in the currency as regards its capability to safeguard wealth in real terms, and by the role it plays in determining the structure of return and risks affecting overall wealth. The latter of these aspects reveals the ability of a portfolio to represent as a whole a slighter risk than the sum of the individual risks represented by those assets, in that assets entailing negatively correlated risks are held.[27]

Evidence of outward constitution is consequently provided by the stability of this asset price. A stable, if not fixed, exchange rate results from private agents' sustained willingness to hold in their portfolios claims payable in domestic currency. Otherwise a weak currency will come under constant pressure for devaluation, which may easily lead to a cumulative process culminating in the abandonment of the currency concerned. A cumulative moment is involved because devaluation causes both the value of and the return on claims payable in that currency to fall. Convertibility in a material sense, i.e. the ability to maintain the stability of a free exchange rate, thus forms the hard criterion of outward constitution.

It might be asked why, in the present context, reference has been made to the factors determining a portfolio equilibrium, i.e. a specific structure of risks and rates of return. But this reference is germane to this context in that it highlights in terms of standard economic theory the fact that the emerging monetary economies have had to compensate for a lack of confidence in the ability of their national currency to safeguard the value of assets. Otherwise they risked loosing the small, but decisive, stratum of owners of domestic wealth. Furthermore, describing the currency situation in this way makes it possible to point out the monetary dependence of economies that have formally become independent: specifically, the risk correlation of key currencies has meant for them that adopting a key currency such as sterling as an anchor and through it linking up with other key currencies such as the US $ was a factor determining confidence in their own currency that could not be influenced. Thus any upward movement in the value of the dollar in countries belonging to the pound sterling area caused considerable uncertainty in the emerging currency areas because this upward movement was accompanied by a fall in the value of the pound sterling.

Even the previously mentioned insurance policy consisting in stabilizing the national currency by tying it to the old colonial currency was therefore only in certain circumstances an arrangement suited to building confidence. This indicates that Friedman's proposal, referred to in the last chapter, is an application of economic liberalism seeking to fetter the Leviathan rather than the outcome of development-policy considerations.

Aside from linking a currency to a certain key currency, there are other factors determining confidence in a currency (Lüken-Klassen/Betz 1989, p. 238): the market share of a currency, which normally reflects a country's strength as an exporter, and the central bank's ability to maintain convertibility and to stabilize the exchange rate. This ability of a central bank to defend a currency very largely depends on the size of its foreign exchange reserves.

These preliminary remarks make it possible to advance a hypothesis expressing this study's fundamental divergence from the monetarist approach: the weakness of currencies is taken as a date for the development-policy options open to countries when they became independent and were seeking to establish themselves as sovereign currency areas. The theoretical wherewithal to underpin this hypothesis is provided by both the foreign-exchange market perspective on integration into the world economy and the exchange rate seen conceptually as an asset price. The writings of Friedman, Shaw, and McKinnon, on the other hand, suggest that currency weakness can be ascribed exclusively to policies reducible to erroneous decisions.

If, as is attempted here, currency weakness is seen as a given date at which policy measures were indicated, it should become evident that the - possibly, or even necessarily, dysfunctional - policies constituted a response to the situation of independence. Whether the policies were possibly or necessarily dysfunctional depends on the anatomy of that specific situation. If, as is argued in the next section, this posed inconsistent requirements as to development objectives, the prerequisites of a functioning monetary economy, and as regards the necessities of political legitimacy, then it must be stated that a policy in consonance with all these demands was not possible. In this case the welfare-economic approach becomes inappropriate in that a harmonious fine-tuning of ends and means was not an option in the first place. Instead, the issue calling for clarification is the constraints involved and the violations of the conditions of development under monetary conditions resulting from them. The critique need not in that case be directed solely against policy, it can also direct its attention to these constraints.

If the weakness of a currency can be defined as meaning a situation in which there is domestic demand for foreign currency but no long-term foreign demand for domestic currency (Lüken-Klassen/Betz 1989, p. 244), then this evidently constituted a primary condition of emerging monetary economies. There were enough established and sound currencies in which nominal assets could be held and real transactions could be conducted.

The weakness of a currency finds obvious expression in the fact that it is not used as a denominator of foreign-trade contracts, i.e. in its lack of contractual capacity (Riese 1989a, pp. 196f.). This can extend from currencies for which foreign investors opt even in the very short term only when high interest differentials are involved, to currencies which have limited contractual capacity but are forced to offer long-term investors an interest differential significantly higher than that available at the international level.[28]

Accordingly, the newly independent nation states were forced to rely on domestic investors. The chapter below entitled "Inward Constitution," discusses the options that were available to motivate these investors to accept claims and liabilities payable in the national currency. However, what was relevant in both theoretical and practical terms for outward constitution was that the then current paradigm of development policy propagated a different approach to coming to grips with this weakness. Prompted by the spirit of the Truman Declaration, the recommendation was made not primarily to increase the demand for domestic investments, but instead to satisfy the surplus demand for foreign exchange resulting from the weakness. The post-Keynesian "two-gap" models (Chenery/Strout 1966; McKinnon 1964) identified, beside a poverty-related savings gap, a development-related foreign exchange gap that, it was argued, might be closed by means of a transfer of resources from abroad.

This simple solution, however, which obviously coincided with the export interests of the industrialized nations, stumbled over the fact that the supposed gaps are not accessible to treatment as quantitative categories. "Closing" them therefore resulted in adverse price effects which, in the process of attempting to narrow them, tended more to widen the gaps. Post-Keynesian theory grasped both the balance of current accounts and the balance of trade as quantitative categories, since it assumed fixed prices in an equilibrium of underemployment, while the Bretton Woods system provided for fixed exchange rates. It thus appeared possible to treat trade deficits and current account deficits as quantities of goods valued at accounting prices and to view foreign-exchange aid as the equivalent of this quantity of goods.

These are extreme implications of a conventional mode of economic theory that treats capital flows as real phenomena and considers foreign trade in terms of the model of a closed economy to which a balance-of-payments element has been added: flows of capital are then merely a reflection "induced" from flows of goods plotted in the balances of trade and current accounts. In contrast, the model outlined here is able to explain why closing the foreign-exchange gap, alias commodity gaps, via transfers of resources proved to be a Greek gift for most countries.

Foreign debt or foreign aid represent a supply of foreign exchange not matched by demand for domestic currency.[29] This not only makes it possible for transfers of resources to sustain the state of currency weakness. It also results in mounting overvaluation precisely when the exchange rates are constant: holding claims payable in foreign exchange becomes increasingly attractive because such a country's foreign-exchange liabilities are on the rise. The ensuing switch to foreign-exchange holdings is bound to result either in depreciation or, at fixed exchange rates, a mounting overvaluation. A constant rate of overvaluation is perpetuated when a resource transfer just satisfies the mounting demand for foreign exchange. This, however, brings with it a growing amount of foreign-exchange stocks in private hands which never return to the monetary authorities.

The overvaluation sustained by the transfer of resources was bound to have an ambivalent impact on the credibility of any new currency. Since these transfers were as a rule conducted at government level, a central bank, constantly faced with the privatization of foreign exchange in view of its weak currency, then had foreign-exchange reserves at its disposal. That doubtless increased the willingness, at least of nationals, to hold the national currency.

On the other hand, this was accompanied by a mounting government debt, even when such transfers were effected at concessionary terms. But mounting government indebtedness indicates to those who hold claims payable in the currency of the country concerned or are considering doing so that the interests of the owners of wealth are not safeguarded in this country. The budget deficit, secured externally by a transfer, has, in monetary terms, an expansionary effect, the ensuing price rises depreciate the nominal claims payable in this currency. From this result the effects on price level and exchange rate neglected by "gap theorists". A transfer of resources supporting this development will undermine confidence in the currency concerned. Any political conflict with the donor countries can lead to an exodus from this currency, since this would threaten to destroy the basis on which confidence has rested.

As regards the commodity markets, a transfer of resources means an increase in the overall monetary demand in that it makes possible a persistent excess demand for foreign exchange - which, in turn, will be likely to crowd out domestic production. This depends, among other things, on the response of domestic monetary policy: when it seeks to counter the expansionary impulse stemming from a resource transfer by means of restrictive measures, the macroeconomic process gives rise to a crowding-out effect. There is, in addition, the direct crowding-out effect resulting from import competition, which can spell the end of domestic producers (Shaw 1973, pp. 214f.).

The expansionary impulse stemming from a resource transfer finds external expression in a deficit in the balances of trade and current account. The import of capital leads to commodity imports, and not the other way around, as the neoclassical and post-Keynesian schools contend. For what is paid for is not, in keeping with a barter logic, what must be imported for reasons of efficiency or for structural requirements; what can be imported in monetary economies is restricted to what can be paid for. If, seen in these terms, a causal relation can be established at all between the two balances, the direction of the causality runs from capital account transactions to the current-account balance (Böhm-Bawerk 1914). Any closing of the foreign-exchange gap would then, however, amount to casting out the devil by Beelzebub.

The current-account deficit has conventionally been explained with the necessity of importing technology and capital goods. It must be noted with Lüken-Klassen/Betz (1989, pp. 243f.) that, in a monetary economy, "*it is not the physical productivity, but the productivity of technologies in value terms that decides on their implementation*". When, however, the exchange rate is overvalued, the price of technology imports is always favorable. A resource transfer thus brings about a "wrong" choice of technologies in the twofold sense that it sustains the price relevant for this choice, the exchange rate, at an overvalued level and furthermore makes it possible to finance the import of such technologies. Viewed in even more general terms, the following may be concluded: a macro-economic reason for the use of non-adapted technologies lies in a weak currency that is sustained by resource transfers.

Finally, the weakness of newly created currencies has also made it more difficult to satisfy the surplus demand for foreign exchange via the market, i.e. by achieving foreign exchange revenues through exports. Furthermore, this requires a net export surplus and not, as traditional foreign-trade theory would have it, an even balance of trade. In view of the export structure held over from the colonial period, however, an export surplus would have to be accomplished largely by means of traditional exports in accordance with existing comparative advantages. What characterizes these exports is that they are subject to sizable price fluctuations and run into low demand elasticity levels. To move away from this division of labor, which offered as little promise to the producers as it did to the economy as a whole, the measures required included extensive investment aimed at altering the traditional features of comparative advantage. Apart from this, tariff policy was needed to create the relevant incentives for structural change.

An export orientation meaningful in terms of development policy is thus reliant on investment. In view of the currency weakness that must - as was argued above - be presupposed, an export surplus can be achieved only by lowering the wages paid in export production and not by strategic devaluation. Yet low-wage employment does not necessarily create development, but is likely to be low-wage assembly work for the industrialized nations. This link between exports and investment points to the fact that outward constitution is an essential contributing factor toward *inward constitution*.[30] For investment aimed at increasing value added in exports implies the formation of productive real assets, which must necessarily go hand in hand with the formation of financial assets.

What is meant here by the problem of internal constitution is: claims payable in domestic currency must increasingly replace tangible assets as an investment so as in this way to achieve a division of labor between producers and households, a concentration of capital accumulation (World Bank 1989, p. 31). This process of inward constitution, through which nominal assets are established as an alternative to tangible assets for the storage of value, is analogous to outward constitution, which succeeds when the domestic demand for foreign exchange is substituted in favor of claims denominated in domestic currency.

That the storage of value in tangible assets must be reduced while simultaneously increasing the share of nominal assets is a fact resulting historically from the circumstance that modern monetary economies emerge from primarily agricultural economies. In preindustrial economies in general, in the former colonial nations in particular, land functioned not only as a resource in production, but also as a store of value or means of asset formation. This double function of land can hamper its productive use since in this way an exploitable resource is "misappropriated" for the purpose of securing and increasing wealth. The difference in the two "uses" is evident in the fact that in production value is created by extensive or intensive processing, while value created due to the asset function of land may result from a mere change in the willingness to hold a scarce stock as compared with possible substitutes. In as much as the stock of land is a quantity more or less fixed by natural circumstances, accumulation, as opposed to cultivation, tends to come about only through an increase in the price component of land value, and not through its quantity component. The detrimental consequence of this may amount, literally, to cutting the ground from under the feet of agricultural production, since the returns yielded by price increases can no longer be earned by cultivating the land.

In other words, one important element of an expanding monetary economy is that the productive households in the agricultural sector more and more choose different media for forming tangible assets as producers and for generating wealth as households. The accumulation of wealth by holding financial claims promises higher liquidity, transaction-related advantages such as better divisibility, and the claim to a current income from interest. The claim to interest is itself a dynamic factor of a monetary economy as opposed to an agricultural economy organized along feudal lines. All production is in that case subject to the stipulation that it serve to increase wealth in the amount of the surplus income earned. The feudal mode of production entails no such condition but is, instead, marked by quantitative reproduction of stocks.

Outward constitution can be assigned a date, i.e. a point in time at which a sovereign currency was proclaimed and from which sovereignty will then have to be verified in economic terms. It does not appear to be possible to date inward constitution in this way. It takes place as a continuous transition from the money-using economy to the monetary economy. The formal characteristic specified for the latter was the institutionalization and economic functionalization of money as a public good. It was in this way, to put it in Keynesian terms, that the *conditions for the liquidity premium* were created. As the "medium of deferred payment" it then limits overall economic production by restricting the lending of the banks to the measure that allows them to maintain their liquidity at any given macroeconomic level of credit relative to the supply of money. In this respect it is the supply of the public good money, and not, as in neoclassical general equilibrium theory, the initial allocation of resources, that defines the budget constraint of the market system (Riese 1989, pp. 20f.).

The transition from the liability-based society of a money-using economy to the credit-based economy of a civil society is, as was indicated in 1.3, fraught with socio-cultural implications.[31] In view of the resistance to be expected, it would appear inappropriate to regard the expansion of monetary relations and the rise of a national economy based on a monetary budget constraint in merely evolutionary terms.

The use of money to fulfill social obligations or in trade showed no natural tendency at all to spread to the sphere of production as a whole (Kindleberger 1984, pp. 180f.). In primarily agricultural economies it can, instead, lie in the interest of potential creditors, i.e. land owners, and potential debtors, i.e. their tenants, to avoid monetary relationships. The extreme variant of this consists in restricting production to the subsistence level, i.e. to prevent from the very start the emergence of creditor-debtor relationships so as to avoid the risk of loss of wealth or sanctions threatened in cases of overindebtedness. Other possibilities would be to replace the contracts of a liability-based economy that require performance in money with feudal relations of dependence in the broadest sense. An obvious reason for this, and one equally valid for both contracting parties, could be to seek to avoid the insecurity stemming from the monetary exploitation of production. Advances of money, production for an anonymous market, and the turning of the products to account it in this market necessarily constitute an intertemporal process in which the basis on which decisions were first taken may change in the course of the process. Feudal services and transactions do not necessarily have an intertemporal character of this sort: if, to take the standard example from the literature on traditional agriculture, tenant and land owner agree to share-cropping, the liability-based relationship begins and ends when the crop is harvested. If work is agreed upon within the scope of feudal relations, which as a rule include the cession of land, the liability-based relationship is permanent and decoupled from the actual market performance of the party obliged to serve.

If, consequently, no tendency toward the development of a monetary economy can be identified, it would seem appropriate to look for measures intentionally taken to promote development in this direction. In the last section, governments were named as a key actor in this respect. Monetary economy appears to have been a means to the end of meeting the financial needs of the modern nation state or of realizing the modernization interests of infant nations following their independence. The pressures exercised by government toward the development of a monetary economy were, to be sure, always linked to the interests of particular social groups, like merchants, the urban trades, or industry.

One proved means of forcing private individuals to produce for the market, and thus to secure payment in money, was to levy taxes payable in currency instead of taxes in kind (Tilly 1975, p. 53; Ardant 1978, pp. 575ff.). This not only forced commercialization of agricultural production, but in many nations led to a further development of the legal prerequisites for a monetary economy: surveying land ownership for taxation purposes led to the keeping of land registry records on the basis of which land ownership could be used to secure loans and land became transferable.[32]

Governments were able to exercise additional, though indirect, pressure toward production under monetary conditions by fostering the development of a financial system in connection with its capital borrowing, although in doing so its debts often had a ruinous impact on the evolving system. This is bound to happen when a government no longer assumes the position of a net creditor. However, the emission of government bonds may also deepen and broaden an emerging capital market. Helping in this way to diminish volatility, government contributes to diminishing any reticence toward the formation of financial assets. For those who take advantage of these opportunities, for example wealthy private citizens and protobanks in the form of wholesale merchants, this may provide incentives to subordinate their economic activities to a uniform and coherent financial rationale. When they begin to pay money for work or demand money for rents, this forces broad segments of the population to offer goods and services in exchange for money. Above all, cash payment for labor is crucial to the emergence of the monetary income cycle.

The question as to whether and how this promotion of a monetary economy resulting from the state's financial needs necessarily ended up in industrial capitalism may remain open at this point. It was in any case with an eye to the industrialized nations that the newly independent countries, including the Latin American nations, wanted to accelerate their own industrialization. This is evident not least in considerably higher investment rates, which, despite all due skepticism about data from the nineteenth century, appear to be indisputable.[33]

The resultant requirements for long-term finance had already proven a great challenge to the industrializing nations of Europe. The governments of the countries developing in England's wake tried to meet this challenge by participating directly in banks and enterprises, supporting the establishment of investment banks, promoting the universal banking system, which might sometimes be referred to as toleration of close arrangements between banks and large-scale industry (Gerschenkron 1962, pp. 11ff.). The latter has even taken on institutionalized forms in Asian countries: conglomerates combining industrial and banking functions emerged, like, for instance, the "managing agencies" in colonial India (Goldsmith 1983a, pp. 53 - 56), the "zaibatsus" in Japan (Goldsmith 1983, p. 62), the "chaebols" in South Korea.

Only limited division of labor between government and private sector on the one hand and industry and financial sector on the other shows how precarious a problem is posed by the long-term financing of production processes like those characteristic of modern monetary economies. The internalization of market relations in the firm[34] is particularly symptomatic for the fact that industrialization along the lines of liberal doctrine is hardly possible.

The commitment of the governments of the new nations seeking to accelerate industrialization was accordingly far-reaching. It was noted above that resource transfers from the North enabled them to ease their role as tax creditor vis-à-vis the private sector. In accordance with their modernization interests, they created other pressures towards a monetary economy, although this was rarely the outright objective of the measures taken: industrial policy was intended to give rise to a sector employing wage labor and generating capital; land reform, later the "green revolution", were intended to promote modernization in the sense of commercializing agricultural production; agricultural policy, which forced farmers to sell to state agencies, was intended to set the stage for market production in agriculture, for low real wages - and thus for expansion - in the sector employing wage labor; finally, the so-called financial infrastructure was to be expanded so as to involve as many population groups as possible in the emerging monetary economy via an increased supply of financial services.

But this contrived establishment of monetary economies led to persistent problems. One severe dysfunctionality of the "compulsion to form a monetary economy" was that the governments ended up in the position of net debtors to the private sector. This made it unattractive to hold claims payable in national currency, or had to be made attractive by means of sizable guarantees and interest payments. This additionally exacerbated the budget problem. The manifest expression of this was the permanent risk of inflation going as far as the erosion of the national monetary system. The consequence was at times a degeneration of monetary development in the sense that a foreign currency became the domestic standard of value, entailing a drop in the share of production meant for sale for domestic currency. The problems of constitution changed into symptoms of a persistent dilemma of development under monetary conditions.

2.2   The Dilemma of Development under Conditions of a Monetary Economy

The problems involved in constitution, it was argued, consist for developing monetary economies in having to establish the national currency as the base for portfolio decisions against both other currencies and tangible assets. It is thus a prerequisite of development in a conventional sense, i.e. dynamic income generation and enhancement of productive capacities. The sequence of the argument presented in the last section will now be reversed with the aim of discussing, to start with, monetary income generation, which again picks up on the problem of internal constitution. The characteristics of emerging monetary economies will be considered here to the extent that they can be formulated theoretically. The dilemma of development under monetary conditions will be discussed in a second step; it can take on drastic forms in the latent contradiction between dynamic income generation and a viable foreign exchange position. To this extent, the following section proceeds from the problem of external constitution and attempts to explain why the imperative of modernization, as it was understood in the context of the Truman Declaration, conflicts with the necessity of a national currency to assert itself against other currency areas.

Monetary Income Generation

In a monetary economy based on division of labor, the actors can be assigned different functions. Income generation as a process and outcome of the interaction of markets results from the respective dispositions of these actors. This is the reason why the various functions and rationales of action will first have to be addressed. An actor may as a person, it is true, assume a number of functions. But this section will largely abstract from this aspect. As long as nothing else is stated, an actor will be identified with specific functions in the monetary market system. The problems of development under monetary conditions will then be recognized as grounded in individual constellations of interests. It can also be shown that financial relationships can themselves be shaped in such a way as to permit contracting parties to pursue extensively differentiated rationales.

The concept of the liability-based economy as well as the make-up of modern monetary economies suggests identifying four *prototypic actors of income generation*: the central bank and the commercial banks, whose interaction determines the money supply, and the households and enterprises, which in the end hold the titles to national economic wealth. For the reasons explained below, it makes sense to subsume the commercial banks under the general concept of portfolio or wealth holders and to class the households, on the other hand, as portfolio or wealth owners.

In an integrated monetary economy adequately differentiated into complementary production and consumption units, these four roles appear to represent a cast sufficient to demonstrate the fundamental creditor-debtor relationships involved in income generation. This is not enough to do justice to emerging monetary economies. It was noted in connection with the problem of internal constitution that, for evident reasons, in preindustrial economies there is not, or need not be, any motivation for a proliferation of monetary relations. Historically, the state was thus the driving force that, as it were, first coerced its subjects to produce in a mode geared to money earnings, and then also to create the fundamental conditions for a monetary economy developing with a dynamic of its own. This makes it necessary to consider at least two further actors, i.e. the government and the firm-households (McKinnon 1973) or productive households typical of preindustrial economies.

In functional terms, the actors can be described as follows:[35]

-    The central bank has the task of issuing that means of payment which is the legal tender in a national economy. For the purpose of the present study it will suffice to impute to it an objective geared to self-preservation. This preservation of itself, the central bank, as an institution is tied to the acceptance of the money issued by it. Acceptance implies that income generation proceeds on the basis of contracts whose definitive medium of performance is the domestic currency. To achieve this, wealth owners must be ensured that they can reasonably protect assets and returns on them through nominal contracts instead of alternative investments. As will be explained below, this requires a hierarchy of the scarcity of money advanced for production over against the resources that must be acquired for that purpose. A central bank must therefore maintain this hierarchy of contrived scarcity, if need be even against the otherwise sanctioned interests of private parties in the market. As a state institution it can formulate this objective without regard to its liquidity or considerations of profitability: it can accept that, in connection with a tight money supply, its claims may in part become uncollectible when banks are forced to close for reasons of illiquidity. To be able to exercise a constraint of this sort, it must be a creditor, not only in formal terms, but in material terms as well. When it enforces its claims they must be extinguished either by redemption or through the bankruptcy of the debtor concerned. That prohibits in particular a persistent acquisition of public debt securities because the public debtor is very limited in its capacity to declare bankruptcy. Furthermore, a restrictive course aimed at sustaining the hierarchy of monetary and resource stringency requires that the central bank's claims be, on the average, of shorter term than those of the rest of the economy. Only in this case are banks unable to acquire liquidity more quickly than it can be withdrawn from them by the central bank. An important consequence of this is that the institutional mix of central-bank and development-bank functions is extremely problematical in that the term structure of assets associated with the latter jeopardizes any effective monetary policy.

It may thus be noted that the asset side of a central bank balance contains short-term claims that, in accounting terms, reflect the money supply on the liabilities side.

- Banks and financial intermediaries, referred to here as portfolio holders, can be identified by the criterion of their "access to the central bank's discount window". They borrow in order to lend, i.e. to contract profitable claims.[36] This results in the risk of illiquidity mentioned in 1.3, for from a microeconomic angle, claims on others must in principle be classified as less safe than one's own liabilities. After all, the legal system of a monetary economy is able to call to account the defaulting debtor, but not to compensate creditors for their losses. If this were not the case, banks would hardly feel a microeconomic constraint to stabilize the hierarchy of advances of money over against the resources available via their own lending policy. - The portfolio holders can enhance their liquidity through measures which tend to diminish profitability. These include in particular the holding of (non-interest-bearing) precautionary funds and a fine-tuning of claims and liabilities aimed at safeguarding liquidity, which lowers their interest margin. It follows from what has been said about the claim structure of central banks that banks are forced to refinance their own credits with the central bank at terms shorter than those at which they lend. They can diminish the degree of risk to their liquidity by refinancing from deposits. The better they succeed in doing so, the longer, *ceteris paribus*, the terms will be at which loans can be provided to enterprises. - One final circumstance resulting from the fact that portfolio holders are at the same time creditors and debtors is that they are affected only marginally by depreciations of holdings due to inflation. In an inflation process, their claims and their liabilities are depreciated equally.[37]

Seen merely in terms of balance, it may be said by way of summary that the ideal-type of the portfolio-holder's asset side displays a precautionary fund of central bank money and claims covering the entire spectrum of terms. The liability side shows the short-term liabilities due to the central bank and longer-term liabilities due to the portfolio owners.

-    Enterprises are the prototypic debtors of the income-generation process. They contract a liability - in the case of self-finance, with themselves[38] - with an eye to turning production to profitable account. Keynes (1936, pp. 135ff.) gave these profit expectations, which determine the advance of money for production, a price-theoretic expression, the "marginal efficiency of capital." It is determined as the internal rate of interest on an investment by discounting the expected returns from the price of the investment goods to be acquired. Comparison of the expected rate of profit with the prevailing interest rate yields the basis on which the decision is made whether or not it is worthwhile to incur debts in order to go into production. It is thus determined neither by the classical accumulation instinct nor by the neoclassical desire for future consumption. Rather, enterprises in a monetary economy weigh off the possible increment to assets against the threat of a loss of assets if their investment expectations are not fulfilled but the debt incurred has to be honored. Since the investing enterprise assumes the position of a debtor, price rises ease the refunding of the money advanced, including the surplus of interest and profit earnings. It thus follows from the Keynesian investment rationale that decisions taken by business foster a cumulative process of rising prices. And in the face of given expectations as to price changes, it makes no difference whether these decisions are made in terms of real or nominal calculations (Heering 1991, pp. 94ff.).

The asset side of a business account thus contains the value of tangible assets reflected on the other side by liabilities with terms as long as possible. Short-term liabilities may also be used to bridge over excess expenditure.

-   Households are considered here in their specific function of portfolio owners. They are, in complement to the business sector, the prototypic creditors in the process of income generation.[39] Their titles of ownership my be held in tangible or financial assets. As regards financial assets, they also face the question as to the currencies in which they should be denominated. These portfolio decisions were discussed above as the two aspects of the problem of constitution. The formation of industrial capital, however, requires that not only financial but also long-term financial claims be held. In functioning monetary economies, these end up with the portfolio owners in that banks or portfolio holders considering their liquidity position seek to prevent the degree of maturity transformation from rising too high. It thus appears plausible on theoretical grounds, again in developed financial systems, to assume that the portfolio owners would not have to worry about repayment of outstanding claims, while the portfolio holders must bear this risk (Lüken-Klassen/Betz 1989, p. 222). Deposit insurance systems do permit such a differentiation of constraints on microeconomic choices. Since insurance guarantees deposits when a bank collapses, the threat of illiquidity due to uncollectible claims is no longer of decisive significance. Instead, the depreciation of long-term claims through inflation is the criterion that can force portfolio owners to cease holding financial claims. In less developed financial systems, the uncertainty whether liquidity can be restored through repayment in due time course is, to be sure, a significant determinant of the decision-making process. If this causes the portfolio owners to reduce the claims they hold in financial form, this potentially restricts the formation of tangible assets that can be accomplished without any weakening of the currency. Investment in long-term government bonds thus functions as a substitute for deposit insurance which is hardly feasible in a developing country. This, however, fulfills its function of raising the volume of financial claims toward the end of forming tangible assets only when government does not accumulate an unmanageable debt burden in the process. This amounts to cutting off development possibilities just as in the case in which there is from the very outset a lack of willingness to hold nominal claims.

When the process of monetary income generation is functioning, the balance of the portfolio owners displays on the asset side long-term claims and, possibly, cash holdings to finance transactions. This is reflected by the net worth on the liabilities side.

-    For the purposes of this study, government as the executive organ of the state is seen as a single coherent actor. In contrast to a central bank, it may not to be treated purely along the lines of a self-preserving institution. Instead, it is defined in relation to other political entities, in this case in relation to other currency areas. The constitution and integration of a national economy was, both for the modern European states and for the nations that became independent in the postwar period, the means of developing a national identity.[40] This concept of the state, viewed here only in its economic function, might be termed mercantilistic. It differs from welfare-economics and more recent politicoeconomic views that discuss it as a grand householder or as a profit-maximizing firm. In contrast, the mercantilist state has genuinely political rationales and hence an instrumental relationship to the economy. It is this that makes it possible to introduce the government as a unique actor forced to pursue its goals under specific constraints. - As was mentioned above in connection with the "pressures to form a monetary economy", government as a tax-collector assumes the position of a creditor. Accordingly, it switches into the debtor role when its spending exceeds the tax claims that can be enforced. It was just pointed out that in underdeveloped financial systems long-term government bonds can represent the primary long-term investment opportunity. But the uncertainty of those who hold claims, possibly to be compensated by a sovereign debtor, reflects at the same time the uncertainty of expected returns on investments. In other words, for the long-term government debt to represent a functional equivalent for financial relations that support development, it must be employed toward the end of long-term capital accumulation. The government can in this way assume a twofold role vis-à-vis the households, i.e. that of the portfolio holders and that of the enterprises. But what enables it to achieve this functional link, its sovereign position as a debtor, can also result in severe functional disorders. This will be discussed in the following section.

The state's particular status is clearly expressed in its balance. On the asset side is money for transaction purposes that it can procure directly with the central bank, plus tangible assets. The latter corresponds to long-term indebtedness and the net worth on the liabilities side.

–   What will be designated here as productive households are units that make up the basic form of organization in predominantly agricultural, pre-industrial economies. In as much as they reproduce under the conditions of a pure subsistence economy, their accumulation of tangible assets is restricted to their capacity to generate net worth. It thus presupposes the deferred consumption that economic textbooks still impute to investors in general. At any rate, this constraint can explain a disproportionate dynamic of income generation between these units representing, in the broadest sense, the traditional sector and enterprises in the formal sector. - In partially monetized market conditions, units of this type are for the most part given only short-term credit because their limited production for the market decouples the connection between indebtedness and advance of money for market production, which is supposed to serve to refund the advance. In other words, even in this case long-term capital accumulation is possible only to a limited extent for such units, since it is associated with a high risk. Maturity transformation has in the end to be effected by the borrower himself. - Aside from this threat of illiquidity resulting from integration into the monetary economy, the impact of depreciating nominal assets is of specific significance for such productive households. On the one hand, depreciation provides relief for them as debtors, if higher costs can be passed on in market prices. On the other hand, depreciation of financial assets means, conversely, an appreciation of their property as a productive unit generating tangible assets. Accordingly, these two effects of inflation tend in opposite directions as regards their integration into the monetary economy. The former may be beneficial to the extent that the marketability of their products permits higher costs to be passed on or that the depreciation of their debts does not lead, retroactively, to higher interest. The second effect tends more in the direction of a withdrawal from the monetary

economy. After all, productive households are not under all circumstance reliant on achieving monetary earnings.

On the asset side, the balance of a productive household accordingly
displays tangible assets corresponding to short-term liabilities or
purely net worth on the liabilities side.

Leaving out the foreign sector, creditor-debtor relations of an emerging monetary economy can be depicted as follows:

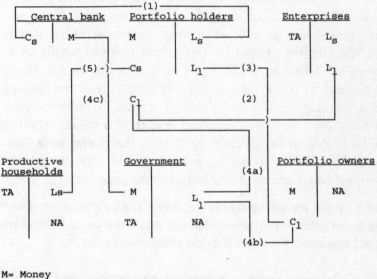

M= Money
C_s, C_l = short- and long-term claims
L_s, L_l = short- and long-term liabilities
TA, NA= tangible assets, (net worth) net assets

Reduced to its elementary processes, income generation in an economy of this type can be described as follows:

(1) Part of the portfolio holders can take on debts with the central
    bank so as to procure the money required to provide loan.

(2) In the most favorable case, they will pass on this short-term refinance as long-term credit to enterprises.[41]

(3) Income is generated in the production process financed from (2); part of this income is saved by the households, in general terms: the portfolio owners, so as to accumulate wealth in this way. In the simplest case this is done via saving deposits in the banking sector, which enables the sector to refinance its loans on a long-term basis.

(4) The accumulation of wealth can, however, also proceed via investment in government bonds. When portfolio holders invest in this way for commercial reasons and not as the result of government decree, this is reflected in their assessment of the investment opportunities offered by enterprises: (4a) can wholly or in part replace relationship (2), in the most favorable case it simply supplements it. It may also reflect low credibility of the banking system in the eyes of portfolio owners, so that (3) is virtually replaced by (4b). Finally, the special feature of a public debtor is that he is able to obtain cash credit from the central bank (4c). Longer-term loans, on the other hand, would conflict with the functional requirements of monetary income generation.

(5) Finally, some income generation comes about as a result of short-term loans provided by money-lenders and other portfolio holders to the productive households in the traditional sector.[42]

Reducing the income generation process to *elementary debtor-creditor relationships* can demonstrate that what is required to proceed with a production process is an advance of money and credit. It is not deferred consumption in the form of savings (Preiser 1963, pp. 65-81). Savings are always income that is not consumed, and it therefore seems implausible to place them at the beginning of the process in which income, as a result, is to emerge in the first place.[43] An analogous argument can be opposed to the classical hypothesis that investment stems from retained profits, deferred consumption on the part of the entrepreneurs. Retained profits also represent a category of income.

Savings of households and business profits are a reflection of investments and, in open economies, of exports as well, the two income-generating categories.[44] It is therefore not possible for higher interest, as McKinnon (1973) and Shaw (1973) argue on a theoretical level, to induce greater savings or any internal accumulation of funds. If, by impeding investment, higher interest rates lead to a decline of accumulation, then the share of income not consumed is likewise bound to decline. The capacity to save would diminish given a constant propensity to save. Only behavioral assumptions impossible to ground at the theoretical level can then give rise to an increasing propensity to save, e.g. for reasons of providing for sustenance during a recession.[45] A rationale that may be formulated on theoretical grounds is, however, that the form in which savings are accumulated is bound to change when interest rates rise. In that case, for reasons of opportunity costs, savings in financial form or a financial investment of retained profits become more attractive than, for instance, investing in real estate or office equipment.

Theoretical considerations of the income cycle thus suggest placing a loan at the beginning of income generation in that a loan can emerge from the "*creatio ex nihilo*" of an expanding money supply. Portfolio holders or banks assume a strategic role in this. The volume of credit is determined by their readiness to take on debts, in this case: to refinance the credit from the central bank at the prevailing rate of interest in assessing profitable investments. This double credit relationship finally depends on money issued by the central bank in that the legal tender is the definitive means for performing contracts. The central bank can keep the currency so tight that no such credit relationship comes about: because the potential borrower is unwilling to contract the debt at the higher rate of interest or, as Stiglitz/Weiss (1981) have noted, because the lender is unwilling to believe that the potential borrower will be able to repay the loan at this rate of interest.

Individual dispositions with respect to asset markets rely on the macroeconomic setting, for they have to be realized within the *system of interacting markets*. In emerging monetary economies, this system may be incomplete or fragmented. But as was argued with respect to weak currencies in a portfolio-theoretic framework (chapter 2), the frame of reference of an integrated economy can nevertheless provide important insights into the obstacles to income generation generated in this way.

In commodity markets, the expectations of portfolio holders and enterprises imply that they count on a formation of prices that will ensure their profits. They achieve this both macroeconomically and with regard to each segment of the commodity market system by keeping the nominal advances tighter than the labor and resources required for the process of production. Otherwise, at a given price level the cost pressure would absorb the surplus earnings included in the sales prices. This constellation characterizes, as will be discussed in the next section, a situation of full employment in which the monetary authorities have the will to sustain a stable price level. Such a case illustrates what was expressed above in formal terms: in a monetary economy the volume of nominal advances, i.e. the credit based on central-bank money, constitutes the budget constraint of the market system. It is neither the manpower available, as in classical economics, nor, as in neoclassical economics, the stocks of resources available, given the willingness of the resource labor to defer consumption and leisure.

In this sense underemployment is the prevailing condition of a monetary economy. But if underemployment is widespread, nominal wages cannot follow a purely competitive principle, since market forces could not ensure that wages would remain above the subsistence level or that the onset of cumulative deflationary processes would be prevented. To this extent, collective representations of the labor supply, such as trade unions or minimum-wage regulations, are not market imperfections in principle but elements of the monetary market system which can be explained in functional terms (Riese 1986, pp. 33ff. and 161f.). This is of course not to rule out the possibility that wage demands, enforceable with institutional backing of this sort, may have destabilizing effects or restrain development.

The hierarchy of asset market, commodity market, and labor market - each understood as the macroeconomic aggregate of respective single markets - can be focused even more exactly.[46] As mentioned above, production is proceeded with only when enterprises or portfolio holders, in view of their credit demands, can count on a formation of prices that will ensure their normal profits. In macroeconomic terms, these expectations to be fulfilled require determination of a price level which permits, on the average a realization of profits. When this is derived formally, it once again becomes apparent why lack of savings, understood here as deferred consumption on the part of households, can never prevent production from proceeding in a monetary economy.

The simplest form of an income-expenditure model - it will be extended presently - is the following one:[47]

(1) $Y = P \cdot y$ (income corresponds to value of aggregate product)

(2) $Y = W + Q$ (income is distributed across wage and surplus earnings)

(3) $Y = C + I$ (income spent corresponds to value of demand for consumption and investment goods in the model of a closed economy without government)

(4) $Y = C + S$ (income is used for consumption and non-consumption)

Y = nominal income, P = price level, y = real income,

W = wage sum, Q = surplus earnings

C = value of demand for consumption goods

I = value of demand for investment goods

S = value of non-consumption, savings in the broader sense

The second two equations have of course been used to infer that $S = I$ constitutes an identity. That is true if S is interpreted not as deferred consumption at given prices but as the value of non-consumption necessarily corresponding to the demand for investment goods. But how is this correlation achieved in the market process? What happens if the value of voluntarily deferred consumption, savings in the narrower sense of the term, is lower than the sum of investment made by the business sector? In the commodities markets this will, at given prices, then entail excess demand. The prices will thus rise and create the correlation of income and spending required ex post, i.e. of consumption and non-consumption as represented by goods and income shares respectively (Keynes 1930, Ch.18).

In such a market situation of global excess demand, windfall profits Q' accrue to the business sector. As can be inferred from this, an investment does not even subsequently require consolidation via additional savings if it is concomitant with a macroeconomic expansion of the money and credit supply. Windfall profits realized due to a jump in the profit-price level P' can just as well bring about the identity of investment and non-consumption required to fulfill the macroeconomic balance identity.

Yet it is not only a discrepancy between S and I that leads to such windfall profits, but net aggregate demand from abroad and from the government budget as well. The aggregate value of goods sold must in the end exceed the wage and surplus earnings $(W + Q)$ formed or counted on in production by this additional demand, which in turn comes about via price adjustment. The windfall profits can accordingly be formulated as:

(5) $Q' = I\text{-}S + Ex\text{-}Im + G\text{-}T$

$Q' =$ windfall profits, $Ex =$ exports, $Im =$ imports,

$G =$ government spending, $T =$ government revenues, i.e. taxes

$S =$ savings in the sense mentioned, i.e. deferred household consumption

The transformation shows that available savings cannot restrain the process of income generation. It arises together with windfall profits as a reflection of the net demand of actors whose income does not correspond to an advance for domestic production.

(5') $S+Q' = I + Ex\text{-}Im + G\text{-}T.$

If planned savings correspond exactly to planned investment, the equilibrium price level, i.e. a price level at which enterprises on average realize their expected profits, must be determined as follows:

(6) $P \cdot y = W + Q$

$$P = \frac{w \cdot L + r \cdot K}{y}$$

$$P = w \cdot \frac{L}{y} + \frac{Q}{y}$$

w = nominal wage rate, L = employed labour

r = nominal profit rate, K = advance for means of production

Since L/y is the reciprocal value of labor productivity a and profits are calculated in relation to unit labor costs (as the approximate value for the advance) the price level at which normal profits are realized is

$$(7)\, P = \frac{w}{a} \left[1 + \frac{Q}{W} \right]$$

from: $P = w \cdot \frac{L}{y} \left[1 + \frac{1}{w} \cdot \frac{y}{L} \cdot \frac{Q}{y} \right]$

If excess demand fueled and made effective by an increase in the money supply are now included, the price level is determined from:

$$(8) \quad P \cdot y + P' \cdot y = W + Q + Q'$$

$$P + P' = \frac{W + Q}{y} + \frac{Q'}{y}$$

$$= \frac{w}{a} + \frac{Q}{y} + \frac{I - S + Ex - Im + G - T}{y}$$

$$(9) \quad P + P' = \frac{w}{a}\left[1 + \frac{Q}{W}\right] + \frac{I - S + Ex - Im + G - T}{y}$$

This equation (9) will assume crucial significance for the dilemma of development under the conditions of a monetary economy to be discussed in the next section.[48]

The first component, resulting from w/a $(1 + Q/W)$, might be termed the "income-price level" P: if it is realized, wage income and nominal profits are generated as planned. The nominal wage level here indicates the lower boundary for entrepreneurial mark-up pricing, and from it results, macroeconomically, the price level. The mark-up, $Q/W = (r \cdot K)/W$, is determined in terms of the interest rate demanded by the asset market, which must at least compensate for the liquidity premium of the portfolio holders. To this extent, this mark-up is not an arbitrary extra profit resulting from an oligopolistic market position, but interest resulting from the contrived scarcity of advances and hence of production processes: $r = Q/K$.[49]

It is for this reason that the profit rate demanded and not the real wage rate is crucial for the decision to proceed with production. The real wages result from the interaction between commodity market and labor market, from the price level consistent with the interest rate required and the nominal wage rate negotiated in the labor market.

The second component in equation (9), which results from (I-S + Ex-Im + G-T)/y, may, analogously, be termed the "profit-price level" P', although the more correct term would be "windfall profit-price level". It is obviously increased by export surpluses and budget deficits. As will be discussed below, this may explain why persistent export surpluses are an unlikely market phenomenon. The price level increases associated with it finally undermine its own basis. That is the reason why specific economic-policy measures are required to sustain a market constellation geared to ensuring export surpluses. - This expression furthermore explains why budget deficits may have effects that stimulate accumulation: they generate extra profits. At the same time, however they display, in monetary respects, a destabilizing effect in terms of shifts in the price level. In debates on economic policy, one of these two effects is normally suppressed, depending on whether the person speaking is a fiscalist champion or a monetarist opponent of employment policies.

This is intended to close the discussion on what determines macroeconomically the realization of individual profits. In the aggregate, this requires a price level corresponding to the mark-up pricing of enterprises, which is only possible when the money supply is comparatively elastic. What remains to be said is a brief discussion of the individual economic decision-making process.[50]

The individual enterprise is faced with an interest rate or a nominal wage rate determined on the asset market and on the labor market. This may be termed the assumption of perfect competition in a theory of the monetary economy. This version of the competitive market assumption also presupposes that enterprises can practice mark-up pricing. The wage rate sets the lower boundary of the unit commodity price that must be achieved, the interest rate determines the required mark-up. On the basis of these data, an enterprise must determine its nominal advances for production, K_j, and select at this activity level a technology from the blueprints of available technologies that is geared to maximizing profits.[51] This formalization of the decision-making process means that suppliers themselves do have motives to enter finite markets. Expressed in terms of economic theory, they offer their products in markets in which they "are faced" with a falling revenue curve. It allows them to calculate the advance in such a way as to be able to realize the point on the curve compatible with the interest rate demanded.

The individual economic decision in favor of an investment is geared to achieving normal profits (see equation (7) above). That does not rule out a Schumpeterian pursuit of quasi-rents through innovation. But windfall profits are a macroeconomic phenomenon that cannot be planned for by an enterprise. That they emerge presupposes a shift of the price level which requires support through an additional supply of money if the credit multiplier is taken as given.

Individual profit to be realized obviously depends on the decisions of other investors. For the advances of money made by all enterprises determine the level of overall monetary demand, the volume of profit earnings, the level of employment, and the equilibrium rate of interest consistent with it.

Aggregate investments do not only have an income-generating effect in the current period, however, they also have a capacity effect in the medium-term. This hampers the realization of normal profits over time. The economic phenomenon of business cycles consists, among other things, in depreciating the stock of capital accumulated in past periods, which includes a reduction of physical capacities. This two-fold aspect of investment, i.e. of generating income and creating capacities, should be kept in mind for the later discussion on how much sense it makes for the government to strive for rapid industrial expansion.

The Dilemma of Stagnation and Erosion of a Monetary Economy

In the last section the process of monetary income generation was discussed in terms of the debtor-creditor relationships underlying it. In this way, one gains a specific focus on the problem of development under monetary conditions. Since these relations, constitutive for the generation of income, can meet the expectations placed in them only if macroeconomic conditions permit, monetary policy necessarily assumes a key role in the development process.

In a first step, it will be argued that income generation shows a tendency toward stagnation under market conditions typical for emerging monetary economies. There then follows a discussion of whether monetary policy, being in a position to influence the macroeconomic budget constraint, can counterbalance this endogenous weakness of income generation. This, finally, will lead to a depiction of the problems surrounding inflation and its tendency to lead into the erosion of a monetary economy.

The possibility, addressed at the end of the last section, that microeconomic rationales of action and macroeconomic conditions of realization may diverge can be observed frequently in emerging monetary economies. Development theory of a structuralist tinge has created a heightened awareness of the factors responsible for this (e.g. Shapiro/Taylor 1990, pp. 872f.): agricultural prices fluctuating due to climatic disturbances, shifting sales and procurement conditions, and economic-policy responses that can exercise an unpredictable influence on the underlying data. A low level of domestic market development entails among other things that producer returns may fluctuate very sharply. Even slight shifts in the number of suppliers or in effective demand can produce sharp effects if markets do not display a certain degree of breadth and depth. All of these features - imperfections when viewed from a model-based theoretical vantage point - exercise a disconcerting influence on lending and investment decisions since they create an element of uncertainty as to the recovery of the advances made, including normal interest.

This does of course not necessarily mean that in developing countries enterprises, or portfolio holders, achieve low returns "for structural reasons." It can, instead, be inferred both from the decision-making process outlined above and the equations denoting the price level that ensures profit-realization that, in principle, every interest rate demanded has a price level compatible with it. This depends on the ratio of surplus earnings to the funds advanced for wages and means of production. If the profit-taking price level, from the microeconomic angle: the relevant prices, cannot be expected to materialize, production will not proceed. There is no such thing as compulsion for full employment of resources or manpower potentials.

The result can be formulated as follows: at any given level of the nominal wages to be advanced, as the approximation value for the overall amount of nominal advances, the volume of investment will be lower than it would be if the uncertainty as to the reflux of payments were less pressing. The real wage incomes necessary to proceed with production are therefore also lower given the volume of advances and the surplus income demanded. If the creditors and the producers are extremely reticent, this can even mean that the real wages that result would have to fall below the subsistence level. Child labor, low worker life expectancy and the like are symptomatic of a market constellation of this sort. If it proves impossible to depress wages, then one strategic variable of an investor's decisions that remains is to so restrict production processes that investments made will at least bring in interest returns compensating for the liquidity premium.

In macroeconomic terms, this view focusing on the strategic role of portfolio holders and enterprises implies that income generation and employment will stagnate given the market conditions typical for emerging monetary economies. Stagnation may characterize a situation of market equilibrium. Having said this, it is important to note that government or foreign markets as sources of additional demand have been disregarded thus far. Identifying an *inherently stagnative tendency* is therefore tantamount to the proposition that it is highly unlikely in such countries that a self-supporting accumulation process will come about. A process of this sort would be fueled by windfall profits, which occur when a surplus ex ante of investments over savings accrues. In other words, since the condition of (Keynesian) investment is that profit-taking prices appear to be realizable, surpassing these expectations by means of Q' profits is bound to have a stimulating effect.[52]

The rise in income generation fueled by such profits implies an outward shift of the macroeconomic budget constraint. This presupposes a mounting volume of advances, i.e. aggregate real credit, which as a rule must be fed via an increase in the money supply. This link between accumulation and monetary policy gives rise to the question of its relation to the stagnation identified, i.e. whether it can contribute to overcoming stagnation or, indeed, to initiating a dynamic of its own.

Windfall profits are realized in the course of shifts in the price level. A *stability-oriented monetary policy* would therefore have to counteract the emergence of windfall profits. The rationale of such a monetary policy consists in creating the macroeconomic conditions for the competitiveness of national production by aiming for a stable exchange rate to ensure a rise in the price level lower than that occurring abroad. This would, by implementing an austerity policy having mercantilistic consequences, create a constellation entailing an undervalued exchange rate. However, the corresponding contraction of the money supply that might be prerequisite to achieve this end would have to force enterprises to accumulate unplanned-for stockpiles, to revise their original investment plans, and to accept "windfall losses".

A monetary policy of this sort will have ambiguous effects on government budget deficits, another potential source of excess demand and windfall profits. Stability-oriented monetary policy would, to be sure, hamper deficit financing in the current period and the one following, thus, in tendency, forcing the deficit down. But this could possibly be affected adversely by additional interest costs for the outstanding national debt and by sinking tax revenues, which would be likely to contribute to a rise in the budget deficit.

The only component of aggregate demand on which a restrictive course would have a definitely positive effect is exports. Foreign demand may compensate for the effects of a restrictive monetary stance to the extent that it outstrips domestic demand for foreign goods and services. A surplus of net exports, however, presupposes as more or less solved the constellation addressed here as problematical, i.e. the creation and maintenance of an undervalued exchange rate. An undervalued exchange rate may be characterized as a device for global protection, since it curtails the volume of import demand and enhances the competitiveness of the export supply. This characterizes a rather peculiar macroeconomic situation and cannot be taken as the standard case, as will be outlined below.

Given a typical developing country's in any case more fragile propensity to invest and its government budget problems, a monetary policy of this type would thus tend more to weaken accumulation and exacerbate the national debt. How sharply investment will drop,[53] depends on the possibilities of adjustment open to the producers. If productive capacities are developed, monetary discipline can force them to take measures aimed at increasing their earnings by shifting to production processes with higher value added. They can in this way come to terms with the aggravated commercial conditions they face. The adverse effects on the level of economic activity might thus remain within limits. If capacities are less developed, then the adjustment options open to them, e.g. organizational and technical rationalization, are restricted, however. In this case the obvious responses are pressure on wage earnings and discontinuation of production processes.

A stability-oriented monetary policy like that recommended by Friedman (1973) obviously has a quite different impact on economies at different stages of development. It may initiate in the one case a wave of innovation, while causing a depression in the other case (Riese 1989a, pp. 201f.). The impacts on enterprises and government outlined here may explain, among other things, why what is practised in developing economies is often not a stability-oriented monetary policy, but repression of inflationary tendencies, as will be argued at the end of this section.

In view of this state of affairs, it might be asked, conversely, whether monetary support of windfall profits, a *permissive monetary policy*, is sufficient to overcome weaknesses in accumulation. This at the same time implies asking where the surplus demand at given prices stems from. In this way the initial scenario is widened to include foreign nations and government as sources of aggregate demand. A permissive monetary-policy course would necessarily have the following impacts on the individual components (see equations (5) and (9) above).

$(I-S)/y > 0$:

It must first be asked where this constellation - referred to above as unlikely - may derive from. The *ex ante* divergence of investment rate and savings rate in the first place says nothing about their levels. At a very low level of financial savings, higher investment by no means indicates that stagnation in income generation has been overcome. Structuralist development economists have, with reference to the "savings gap", pointed to a low level of savings to explain the necessity of transfers of resources.

The analysis presented here more suggests tracing a low savings back to a low degree of acceptance of the domestic currency. Accordingly, a constellation of this sort would be expected precisely in an inflation process supported by a permissive monetary policy. After all, the medium-term capacity effect of investments resulting from this exerts pressure on normal profits. If, in other words, an *ex ante* investment surplus is the result of a constellation of this sort, what is indicated would not be a permissive money supply. It would result, as is explained below, in an erosion of the monetary economy concerned.

The criterion for an investment surplus relevant for development is its subsequent impact on labor productivity. That implies a development of productive capacities that lowers the income-price level and increases real wages in consequence of the macroeconomic process. It can, however, be ascertained only after the fact whether the advances are employed in this way and whether an income-generation process is developing which would give rise to endogenous technical progress. Monetary-policy support of such investments can have no influence on this in that its macroeconomic character makes it impossible to distinguish between desirable investments and immiserizing growth.

(Ex-Im)/y > O :

Foreign exchange revenues stemming from export surpluses trigger an expansive course of monetary policy when they become reserves with the central bank. In this way, however, they undermine, as was noted above, their own base. Price rises at a given exchange rate exacerbate a country's competitive position in the world market. A permissive monetary policy is thus hardly compatible with a market constellation of persistent export surpluses.

Instead, monetary policy can support such a constellation desirable in terms of development policy via strategic capital exports. An increase of the central bank's stocks of foreign exchange sustains undervaluation of the domestic currency by creating an "artificial" demand for foreign exchange. It must, however, at the same time neutralize the expansive monetary impulse caused by the increase in stocks of foreign exchange in order to prevent rises in price levels. In other words, any "stockpiling" of reserves has to be accompanied by a rise in the interest rate set by the central bank.

The possibility of pursuing an undervaluation strategy of this type does, however, depend on foreign exchange ending up with the central bank in the first place, instead of being privatized. It is precisely heavily indebted countries, i.e. economies which should be achieving sustained export surpluses, that are incapable of a strategy of this sort. The fragile acceptance of their national currency turns foreign exchange into a sought-after reserve media of the private sector. - A somewhat different problem, one relevant above all for middle-income countries, emerges from the circumstance that capital imports are attracted when it proves possible to sustain undervaluation and a stable price level. The emerging tendency toward appreciation of the exchange rate counteracts the current-account surplus.[54]

In sum, it is not an expansionary monetary policy feeding windfall profits from export surpluses that contributes toward overcoming weaknesses in accumulation. This is more the field of a mercantilist monetary policy that shapes the exchange rate and the price level in a way that favors exports by sterilizing the expansionary impulse stemming from influxes of foreign exchange. The export surplus can then support domestic market development by increasing the credibility of the domestic currency and creating latitude for imports relevant for development. Import-policy measures, in particular selective tariffs, must reinforce the latter effect by influencing relative import prices.

$(G-T)/y > 0:$

In principle, a budget deficit produces effects similar to those of a high level of domestic demand for consumption goods. It can improve the marginal efficiency of capital if it, as effective demand, has a favorable influence on investment prospects. This is, however, only true to the extent that the expansionary monetary course associated with it is not translated primarily into rising imports. The price-raising effects will additionally jeopardize the exportability of domestic products. A budget deficit thus tends in two ways to produce detrimental foreign trade effects tending to neutralize its stimulating potential. Moreover, if a budget deficit supported by monetary policy is linked with a current-account deficit, this is sure to jeopardize monetary stability. A continuous supply of domestic currency in the face of persistent demand for foreign exchange is bound to weaken the national currency. Even if portfolio preferences for domestic claims are taken as given, such claims will be subject to depreciation since claims payable in foreign exchange are increasingly sought after owing to their growing relative scarcity.

The preceding analysis interprets government demand as being equivalent to consumer spending in that it primarily affects profit expectations. It could be argued, however, that government spending G might also be employed for investment. This objection might be countered by claiming that government spending for investment is covered under I, while current expenditures are covered by G. But such a technical solution hardly provides a neat solution in that it is, at the least, faced with problems associated with obtaining adequate data in practice. What is even more dubious in this line of reasoning is that, in economics, it is not at all trivial to distinguish between government spending which adds to existing capital stock and government spending which serves consumption. This is particularly true when this distinction is made to condone the use of printing presses in the one case while damning it in the other. Government expenditures earmarked for investment, e.g. measures related to infrastructure or energy generation, must be qualified as consumption-related spending as long as they are not used to manufacture products capable of being sold in the world market. Thus a distinction as to whether government expenditures meant to be investment-related are G or I can be made only after the fact. It is a market result. For the reasons named, a monetization of budget deficits promotes their consumption-related character.

A permissive monetary policy thus hardly appears suited to provide effective support for income generation in emerging monetary economies. As regards investors, it will most likely support those who seek easy profits realized through continuously rising prices if the control exercised is not an effective one acting in favour of development policy. It furthermore jeopardizes the achievement of export surpluses and diminishes - partly as a consequence - the development potential of fiscal measures.

If, in other words, a monetary policy meant merely to support expansion gives rise to questionable effects, a *policy of easy money* would seem to offer even fewer prospects of initiating a process of real income generation. A weakness in accumulation is in the end caused by pessimistic expectations of returns on the part of investors. It must be assumed for methodological reasons that portfolio holders rate investment projects in roughly the same way as their potential borrowers. If the central bank eases refinancing for the banks in a situation marked by weakness in accumulation, this will do little to improve the quality of investment opportunities.

The liquidity preference theory of interest states that an expansionary monetary policy will by no means necessarily trigger a downward trend in interest rates. If banks prefer unqualified liquidity or are unwilling to assume the risk of losing assets due to lending, the more favorable refinancing may result in effects entirely different from those intended.

The banks will then, on the one hand, still have the option of counteracting the attempt to expand the money supply. They can simply use money offered at favorable terms to settle old liabilities with the central bank. This transformation would eliminate part of the old money stock, the supply of money outstanding would remain the same. This possibility of controlling an expansion of the money supply is, after all, the crucial feature of a two-tier system of liquidity supply: it provides the mechanism by which moneyed interests assert themselves. The money supply thus becomes endogenous to the extent that it is controlled by the liquidity preference of the portfolio holders, i.e. the banks (Lüken-Klassen/Betz 1989, p. 223).

On the other hand, an expansion of the money supply that in the end fails to diminish the liquidity preference or increase the marginal efficiency of capital will tend to weaken the currency. When a given portfolio mix is held voluntarily, an additional supply of domestic currency implies that it must be depreciated in relation to other portfolio components if it is to be absorbed. The extreme case is that favorable refinance of loans merely paves the way for a beneficial flight into tangible assets, which tends to drive prices up. Or it finances a flight of capital, which intensifies pressure on the exchange rate or fuels its overvaluation.

The *part played by monetary policy in the process of development and accumulation* can now be summarized as follows: its relevant use, i.e. its use in line with development policy, is precisely not to fuel unreservedly an accumulation process driven by shifts in the price level. Its relevant use aims, instead, at creating macroeconomic conditions favorable to making inroads into export markets and developing the domestic market. Exchange-rate stability is one of the most important conditions, though not one always within reach of monetary policy. This requires a tight monetary policy, which, however, calls for high standards of adaptability on the part of producers if it is not to stifle income generation. A monetary policy consistent with development under monetary conditions thus by no means facilitates this process. On the contrary, it is a conditioning factor of this process in addition to being bound up with issues of political legitimacy and sociocultural considerations. This is in the end only the consequence resulting from the fact that the money supply represents the budget constraint of the market system in a monetary economy, and not the lubricant of transactions in a barter economy.

The primary task of monetary policy becomes clearly evident in an inflation process. For inflation processes, it will be argued in what follows, tend to dissolve the debtor-creditor relationships constitutive for income generation and lead to an erosion of the monetary system. Nowhere else is the conditioning - i.e. the condition-imposing - role of monetary policy in the development process so manifest: constitution in the sense of acceptance of the national currency must be its primary objective, because the willingness to hold domestic financial claims is the *conditio sine qua non* of monetary development.

In the face of lingering erosion, one possibility of effecting a reduction of claims is to repress income generation. Such a halt to erosion is implied by the standard IMF package, although this is not conscious IMF policy. But repression is not necessarily adequate to establish the stock equilibrium of nominal holdings as required and may, as will be discussed below, even accelerate the erosion process. The alternative is a drastic incision into wealth of the sort represented by a currency reform.

In monetary economies, inflation is a phenomenon always present in latent form, i.e. present in the form of abetting factors that, however, must combine in specific ways in order to materialize. This is due, first, to the peculiar manner of dealing with quantitative shortages in a monetary economy. In the face of a tight supply of labor or resources, any attempt to secure normal returns on the nominal advances for production will lead to rising prices. These can, under conditions to be discussed below, trigger a process of inflation. If it proves possible to pass on rising prices and thus to secure claims to interest and profit, this does not necessarily entail a restriction of production. In a barter economy, a stringency of this type would have to diminish directly the physical or priced surplus.[55] It does, it is true, become more attractive to implement labor- and resource-saving technologies or to utilize sources not yet tapped to increase the supply when the "second" budget constraint of labor supply and resources becomes tighter in relation to the "first" budget constraint. This will be the response of enterprises if they do not succeed fully in passing on rising costs in higher prices. Apart from restriction of production, another possible adjustment strategy is to recruit labor from abroad and exploit as yet untapped primary resources.

A second reason for the pervasiveness of the phenomenon of inflation in monetary economies is closely linked with the first: if the primary factor restricting production is represented by advances of money, it then would appear simple to abrogate this restriction whenever the need occurs, until the second, quasi-natural, budget constraint makes itself felt. This consideration suggests itself in today's monetary economies, where the state issues a general means of payment as a public good. This seems to be an even more obvious option when a country's income level is low and a pressing need to expand production can be identified everywhere. A call to remove all monetary obstacles impeding the generation of income then sounds only too convincing. It is tantamount to a call for a policy of easy money. This, as was noted above, is restricted by decisions of portfolio owners relating to their asset holdings. If the money supply is increased to finance investment, they will have to hold this money voluntarily as the base of their nominal claims. The portfolio rationale per se always causes a weakening of the asset, e.g. currency, whose supply is in the process of being expanded relative to other assets.

This weakening is intensified when price effects gain prevalence vis-à-vis a quantitative expansion of production and employment in connection with an income generation stimulated by monetary means. After all, it does take more time to make labor and resources available or to raise their productivity than it does to make money and credit available. The fact that the second budget constraint takes on a more binding character in relation to the first finds expression in partial price rises that can result in a process of inflation. In this way, not only the asset market, but commodity and labor markets as well, generate monetary destabilization.

A final factor assuring the virulence of the phenomenon of inflation may be seen in the rationales of the actors themselves. In characterizing the actors, it was pointed out that neither enterprises nor portfolio holders experience direct negative effects from price rises. Not the enterprises, because they are debtors and have on the average better chances realizing their prices in an inflation process. Not the portfolio holders, because their claims depreciate no less than their liabilities, and in the face of higher prices their claims become more secure on the average. At best, indirect effects can cause a more reticent - and hence stabilizing - lending policy on the part of the portfolio holders. On the one hand, the depositors will shorten their deposit terms or even withdraw deposits, which, ceteris paribus, diminishes bank liquidity. They will presumably bear this in mind in their lending policies. On the other hand, the central bank must be expected to react during a process of inflation. Its restrictive policy can mean that the claims held by banks will become uncollectible. This anticipation can lead to cautious arrangements to the extent that, owing to it, the threat of illiquidity in connection with lending policy may at this point loom greater in the eyes of the banks. Both factors can, incidentally, explain why interest rates rise in connection with inflation.[56]

Apart from these indirect effects, however, the market position of enterprises or portfolio holders implies that price rises are for them beneficial or neutral and that the motives behind their activities will not run counter to a process of inflation. This aspect in the end provides the rationale of a state central bank that can counteract the endogenous tendency toward inflation without, like a commercial bank issuing notes, putting itself at risk.

If, in other words, there are at least three reasons for inflation to be virulent in all modern monetary economies - the specific modes in which they come to grips with shortages, their budget constraint, which is manipulable as a matter of principle, the rationales of their crucial actors - what has to be looked into is the conditions under which inflation is actualized. More precisely: under what conditions do rises in individual prices or shifts in the price level lead to a *process of inflation*? The theoretical problem involved in explaining this consists in indicating when rising prices lead to a continuous rise in price levels perpetuated in the market process (Riese 1986, pp. 82-84).

In keeping with the theory of income generation outlined in the last section, inflation can also be explained from the interaction of the investment, commodity, and labor markets. This can be demonstrated with the aid of equation (9), which will be cited here again:

$$(9) \quad P + P' = \frac{w}{a}\left[1 + \frac{Q}{W}\right] + \frac{I - S + Ex - Im + G - T}{y}$$

This equation breaks down the price level resulting in the commodities market into two components: the independent variables determining income component P are the nominal wage rate representing the labor market and the profit rate representing the asset market. Profit component P' reflects a high effective demand in the commodities market; it can be realized by providing additional finance.

Reference has already been made to the fact that a monetary budget constraint implies that labor and resources are normally in excess supply, i.e. underemployed. Full employment, as an outcome of the market process and not as a result of successful income policy, therefore characterizes a situation of disequilibrium in that it indicates the second budget constraint as a binding constraint. A situation of full employment is achieved in the course of a phase of continuing and dynamic accumulation. It is, for the reasons discussed above, driven by the fact that windfall profits exceed entrepreneurial expectations of normal profits. Continually shifting the monetary budget constraint outward finally leads to a wage-effective exhaustion of the potential labor force.

From a theoretical point of view, it is thus not plausible to point the finger at mounting wages as the factor triggering inflation. Empirically, a situation may occur in which the politically backed market power of the trade unions may prove able to push through wage increases that cannot be explained from the employment situation. This explanation can, however, raise no claim to general validity, as it does in post-Keynesian and structuralist inflation theory.[57] The triggering factor must, instead, be sought in a jump in the profit-price level. This factor shows, to use a dubious term, the market power of the investors, for they decide whether or not to proceed production. If wage-earners attempt to push through nominal wage hikes that cannot be passed on in commodity prices, the investors can turn down production and employment. Besides, the achievement of windfall profits points to the fact that such a shift in the price level is conditional on monetary factors: even a one-time jump implies *ceteris paribus* that the banks must have created additional credit if, in the aggregate, it is possible to push through rising prices.

Inflation as the process of a rising price level must be fueled by an increased supply of the means of payment, an increased supply of media of barter cannot sustain it. An acceleration of velocity or the credit multiplier are subject to limits when the money supply remains constant.[58] The possibility of inflation is therefore conditional on an increase in the supply of money, which provides the framework for continuous price rises. This fact is suppressed by all those theories of inflation that merely indicate triggering factors - like the market power of the unions, petroleum price hikes, or currency devaluations - but without making note of what sustains such price rises.

But only when monetary support is met by an endogenous market response does a one-time shift of the profit-price level lead into inflation. This is where the labor market has a significant role to play. In view of the underemployment normally prevalent, a rationale of "wage bargaining" on the part of the labor supply can be formulated only in heuristic terms. It appears plausible - for being based on the weakest assumptions possible - to impute to the labor supply a rationale of safeguarding real wages (Keynes 1936, pp. 5ff.; Riese 1986, p. 162). This is true both of individual suppliers of labor and of their representatives in the guise of the legislative or the trade unions. Since a jump in the price level is synonymous with a drop in real wages, they will seek to push through a nominal wage hike. If they succeed, enterprises will see themselves faced with the challenge of raising prices so as to safeguard profits. If this proves possible due to a perfectly elastic response of the money supply, it will result in a jump in the income-price level. This in turn may pose a challenge to the suppliers of labor, who will try to safeguard their real wages.[59]

If the central bank is concerned to suppress this price-wage spiral, more precisely the P'-w-P mechanism, all it can do is prevent increased wage costs from being passed on. The determination of nominal wages is after all not an instrument of central-bank policy. It must therefore cause the enterprises unforeseen losses by contracting the money supply. That will counteract the formation of a price level permitting the realization of an ex ante surplus of investment over savings, i.e. windfall profits. Given a high liquidity potential, it may take some time for austerity to take effect. It will be the unemployment brought about in this way that will then prevent wages from mounting any further.

To what extent can this outline of an inflation process be *transferred to an emerging, less integrated monetary economy*? Two basic theoretical elements appear to lend themselves to an immediate application to development economics, i.e. the assumption of mark-up pricing by enterprises and the existence of unemployment. Moreover, in the end, distinguishing between a triggering factors and process-sustaining mechanisms allows for enough flexibility to consider features specific to developing countries.

In such countries shifts in the profit-price level often result from budget deficits that can be reflected in an investment volume exceeding voluntary savings. As was argued previously, a constellation of this sort may be explained by the fragility of income generation in a developing monetary economy itself, which implies that government expenditure takes on a "stopgap function". The two expansionary monetary impulses are, however, typically compensated for wholly or in part by a current-account deficit that, as it were, inflicts losses on domestic producers.

In countries at this stage of development, some kind of minimum-wage legislation usually substitutes for labor supply as a market phenomenon. The price-wage spiral is set in motion here, if safeguarding the real minimum wage can be assumed to be intended by the legislative. There can be wholly tangible reasons for the legislative to raise wages in this way, as is demonstrated by public responses to adjustment programs. In this case protest replaces the union demands advanced in wage negotiations. The resulting continuous price hikes are then quite analogous to the interaction of profit- and income-price levels discussed above.

It is also conceivable, however, that the inflation process does not result from this interaction typical of an integrated system of markets. In economies of this sort, a shift of single prices can entail sizable reactions, especially since they make sensitive shortages more likely. Notorious examples of this are rises in agricultural prices due to negative climatic factors, devaluation forcing up import prices, or state demand coinciding with shortages. If these shifts in single and thus relative prices lead to attempts on the part of business to pass on increased prices, or attempts on the part of labor to demand higher wages, this can set in motion a process of persistent absolute price rises.

In countries in which money constitutes an important store of value and is thus hoarded, there is for the most part a high liquidity potential. The breaking up of hoards in connection with an inflation process can fuel this process for a time. Dishoarding can even accelerate when a restrictive monetary course leads to an increase of interest rates on formal financial investments. Inflation control must thus proceed very restrictively so as to diminish this "liquidity overhang".

In the end, nominal wage policy is not an instrument of monetary policy in developing countries either. At best, government can refrain from adjusting minimum wages. In view of the economic situation of those concerned, who after all include the poorest of the poor, it constitutes an extremely harsh measure when nominal wages are either not adjusted or adjustments are postponed in the face of a rising price level. This is aggravated by the fact that a wage freeze decreed administratively, i.e. centrally, offers a relatively visible target of protest as opposed to decentral pressure on wages exerted by firms.

These conditions hampering a restrictive monetary policy do not necessarily mean that monetary inflation control is economically unfeasible in countries of this sort. Here too, the monetary authorities, represented for the most part by the ministry of finance and a central bank subject to government directive, can force through a decline of the overall credit supply. This, it is true, first affects the sectors integrated into the monetary economy, which normally make up the focus of development-policy efforts. A shortage of liquidity can lead to innumerable business and commercial bank failures. In most such countries unemployment entails further proliferation of an already widespread poverty. It is quite understandable that fierce resistance to any policy of inflation control will be the consequence.

The terse statement that inflation control of a monetary type may work hence does not imply that it can be pushed through politically and socially. Many countries have therefore attempted to replace the macroeconomic market mechanism. One option is offered by the corporatist solution of income policy: representatives of employers and employees reach political agreements that as a rule include employment guarantees on the one hand and wage restraint on the other. This of course presupposes a high level of social group formation unlikely for new nation states. An income policy of this type also requires that the inflation problem be, to one extent or another, already under control. Otherwise the parties to such agreements can hardly be expected to be able to comply with its formal terms.

A centralist or statist variant used to get around the macroeconomic market mechanism is the *attempt to repress inflation*. Wage and price controls as well as a fixed exchange rate suggest themselves as methods to this end. In the face of high liquidity concomitant with repression, this will lead to sellers' markets, i.e. to rationing on the demand side. In consequence, the state will also have to intervene in the allocation of goods, for otherwise the price controls are doomed to failure from the very start by emerging black markets: no one will be willing to offer goods at the controlled prices.

Even if it should prove possible to repress the emergence of black markets to such an extent that supply via official channels does not collapse across the board, this nevertheless places a monetary economy in the worst of all possible worlds: the measures required suppress the stimulative impulses brought about by rising prices, but without eliminating the condition that leads to their emergence, the high liquidity potential. Stagnation will then go hand in hand with the price rises checked at such cost in effort.

Repressed inflation can also initiate a process of government indebtedness with a dynamic of its own: if a complete withdrawal of producers from official markets is to be avoided, the difference between commercial and administrative prices must be subsidized in some form; the prices for public services are unlikely to be able to cover costs if they are set with an eye to diminishing inflation; population groups especially affected by partial price rises and rationing while inflation is repressed will likely have to be compensated; finally, black-market activities reduce the tax base. This growing discrepancy between government revenues and expenditures makes it increasingly urgent to control inflation by monetary means.

Not only as a result these implications of inflation, but also for reasons of a more fundamental nature, repression of inflation is unsuited to achieving the *goal of inflation control*. As was noted in the discussion on monetary income generation, it must chiefly serve to motivate portfolio owners to hold nominal assets in domestic currency. Willingness to hold claims must be harmonized with a willingness to take on liabilities. No one wants to be a creditor in a depreciating currency, although the reverse is the case for debtors. Successful anti-inflation policy thus implies that debts will become more oppressive, while claims become more attractive.

It is precisely this move towards a stock equilibrium of asset holdings that cannot be achieved by repressed inflation. Its measures are applied only against the demand for transactions balances, the demand for money as a means of exchange, in that they attempt to ensure a stable real purchasing power of the currency. But the more severe the imbalance in the desired asset holding becomes, and the less credible the administratively backed price stability grows, the closer the day of exodus from the currency into tangible assets and foreign exchange will approach.

Administrative repression can thus not be employed as an alternative to monetary anti-inflation policy. The latter should start as early as possible, because inflation, owing to its different impacts on creditors and debtors, can change very rapidly into a cumulative process. The exodus from domestic monetary claims finds expression in a rising velocity of circulation that accelerates price increases. The enterprises and even the portfolio holders may, on the other hand, thus be induced to build an ever higher credit pyramid since their expectations are in this way more than fulfilled.

The *erosion of the monetary system* is an inevitable outcome of this process in which the nominal wealth formation of the households in the broadest sense of the term and the formation of tangible assets on the business side drift further and further apart. The flight into tangible assets and foreign exchange, financed by an explosion of credit, leads to shortages of goods, to exorbitant price rises for storable goods, and, finally, to a breakdown of debtor-creditor relationships.[60] In a situation like this, repression of income generation due to monetary anti-inflation policy can mean that this discrepancy will even widen, accelerating the breakdown: in view of the risk that debtors may default, claims are more frequently called in, while debtors seek to avoid the illiquidity threatening them through recourse to emergency borrowing. This leads not to a reconstitution of the monetary economy affected, but to its dissolution in a financial crisis. The process of erosion can be demonstrated cogently in the resulting balances of the three actors concerned (Lüken-Klassen/Betz 1989, pp. 247f.).

If government does not intervene, long-term claims are no longer held in order to permit a long-term accumulation of tangible assets (2). The portfolio owners hold deposits only to have access to cash for transactions (3). The central bank thus ends up with the function of the portfolio owners (1).[61]

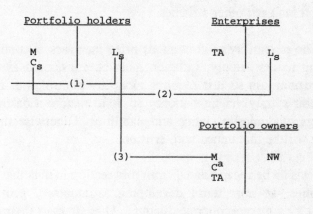

C^a = claims in foreign exchange
(see above for remaining abbreviations)

What has been argued in this section can now be summed up for an emerging monetary economy: it was first noted that in emerging monetary economies there is an inherent tendency toward stagnation. This was inferred essentially from the uncertainty with which intertemporal creditor-debtor relationships, the reflux of nominal advances, are incumbered at this level of development. In addition, given the fragile constitution of the national currency, there is widespread reluctance to incur and hold nominal domestic claims. At least that part of income generation will therefore take place at a low level which stems from private economic or exclusively commercial motives. Nor has an expansionary monetary policy been found suitable to overcome this weakness in accumulation. It has a tendency to exhaust itself in price effects.

Yet despite, and precisely because of this stagnative market tendency, the problem of inflation is virulent. In spite - in that causes exogenous to the economic process are likely to give rise to price increases. Precisely because of - in that it both appears opportune in terms of economic policy and justified by microeconomic rationales to use, or to perceive, price increases as stimulative. They can become factors triggering inflation when profit inflation and income inflation fan each other's flames.

Since the possibility of continuous price increases is conditional on a growing money supply, inflation must be considered as a monetary phenomenon. As such it requires monetary control, i.e. reduction of the credit supply via tight money so as to restore a balance between holdings of domestic claims and liabilities. Otherwise the monetary system will be threatened with erosion.

The thesis to be recapitulated from this section is thus that developing economies, at least those developing as monetary economies, are marked by a macroeconomic dilemma. One effect of their level of development is that incentives toward income generation in the private sector are low. But they are nevertheless urgently confronted with the problem of inflation typical of monetary economies. If its stimulative effects are instrumentalized, i.e. fanned through monetary policy, this can, in the extreme, mean that the economy affected will be threatened with erosion. It would thus be thrown back to the problem of constitution.

This formulation of the problem of development is more adequate to an understanding of why governments have taken on special tasks in the monetary economies of newly independent nations. The following section will discuss the question of how suited this may be to coming to terms with the dilemma described.

2.3   The Role of Government

What was stated above might be summarized as meaning that the development of a monetary economy is not conceivable without the visible hand of government. In discussing the problem of constitution, an attempt was made to show that this development is associated, historically and systematically, with the emergence of the nation state. A monetary macroeconomy is not an outcome of decentral evolution

(Knapp 1918, p 130ff. and passim; Bücher 1920, pp. 135ff.). That is the reason why in economic theory the state does not appear only after the fact - be it as a disturbing factor, be it as a repair shop of the market mechanism - but is crucial for the establishment of a monetary economy.

Monetary income generation, it was argued, is constrained by the volume of the nominal advances for production, which in turn is based on the supply of fiat money. Depending on development level, the government is confronted with additional tasks owing to the fact that income generation tends to stagnate in less developed monetary economies,[62] or is driven and sustained by an inflation process threatening its existence.

This study will, in what follows, of course not presume to develop a theory of the state in the monetary economy. The intention is, instead, to develop some initial thoughts on how it might be possible to consider this essential actor in a monetary economy.[63] The changing role of government in the course of development might also reveal an important link between the theory of the developed monetary economy and the theory of the emerging monetary economy.

Government in a Monetary Economy

Several propositions and points of focus underlying what has been said thus far are relevant to the question of how government is to be included in the picture:

It was stated implicitly that the *norm of a monetary economy* requires that claims of portfolio owners be safeguarded. By no means is this meant normatively in the sense of moral desirability. Rather, what is meant by the norm of a monetary economy is the condition for it to proceed, an objective requirement and yet one that is not automatically fulfilled. The existence of inflation violates this norm. The resulting erosion of the monetary system consists in the fact that the security of nominal values may become so precarious as to indicate an imminent collapse of income generation. If this risk is to be avoided, government will be forced to gear its economic policy to this norm.

The demand that wealth be protected denotes the factual force of the normative in that the formation of financial assets represents the pendant of any productive formation of tangible assets. This merely states in terms of stocks held what is implied by the fact that advances of money, i.e. investment, determine possible income generation over a given period. The primacy of the monetary budget constraint implies that resources and labor are available in relative excess. Employment interests are thus subordinate to investment interests. This means for government - and not only for a democratic government - that its political legitimacy is permanently at risk. Put differently: the norm of a monetary economy represents, in terms of political legitimacy, an exacting demand fraught with potential conflict.[64] The latent conflict between norm and legitimacy regularly becomes manifest when harsh adjustment measures seek to restore this hierarchy of interests.

The theory of monetary economy outlined here has placed the *dynamics of accumulation as a problem* distinctly above the issue of allocation efficiency. This can, to come straight to the weaker argument, first be explained formally. As was indicated in connection with the choice of technologies, the option of discussing certain allocation decisions is not open to an economic theory that argues in categories of value.[65]

It is, however, of more significance that the concept of efficiency appears unsuited to considering the problems of monetary development. Efficiency is a microeconomic concept. In consumer theory it is a measure of the degree to which individual preferences have been fulfilled, given the budget constraint of the household. In production theory the concept covers the relationship between input and output. Its use in modern economic theory presupposes that, in normative terms, all economic activity must be geared to this end and that, in positive terms, any beneficial market result must be traced back to the efficient interplay of individual decisions. The concept thus refers to a relationship between variables, not to their level. Moreover, this approach reduces the various constraints with which microeconomic activity is faced to a budget constraint. The cognitive interest guiding this study is, however, directed toward an explicit discussion of the constraints to which the actors in an emerging monetary economy are subject.

Thus government comes into focus as a decision-making unit pursuing its own rationale and subject to constraints other than those facing other microeconomic actors. As such, government is not interested in efficiency, for efficiency in no way expands its scope for maneuver. Yet economic theory has until now introduced the state as operating on this rationale (Krueger 1990), i.e. as a householder ("benevolent dictator") or as a monopolist firm ("rent-seeking bureaucracy").

Finally, the focus on accumulation is also, in contrast to allocation, well suited to gaining a clearer view of government's difficulties in maintaining its political legitimacy: dynamic income generation can and will as a rule conflict with the functional requirements of a monetary economy, while efficient allocation does not.

There is one last topic of the discussion conducted to this point that is relevant to the role of government in a monetary economy. The state is not simply introduced because it exists, in order then to ascribe to it goals analogous to those of other actors. Historical retrospect and systematic considerations were intended to demonstrate that the government's room for maneuver as a political entity is dependent upon how stable and prosperous the national economy is. Most nationalist movements have been driven by the expectation that they would achieve additional degrees of freedom via constitution and integration of a monetary economy, i.e. through economic sovereignty. But it has turned out that functional requirements impose considerable restrictions, precisely in a world of unevenly developed currency areas. While economic policy interventions may indeed be called for repeatedly in cases where the functioning of the monetary cycle is fragile and prone to crisis. But the *policy intervention must then be one conditional on market forces* if the government is not to be tripped up by the evasive reactions of other economic actors or to run the risk of the country they rule being downgraded in the hierarchy of currency areas.

In the next section an attempt will be made to conceptualize these positionings of a political economy: the "regime" of a monetary economy refers to the composition of economic policy as conditioned by the functioning of the monetary system. Differences between regimes can be traced back to the circumstance that the pressure of legitimacy may make itself felt more or less strongly. In economic terms, this doubtless depends above all on how difficult and precarious it is to adhere to the norm and to develop a dynamic of income generation.

Regimes of a Monetary Economy

For the present purpose of pointing out problems involved in development under monetary conditions in theoretical and exemplary terms, it is sufficient to distinguish between a commercial and a redistributive regime. The *concept commercial regime* was inspired by the discussion, conducted elsewhere, on the question of what in essence characterizes a monetary economy and must thus be introduced in connection with the transformation of planned economies (Riese 1990). To this extent the concept "commercial regime" represents the construct of an ideal type that lends pure expression to the features of a monetary economy and the economic policy appropriate to it. As such it can represent only the frame of reference for redistributive regimes and their chances of development. The plural indicates that redistributive regimes may be differentiated as to level of development, intensity and thrust of economic policy interventions, institutional organization, etc. The following discussion is, however, limited to a characterization of the two extremes, i.e. the redistribu-

tive regime consistent with functional requirements and the redistributive regime that violates them and accordingly displays signs of
degeneration.

The *concept redistributive regime* proceeds from a term in common
use in the fields of economic history and social anthropology. Polanyi
(1979, p. 219) designates reciprocity, redistribution, and market exchange as basic "forms of integration" by which economies "attain
coherence and stability". The redistributive mode of economy
emerges with the centralization of governance (Sahlins 1972,
pp. 130ff.). This was manifestly also the political process in which
monetary economies originated: they were constituted together with
the modern European nation state, or in connection with the independence of former colonies in the pre- and postwar period.

Polanyi (1979, pp. 224 and 226) also considers the modern welfare
state and the Soviet system to be redistributive regimes. He sees their
common feature in the fact that their center appropriates a major
share of aggregate income and then redistributes it. The use of the
concept made here does, however, diverge in crucial aspects from
that of Polanyi and his school. It is intended to contribute to an analysis of market and policy constellations in the system of monetary
economies, and not to be applied to various modes of production at
divergent levels of aggregation and historical localization. The concept of the redistributive regime refers to the phase, possibly enduring, in which a monetary macroeconomy is to be established with the
active involvement of government.[66]

Owing to this specific approach, a regime of this type is not interpreted as a mode of production in which the economy is still
"imbedded" in politics (Polanyi 1979, p 156). The higher intensity of
intervention that it is apt to display when compared with a commercial regime need not necessarily be interpreted as a priority of politics. It can be interpreted as a government response to challenges
posed by the economy as a differentiated social system which follows
a logic of its own. In highly interventionist states, such responsive-

ness may lead to a paradoxical economization of politics as a whole. These regimes are quick to legitimize themselves by pointing to the evident dominance of their political objectives. But if government claims responsibility for everything, it can be held responsible for everything. This confronts the political sphere with considerable pressure for economic success. It is entirely possible for highly interventionist politics to become "imbedded in economics".

Following these preliminary remarks, it will now be possible to contrast the *commercial and the redistributive regimes of a monetary economy*, which will involve reexamining some motifs that have already been addressed. Conclusions for economic policy will be drawn from the fact that a monetary economy is an economy proceeding through accumulation of nominal assets, an economy confined to national development, and an economy based on individual creditor-debtor relationships. This will be followed by a discussion of a redistributive regime in the stage of degeneration.

-   The norm of a monetary economy is to protect claims on wealth. From this follows a hierarchy of budget constraints. The norm(al) case is thus that available resources, labor, and intermediary goods will never restrict production. Enforcing the claim to a surplus income also implies that wage incomes will not suffice to purchase the commodities produced. Both consequences can be summarized in the proposition that a monetary economy tends to develop buyers' markets (Riese 1990, p. 24). Restricting production by a nominal constraint, i.e. stringency of money advanced in relation to the returns expected, thus implies a tendency toward quantitative "abundance". Planning for "normal" stocks, which also require advances, becomes part of equilibrium production, i.e. production that meets expectations. The hierarchy ensuing from the norm of a monetary economy finds expression in a stratification of the economic "trinity of production, consumption, and wealth" (Riese 1990, p. 37): production is controlled by considerations regarding wealth formation, consumption results as a derivative of this control.

The commercial regime of a monetary economy might be character-ized as one in which the norm requiring protection of claims on wealth can be raised to the level of a maxim governing economic policy. In the long run, this hardly appears possible if the ownership of wealth is not broadly distributed. The interests of wage-earners and the interests of owners of assets may then coincide in one and the same person. In this case latent conflicts between both interests are less likely to give rise to social and political unrest in that the func-tional distinction is not a personal distinction. This is doubtless not the least important reason for governments to promote small savings programs, "creation of private wealth in workers' hands", and the like. For in this case monetary norm and political legitimacy place parallel demands on economic policy, and the predominance of busi-ness and monied interests over employment interests is capable of winning majorities.

A redistributive regime, in contrast, is confronted with incompatible demands placed by norm and legitimacy, or establishes itself against the background of a conflict of this type. For the reasons named, in only small number of monetary economies is income generation so self-supporting that it is possible to protect and increase claims to in-tangible wealth and at the same to do justice to employment inter-ests.[67] Economic policy intervention in favour of employment need not violate the norm when stimulation of income generation serves the interests of those who hold the titles to productive assets. This typically implies measures such as protection, the build-up of industrial conglomerates, government-supported collaboration between banks and big business etc. (Gerschenkron 1962). From a liberal point of view, these may be highly objectionable on efficiency grounds and owing to their violation of the capitalist order, but at the same time they are consistent with the norm of a monetary economy at a given level of development.

With reference to the economic trinity, the difference between com-mercial and redistributive regimes can be expressed as follows: in commercial regimes production is controlled by the rationales of private enterprise. In redistributive regimes, government controls a sizable share of production. One obvious expression of this is that government spending to a large extent defines the macroeconomic budget constraint. The rationales of owners of wealth can in this case exert control only when economic policy is geared to a rationale that is not necessarily its own. This requires in particular that the government's budget line be observed. The special status of government, i.e. its comparatively low risk of illiquidity, turns this into a deliberate effort, typical market sanctions being less effective here. This is the source of the paradox mentioned above that the more the state intervenes in the economic process, the more the former can be bent to the latter's inherent logic. Ultimately, private agents still have the economic sanction mechanism of a flight from the currency. Governments are therefore well-advised to internalize market reactions, because otherwise they tend to vanish, at least from the perspective of government.

- Every monetary economy is a national monetary economy. It is necessarily related, via the exchange rate, to other currency areas. The exchange rate is determined by the decisions of portfolio owners to hold an aggregate stock of assets. Exchange rate fluctuations result from shifts in currency holdings which lead to changes of supply and demand in the foreign exchange market. The acceptance of a currency, precisely because it is based on decisions to hold stocks of it, is not consistent with fluctuations of its foreign-exchange value. Since the degree of acceptance affects what has been termed the inward constitution of a monetary economy, economic policy must, for reasons internal and external, be geared to stabilizing the exchange rate. For the private sector, this ensures convertibility in the material sense, i.e. the possibility of switching out of the respective currency without sustaining major financial losses. The simple knowledge of such flight options is bound to have a stabilizing effect on confidence. Macropolicy aimed at defending and stabilizing the exchange rate is therefore crucial. Its relative success largely conditions the ability of a monetary economy to assert itself in the hierarchy of currency areas.

In a commercial regime this entails the priority of monetary policy (Riese 1990, p. 92). On penalty of depreciation or persistent overvaluation, with the attendant consequences for debt, the money supply must be controlled in such a way that it remains in tune with private-sector preferences as regards the volume and structure of assets. In economies with weak currencies, interest policy is normally not a surrogate for quantitative measures. It is significant for short-term stabilization, for smoothing out exchange rate fluctuations (Lüken-Klassen/Betz 1989, p. 240).

Roughly the same holds for a redistributive regime. It will, however, have to restrict formal convertibility in order to counteract the consequences of a tendency toward overvaluation. Limited convertibility might, on the one hand, constitute a response to the circumstance of a country finding itself at the lower end of the currency hierarchy. In the long run at best, it will have other means at its disposal to stop any decline of its currency threatening as a result of a lack of acceptance. On the other hand, restrictions on capital movements may prove temporarily necessary in order to achieve a relatively higher level of accumulation in the broadest sense of the term. It is possible, through controls on the movement of capital, to overvalue the exchange rate without incurring outflows of foreign exchange. The extent of overvaluation thus possible is determined by the amount of transaction costs needed to circumvent the controls. Furthermore, selective protectionism must be employed to provide the generally import-stimulating effect of such overvaluation a direction meaningful in terms of structural policy. Restrictions on convertibility would nevertheless be possible and justified in terms of development strategy only for a transitional phase. If no recognizable efforts are made to create convertibility, the result will be a loss of confidence, evasive reactions, and thus rising, not sinking, overvaluation. Moreover, controls on the movement of capital can never prevent a flight from the currency, since tangible assets always remain as an alternative to foreign exchange. While this alternative may be preferred by governments, it inhibits the process of monetary constitution just as much as does flight into foreign exchange.

In the face of unstable acceptance, monetary policy will not have the control capacity it has in an established monetary economy. Administrative defenses of the exchange rate assume a functional role if they serve the end of warding off a vicious circle of low acceptance - depreciation tendency - foreign exchange outflow - a further drop in credibility.

In addition, monetary policy in a regime of this type should never be considered in isolation from budget policy. As a brief glance back to the "financial revolution" (chapter 1) should demonstrate, central-bank policy will gain independence as soon as it proves possible to establish a monetary macroeconomy; it cannot be presupposed. The priority of budget policy resulting from this sequence thus requires that fiscal measures be used to support the end of exchange-rate stabilization. That prohibits, for obvious reasons, an expansionary spending policy financed from monetized deficits. This would intensify even more the trend toward overvaluation and could give rise to sudden crises of confidence.

-    A monetary economy is based on debtor-creditor relationships under civil law. Since any person is free to enter such contractual relationships, there must be guarantees preventing one side from being exposed systematically to the negative effects of unforeseen developments. Otherwise such debtor-creditor relationships tend not to emerge in the first place. Apart from precautionary measures under civil law,[68] it is monetary policy that has the task of vouching for a symmetry of debtors and creditors. An orientation in terms of price-level stability can be justified in that it protects creditors from depreciation of their property and the debtors from appreciation of their liabilities (Riese 1990, pp. 81f.). The objective of monetary policy must thus be to prevent both inflationary and deflationary processes.

In a commercial regime, monetary policy acts within a two-tier system of liquidity supply. A central bank, created by the state yet independent, supplies money proper. The private banks create credit and control the money supply. Characteristically, these actors have no genuine creditor or debtor rationale. The central bank does assume the position of a creditor, but it is precisely its state character that relieves it of any rationale of this sort - which is why it can take restrictive action without any consideration of losses on the claims it holds. As portfolio holders, the banks are both debtors and creditors, and their liquidity preference results from the fact that, microeconomically, their position as debtor is the weightier of the two. It is then the task of monetary policy to maintain the symmetry by seeking to influence the credit production of the banks by means of the supply of fiat money.

In redistributive regimes, monetary policy is, as was mentioned above, subordinate to budget policy for reasons related to the development level and political legitimacy. If the latter temporarily assumes monetary-policy functions, it must thus exercise caution lest its monetary effects destroy this symmetry of creditors and debtors. Budgetary policy can succeed in this only when government is not in the position of a net debtor vis-à-vis the rest of the economy. Otherwise it is evident that it, as the monetary authority, would primarily protect its interests as a debtor. Government could do so by preventing an upward revaluation of its debt by lowering the price level or even by easing the burden through inflation.

The monetary constitution of a redistributive regime will, typically, not provide for an independent central bank. An adequate substitute for this can be provided by legal regulations limiting the quantity and the terms of government borrowing from the central bank. The ministry of finance would thus be given a position comparable to that of the banks. Yet the two-tier system of liquidity supply appears to be an unrenounceable component of the monetary constitution. A for the most part nationalized banking system can remain functional as long as it acts under an effective microeconomic budget constraint and controls the money supply in accordance with liquidity preference and profit expectations. But when these possessory interests lead to a situation in which the banks assume a dependent position and thus become the long arm of redistribution by the center, creditor interests are no longer safeguarded.

This general characterization of the conditions to which economic policy is subject indicates that redistributive regimes tend to be inconsistent. That results from the fact that in a regime of this type the government assumes the functions normally exercised by the private sector in order to achieve or to advance its objective, which in the broadest sense is developing the national economy. Its sovereign position causes it to be subject to other economic sanction mechanisms than those applying to private agents. Since these are less direct, the political objective tends not only to replace private-sector functions transitionally, but to overrule them permanently. The *deformations* resulting from this can be recognized in the fact that what is achieved is the opposite of what was aimed at, i.e. stagnation of income generation or even a break-down of the debtor-creditor relationships constitutive of it.[69]

Attempts have been made to dissolve the conflict between norm and political legitimacy resulting from the hierarchy of interests via welfare-economic objectives. This understanding of government responsibilities would permit extensive economic interventions to determine socially efficient solutions to the alleged trade-off between equity and private efficiency. In the present context, stagnation of private-sector income generation would suggest that government attempt a "big push", creating industrial capacities and employment via public investment. The existing private-enterprise economy would, in view of this objective, have to be regulated in such a way as to achieve production with a maximum rate of social returns. This would reverse the economic trinity in that welfare-economic needs, "social consumption", would control production. The accumulation of assets would then appear as a derivative.

This form of accumulation - accumulation of claims to assets in the broadest sense of the term - is by no means a negligible process here, as is shown by the notorious phenomenon of "rent-seeking". The possibility of achieving rents is, for example, offered by regulatory systems that seek to control production, and in doing so create pecuniary assets such as licences and the like. But an expansion of production, as a rule associated with monetary expansion, tends to eliminate creditor claims to interest. Social returns are, unfortunately, not a market phenomenon, but a sociological concept. They do not accrue, in pecuniary terms, to private agents. Widespread retreat of producers and owners of assets can be prevented only by highly attractive conditions, such as reservation of market segments, subsidies, government guarantees on private debt, etc. Or the government will more and more have to take over production in order to remain true to its objective of acting as a benevolent dictator. Yet not even public enterprises are able to count on social returns. Both variants will therefore, in the middle term, lead to severe budget problems.

An extreme expression of this deformation is the phenomenon of sellers' markets, atypical of monetary economies: at given prices, money or monetary income would be less scarce than goods. Sellers' markets may be the consequence of regulation, pointing in the direction of throttled, stagnating production. Or they may be the consequence of a "misappropriation" of goods for the purpose of capital accumulation, a flight into tangible assets. Sellers' markets would thus be the observable phenomenon reflecting the stagnation or even the erosion of the monetary economy concerned. They would be tangible proof of the failure of a policy that wishes to place the satisfaction of social needs above capital interests, but within the framework of a monetary economy.

As far as foreign trade is concerned, a regime of this sort will tend largely to seek insulation, not merely to protect itself temporarily. Otherwise its welfare-economic objective would be thwarted from the very start by the foreign-exchange constraint. Yet the loss of confidence associated with protection of this sort will give rise to what strict controls on the movement of capital, inconvertibility, and centralization of foreign trade sought to prevent: a dualism of currency uses in the sense that transactions between private persons will be contracted only in foreign exchange. In the most extreme case, private economic agents will hold only enough domestic monetary claims to cover the taxes they owe. Income generation would thus come under such pressure, even from the foreign-trade sector, that it would virtually collapse.

Finally, in a redistributive regime normed not in monetary but in welfare-economic terms, the government would most likely have to assume the role of a debtor. That, however, would prevent, as was noted above, budget policy from representing the functional equivalent of monetary policy. For one thing, a pressing debt burden suggests the seemingly "inexpensive" course of monetizing budget deficits. That is inconsistent with the fundamental principle of credit relationships, according to which debtors can never generate the medium in which a contract is to be performed. For another, monetary policy, alias budget policy, will then no longer preserve the symmetry between debtors and creditors, but seek to relieve itself of its debtor role.

This can give rise to a complete deformation of the monetary constitution by supplementing the monetization of budget deficits by a central bank with a dependent banking system designed to create privileged access to finance. With reference to government as debtor, this would thus institutionalize a passive system of money and credit supply. The remaining borrowers would therefore have to be rationed, with attendant "crowding-out" effects, or the dissolution of the monetary system would accelerate. Such a production of claims controlled by debtors is not compatible with claims held by creditors.

Once again, the latter have the possibility of opting out of the currency. The effects of these sanctions are not so direct as, for instance, refusal of a credit line, which can force a microeconomic debtor into illiquidity. Its effects are, however, no less disastrous, and disastrous for the whole of society, and will ultimately require a replacement of monetary control with far-reaching administrative measures.

3 Implications for Development Policy

The analysis dealing with the question of what development under monetary conditions implies and the problems it entails will be summed up below, the intention being to draw from it some general conclusions on development policy. To facilitate a discussion on the economic policy meaningful under the specific constraints it implies, the underlying assumption will be that a given country either is developing or wishes to develop under the conditions of a monetary economy.[70] For that reason, no alternative paths to development will be indicated, although this is not meant to imply that such alternatives are not conceivable or desirable.

The constraints result from the circumstance noted above in various contexts that development under monetary conditions requires a growing degree of social coherence achieved via debtor-creditor relationships, and that its reference variable is the domestic currency. Proclamation of a national currency was seen as equivalent to the self-imposed objective of development along the lines of a national monetary economy. In this constitutive act, the government concerned has linked its capacity to act to its ability to create and sustain macroeconomic coherence.

In analogy to the problems involved in internal and external constitution, government development policy too can be viewed from a domestic angle and an external angle. Most participants in the discussion over development strategies will no doubt agree that the emphasis cannot be placed on one aspect alone, on "import substitution versus export promotion" (Krueger 1985), but that the important issue is to define the relationship of these aspects to one another. The proposition that monetary economies develop as national economies implies a priority of domestic development, the yardstick for which is the marketability of the goods produced; i.e. it implies that such development should be supported by means of selective integration in the world market.

This discussion, which restricts itself to macroeconomic relations and seeks at the same time to point out the limits of any such approach, is followed by some thoughts on development-policy implications for the financial sector. In the end, monetary development theory begins with the discovery that this sector is of strategic significance. The literature until then contained little more than isolated theoretical references to the role of banks in the industrial revolution (Gerschenkron 1962; Goldsmith 1969). This study even goes so far as to assign to the portfolio holders a constitutive status in the two-tier system of liquidity supply of modern monetary economies. But this is not to imply that encouragement of the financial sector is more fundamental in import than the "classical" development policies of combatting poverty, modernizing agriculture, or industrialization. From the fact, mentioned in connection with inward constitution, that monetary economies were preceded by money-using economies it might even be inferred, perhaps somewhat exaggeratedly, that the so-called financial infrastructure will develop without any direct encouragement if the options available for supplying credit are enhanced both qualitatively and quantitatively. The emphasis would thus be placed more on the side of the demand for credit than on the side of credit supply.

3.1 World-Market Integration as a Means of Developing Domestic Markets

The development problem was split up analytically into the problem of constitution, i.e. the necessity of establishing the national currency as the basis of long-term creditor-debtor relationships, and the dilemma involved in the fact that a developing monetary economy tends sharply in the direction of stagnation or erosion. In what follows, this view of the problem of development will provide the criteria used to appraise policies consistent with functional monetary requirements.

A national monetary economy, i.e. a domestic market as such, is characterized by a currency of its own.[71] Today's developing countries are, in monetary regards, marked at the same time by weak currencies in the sense that they are faced with a situation involving a lack of long-term demand for domestic currency and excessive demand for foreign exchange. What follows will no longer pose the question as to how, in principle, this imbalance in the foreign-exchange market can be effectively addressed, but will ask how this can be done with a view to development strategy and how it is to be evaluated. This also includes the question as to how in principle the productive capacities of a soft-currency country can be bolstered, a process which, under monetary conditions, will find expression in a reduction of the differences in real wages for comparable labor services.

In principle, the excess demand resulting from currency weakness can be reduced by means of interest-induced capital imports, foreign-exchange assistance ("resource transfer"), through devaluation and export surpluses. One pair or the other of these options made up one component of the two fundamental development strategies of the postwar period; as a rule, neither of them is seen today as precluding the other. The IMF adjustment programs, which on the whole represent the practical shape of prevailing development concepts, take all four options into account. This is intended to alter a country's economic structure in such a way as to rule out any recurrence of fundamental balance-of-payments disequilibria. Discussion of the two basic development strategies has given rise to a general assessment of this eclectic approach (Wolff 1987, p. 18).

Interest-induced or concessionary capital imports form the backbone of the post-Keynesian strategy of "growth cum debt", which set out to close the alleged structural gaps in the volumes of savings and foreign exchange and in this way to create the conditions necessary for growth. The expectations associated with this strategy found succinct expression in the debt-cycle hypothesis; its proposition was that the development financed with a transfer of resources would initially entail a major debt burden, but that the country concerned would be enabled precisely in this way to repay this debt and itself assume the role of a creditor nation providing such transfers. At the beginning of the 1980s, however, what emerged was "the debt crisis as the terminal stage of long-term 'growth cum debt' processes".[72]

The concept presented here, which centers on the disposition of assets, in formal terms: decisions on holding claims, makes it possible to explain why a strategic foreign debt is a precarious matter, even when the best possible use is made of it. Loans fixed in a foreign currency weaken the national currency because they establish and cement a future demand for foreign exchange. That increases the legal-tender qualities of foreign currencies and makes it appear less safe to hold claims payable in domestic currency for fear that such currency will lack the capacity to safeguard wealth-related interests. The future demand resulting from the debt makes devaluations seem more or less certain - which in turn triggers shifts in portfolio structures that then confirm expectations. This results in a depreciation of the exchange rate which, in the extreme case, must be prevented by administrative means. Any export surpluses achieved will then come under pressure toward maximizing foreign-exchange holdings instead of adhering to a policy of integration in the world market governed by development-policy considerations. Concessionary loans, i.e. transfers of foreign exchange, can, under certain circumstances alleviate this constraint in that the more favorable terms under which they are provided make it less likely that interest and redemption burdens will lead into a debt dynamic of their own.

This is not to rule out from the very start the possibility that it can, in the framework of an overall development-policy concept, make sense to contract strategic foreign debts. Crucial conditions for success are, however, on the one hand that they be used to finance products that bring in foreign exchange and on the other hand that precautionary monetary-policy measures be taken to counter currency-weakening effects. Internally, this requires a rise in interest rates that will enhance the attractiveness of domestic financial claims.

Stated in categories of the development problem as broken down above, the critique of the "growth cum debt" strategy can thus be formulated such that its intention was to force externally financed accumulation at the expense of monetary constitution. The state of currency weakness was perpetuated in this way. Conversely, in order to remain compatible with development, a strategic foreign debt entails interest-rate measures tending more to weaken accumulation.

Devaluations and a far-reaching system of export incentives are, on the other hand, crucial elements of the neoclassical strategy of the international division of labor that sees chances of success in "correct" relative prices and a large measure of openness to the world market. This is intended to achieve a comparatively advantageous utilization of resources, which is expected, in ways not specified in more detail, to give rise to "dynamic effects (...) and not merely static profits by means of improved allocation" (Krueger 1985, pp. 20 and 23).

From the perspective of this study, the advantages of an export orientation can be explained on the one hand simply in terms of accumulation theory: as has already been pointed out, and is indicated by gross saving and investment accounts, exports and investment are the income-generating categories. A surplus of these elements over savings, depreciations, and transfers of wealth abroad represents the growth of an economy's net worth in a given period. It is also possible to indicate the specific reason for stabilizing confidence in the national currency in favor of a mercantilistic strategy geared mercantilistically to gaining inroads into export markets: paradoxically, foreign-exchange earnings strengthen the acceptance of a national currency in that holdings of foreign-exchange provide a certain safeguard for an option to switch out of the domestic currency. Export orientation thus appears advantageous in terms both of the problems of stagnation and of constitution.

Yet two qualifying remarks must be added here: first, investments and exports are macroeconomically equivalent categories only as far as their income-generating function is concerned. The reversal of trade balances when heavily indebted countries are compelled to make net repayments, or the historically important cases of export enclaves indicate that an accumulation process driven primarily by exports is less beneficial to development than a process fueled by investments yielding market interest rates. Whereas the type of accumulation represented by the export enclaves tends to use cheap labor and resources as a means of offering products at competitive world-market prices, it is difficult to imagine sustained investment without any shifts in the conditions of production. Any striving on the part of domestic producers for market niches and market shares implies endogenous technical progress increasing the productivity of the manpower employed and, in overall economic terms, forcing up real wages. This ambition is - at least for the average supplier in a developing country - subject to far greater restraints in the world markets. Consequently, if productive capacities are not provided with additional support via economic policy, export growth can quickly turn into growth of poverty.

In most developing countries, this has meant placing a phase of import substitution before the phase of forced world-market orientation. In view of the structural discontinuities occurring in such periods, it is not surprising that the result has been misinvestment, attendant overindebtedness, and other "policy errors" of the sort. Despite this uncertainty implied precisely by development under monetary conditions, it must be noted that "export orientation right from the start" would as a rule have implied surrendering to a colonial pattern of the international division of labor.

Besides, this indicates a limit inherent in macroeconomic policy, the foreign-trade instruments available to it being restricted to the exchange rate and the interest rate. It can be used only to support a shift in comparative advantages in primary production and simple goods manufactured by unskilled manpower. The shift itself must be encouraged through structural-policy measures, in particular adequate educational tariffs.

The second qualifying remark concerns the question as to the "right" exchange rate. If export orientation is to contribute to an enhanced acceptance of domestic currency, and not merely to improved income generation, seeking to achieve this goal via a strategy of devaluation is problematical. A strategy of this type is often implicitly demanded when a regime of flexible exchange rates is recommended. As was noted above, safeguarding wealth is hardly compatible with a fluctuating value of domestic currency, especially since a developing monetary economy is not apt to have many possibilities to conduct hedging and other futures transactions in foreign-exchange markets. Even controlled or announced devaluations need to be compensated for by raising interest rates accordingly, which will have negative effects on domestic accumulation, as has already been discussed at length.

What has been said also sheds light on the measures implemented in normal IMF adjustment programs intended to enhance world-market orientation through devaluation and export promotion and to improve the situation of the county concerned by providing it with credit in foreign exchange. If structural effects are to be achieved, the first course requires an undervalued exchange rate, while the transfer of resources would have precisely the opposite effect. This situation is often aggravated by a formal or informal injunction to liberalize any existing protectionist biases, which also means removing barriers to imports. Taken together, any package of this sort will thus most likely enable the country concerned to take on new debts again, while it is at the same time exposed to contradictory signals as far as its ability to export is concerned. It is in this way difficult to avoid new balance-of-payments crises.

The problem of the currency weakness facing developing countries that is assumed here, with some justification, to be a datum implied that there is, in any strict sense, no such thing as a "correct" rate of exchange. It follows from the conditions of constitution that devaluation can at best be used for a one-time adjustment, not least because of the inflationary impulses triggered by it. Macroeconomically, an export orientation of domestic products can thus be achieved not through a devaluation strategy, but through a *strategy of undervaluation*. As long as the exchange rate remains stable, the only option open to a soft-currency country is to enter into a constellation of this type by keeping the rate of price-increase at a level lower than that prevailing in the key currency areas. That as a rule requires a monetary policy more restrictive than that practiced in these reference countries.

It is important to emphasize the relational character of an undervaluation strategy of this type because it points to the dependency faced by weak-currency countries. It also points to the far greater difficulties, or reduced latitudes, such countries encounter in pursuing a development strategy stimulated by monetary policy, now that the economically influential industrial nations have, since the 1980s, switched to a comparatively strict policy of inflation control. Countries with in any case weaker productive capacities and low real incomes would, in comparative terms, have to subject domestic producers to even more severe hardships as regards the returns they could achieve if they are to enter into a constellation of global undervaluation relative to the countries whose currencies they must earn in order to strengthen their own.[73]

What therefore follows from these considerations on monetary development theory, which were consciously kept on a general level, is that the trinity consisting of undervalued exchange rate, restrictive monetary policy, and selective protectionism makes up a macroeconomically consistent strategy of world-market integration. Its development orientation is demonstrated by the fact that it can contribute to developing a domestic market - or, formulated in the key terms underlying this study, that it is in a position to reconcile the constraint implied in meeting the conditions of constitution with the attempt to increase accumulation.

3.2   Macropolicy as a Means of Developing Domestic Markets

The strategy of world-market integration outlined above is beneficial in terms of its effects on income generation and the development of a manufacturing base, although it places - at given wage levels - heightened demands on the returns required from domestic investment. For the domestic interest rate must be attuned to an undervalued exchange rate if it is to create or sustain the balance between the holdings of financial claims and liabilities needed for stable price levels. The attendant rise in interest rates would have the effect of providing domestic support for export orientation. The enhanced willingness to hold domestic currency resulting from earnings in foreign exchange would compensate for this.

In Keynesian terminology, this compensatory effect could be seen as resulting from a reduction of the liquidity premium. The liquidity preference was discussed in connection with income generation, above all with reference to portfolio holders, i.e. for the most part the banks. In relation to them - and to other actors as well - it is, in terms of price theory, the expression of how sure creditors are of returns on their holdings.

But in order to be able to speak of a liquidity premium in the first place, the problem of constitution must not be virulent. The currency in question must have been accepted in some measure as the basis of domestic financial relationships - raising this measure of acceptance toward the end of accumulating productive tangible assets is the priority goal involved in developing a domestic market. Constitution can, as was noted above with reference to historical experience, be encouraged by means of government financial policy. Tax revenues and borrowing as a means of financing the budget can represent a - direct or indirect - contributory or constraining force acting in the direction of a diffusion of monetary relationships.

Assuming that constitution is at least not in acute danger, the issue that will be discussed in what follows is the role that macropolicy can

- aside from its contribution to a development-oriented world-market integration - play in domestic economic development. It will therefore be necessary to demonstrate how the traditional goals of a policy of easy money and fiscal control of demand can be achieved and why they are faced with constraints. Restricting the discussion to macropolicy, and thus neglecting structural and regulatory policy, follows from the subject of this study: the investigation of the specifically monetary character of development is focused on consideration of liquidity-creating, absolute prices and policies affecting such macrovariables as interest and exchange rates. Structural-policy measures, on the other hand, are defined by the fact that they seek to influence relative prices in such a way as to foster manufacturing processes marked by higher labour productivity. Although the non-neutrality of money implies that macropolicy can alter relative prices, and hence allocation as well, this is not its actual direction of thrust, nor is it in possession of the specific tools needed for this purpose.

Macropolicy is, in the broadest sense of the term, monetary policy (Riese 1986, p. 186). It was pointed out in the last chapter that exchange-rate policy - above and beyond the choice of a specific exchange-rate regime - is exercised by controlling the money supply, i.e. through foreign exchange deposits and by adjusting the central bank's interest rate accordingly. Fiscal policy affects liquidity - directly via deficit financing, indirectly via influences brought to bear on effective demand. It may also alter flows of revenues and expenditures in such a way as to change the overall demand for credit.

As was pointed out in the last chapter and in the discussion of the strategy of undervaluation, an easy-money policy implemented via expansion of the money supply is not an option. The same is true of a fiscal policy financed from monetized budget deficits. It will become apparent in what follows that macropolicy that wants to contribute to developing a domestic economy has, aside from its role in shoring up world-market integration, a chiefly defensive function, i.e. to safeguard the framework for an expanded generation of income.

The barrier to monetary income generation is the interest rate demanded in the financial markets. This can also be maintained for a theory of the emerging monetary economy in which a sizable share of production is controlled by subsistence needs and not directly by yield rationales. To the extent that sustaining their production requires them to enter into monetary relationships, for instance in order to purchase seed, the productive households concerned are, passively, subject to control via interest rates. The existence of money-lenders and other informal dealers and the widespread displeasure over their exploitive conduct are witness to this fact. The demand among such productive households for credit is, not least because of the levels involved, relatively inelastic with regard to interest. This makes possible the extreme forms of economic control to which such debtors are subjected; these can range from excessive interest claims to what amounts to debt-related bondage for entire families. This type of stifling control via interest rates at the same time sustains the condition under which it can be exercised, i.e. a very low level of income generation, doubtless an essential reason for a low level of interest-rate elasticity in the demand for credit. The subsistence level of traditional production methods thus not only makes it possible to demand excessive interest, but it is precisely partial integration into monetary conditions that maintains this low level. Typically, however, macropolicy fails to reach this segments of a national economy. The next section will discuss the contribution that can be made via encouragement of the financial sector.

All that macropolicy can seek to attain is a general cut in interest levels. In doing so it must at the same time seek to avoid destabilizing evasive reactions that threaten when legitimate claims to wealth are violated. This prohibits any direct, administrative regulation of interest rates or profits. Instead, macropolicy must seek on the one hand to influence the willingness to provide credit and on the other hand to heighten the readiness to take on debt toward the end of accumulating productive tangible assets. Expressed in Keynesian terms, this means that market-conditioned policies are geared to lowering the liquidity premium and raising the marginal efficiency of capital. Policies defined in this way are, in substantive terms, market-conditioned or functional in that there are limits to the control that can be exercised by the state in a monetarily mediated economy, although such an economy can at the same time be reliant on stabilizing intervention by the state. Since that latter is for the most part not meant when policies "in conformity with the market" are spoken of, the term "market-conditioned" was chosen here instead.

Uncertainty about investment returns or the risk of illiquidity explain a relatively high liquidity premium to the extent that there is little willingness to defer the power of disposal over money in order to take on financial claims. If they are to do so, creditors will demand high rates of interest - if they are prepared in the first place to enter into longer-term financial relations in fragmented economies exposed to exogenous factors like climatic factors and subject to influences stemming from the world market. Market-determined interest rates are (or would be) accordingly high, while the due dates agreed on remain short, and financial depth, i.e. the share of financial assets in the overall accumulation of wealth, remains low. By setting itself the goal of *lowering the liquidity premium*, i.e. above all in employing a monetary policy geared in the long run to price-level stability, macropolicy can contribute to lowering interest rates.

The reverse side of this policy applied on the lending side is a policy aimed at *raising the marginal efficiency of capital* by influencing the demand for investment credit. Under the conditions just outlined, individual enterprises are also uncertain of recovering money advanced for production through sales in markets with inadequate depth and breadth. The returns demanded on a given investment volume are accordingly high. By improving profit expectations, to which, above all, fiscal support of demand in the face of a threat of depression can contribute, macropolicy can reduce the profit rate required to advance a given volume or increase the volume of investments realized at a given market interest rate.

The concrete shape given to policies so defined is, however, dependent on specific market constellations. The difference between a macroeconomic development policy that seeks to influence the expectations controlling market variables and a policy that aims directly at market variables can, however, be illustrated analytically. Liquidity preference and marginal efficiency can be expressed formally as functions. More precisely; At a given level of confidence or long-term expectations (Keynes 1936, Chapter 12), they determine the supply of or the demand for credit for investment as a function of the liquidity premium and the expected profit rate, respectively.

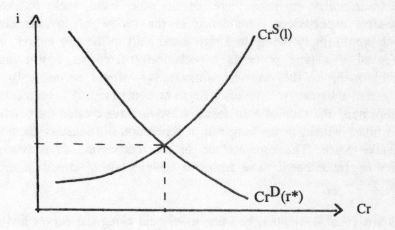

l = liquidity premium, r^* = expected profit rate, i = nominal interest, Cr = credit for investment purposes, indices D and S = demand and supply

A macropolicy measure can now seek to achieve an interest rate cut at a given level of expectations, which would mean movement to the left along the credit-demand curve, to the right along the credit-supply curve. This can entail an enduring effect in relation to the original situation only if the interest level prevailing in the credit market has been above the equilibrium level. That is one possible interpretation of the direction of thrust of structuralist macropolicies, which proceed on the assumption of imperfect markets, interest rate rigidities resulting from oligopolistic behavior patterns, etc. An easy-money policy and a selective allocation of credit in favor of smaller investors can then result in the desired market effect of a low interest rate at a higher rate of employment. Neoclassical macro- and liberalization policy must assume the reverse situation, namely a real interest rate too low due to state intervention: an interest rate hike, achieved via a tight money supply and deregulation, would then increase the effective volume of credit available.

The macropolicy envisaged here, on the other hand, seeks to alter long-term expectations, confidence in the reflow of investments, which would imply the desired right-hand shift in the two curves. A policy of this type proceeds hypothetically from an equilibrium which, owing to the prevailing uncertainty, would permit only a comparatively small volume of credit to be contracted. If it succeeded in improving the state of confidence, it would have created the conditions under which, in the long run, a generation of monetary income can take place. The time-horizon of macroeconomic development policy suggests that it must aspire to achieve lasting effects of this sort.

This analytical distinction between movement along the curves and a shift in the curves can at the same time make visible the limits of macropolicy control. Certain measures have a contrary effect on the curves in question or result in an undesirable shift. Thus, for instance, a permissive monetary policy supporting an investment surplus can have an adverse effect on the state of creditor confidence, leading to a situation in which willingness to accumulate financial assets will even diminish and the interest rate is by no means bound to fall. An interest rate that remains invariable despite economic-policy measures is therefore not always, as is suggested by structuralist theory, grounded in sluggishness and rigidity. Instead, highly flexible responses on the part of those who see their claims to wealth impaired can lead to a supposedly rigid interest rate level. The neoliberal counterrevolution is certainly not entirely wrong in pointing to these rigidities stemming from intervention.

Owing to such ambivalent effects, which could be illustrated with even more examples, the matters addressed - decrease of the liquidity premium and increase of the profit expectations of potential investors - can provide only a criterion as regards the measures that can be ruled out with certainty or in a given market constellation. Thus, for instance, administrative interest-rate cuts no less than a fiscal policy financed from monetized budget deficits may be ruled out from the very start because they clearly violate legal claims to wealth. A "stop-and-go" policy, i.e. one alternating between expansion and restriction, will likely have a disconcerting effect on the expectations of creditors and investors.

It must, however, be pointed out in drawing the line between this approach and a post-Keynesian theory of economic policy that considerations of liquidity preference and marginal efficiency, necessary for functional reasons, are distributed asymmetrically. Stagnant income generation supported or sustained by a stability-oriented policy does not conflict with the functional requirements of a monetary economy. An expansion fed or stimulated by macropolicy can, on the other hand, without doubt lead to the dissolution of the monetary context. To this extent, the underlying idea here is not to achieve a "trade-off" between creditor side and debtor side, between liquidity premium and profit expectations. Instead, macropolicy can function only if it is ensured that the liquidity premium is not eroded.

In other words, the only unambiguous use that can be made of macropolicy in developing a domestic market is to safeguard the coherence of the framework in which the generation of income takes place. This demands a sufficiently "desirable", i.e. scarce, currency. As was discussed in the last chapter, this implies preventing both deflationary and inflationary processes. This relatively sobering statement of account on what can be achieved by a genuinely government, i.e. macroeconomic, policy for a closed national economy has therefore lead to the conclusion that in the development process the government should *directly substitute for the monetary actors*.

This has generally been rejected with an explanation of why economic policy is bound to be market-conditioned in a monetary economy. Yet the risks emerging from the substitution - both to government's capacity to act and to overall economic coherence - can be indicated more specifically. What follows is a discussion of the substitution of the prototypic debtors and creditors of a monetary economy, in functional terms: the enterprises and households. The possibility of substituting the portfolio holders, i.e. the banks, will be discussed in the next section in connection with the development of the financial sector.

The problem involved in substituting functions of enterprises has two aspects. It on the one hand results from the fact that, as a political structure, government has rationales that differ from those of profit-making enterprises. The goal of primarily developing a national economy, and only as a secondary effect profitable state-owned enterprises, implies that publicly owned companies may be subject to a "softer" budget constraint. In this case deficits are in part covered by budget funds or reduced by means of hidden subsidies such as privileged access to credit. This conventional objection to state entrepreneurship carries some empirical weight, although it has more the character of a plausible consideration of questionable theoretical validity. After all, a state-owned company can be subjected to a severe budget constraint without losing its public character. - The other aspects therefore concern the inconsistencies stemming from the position of such an enterprise. One inconsistency stems from the fact that as an entrepreneur the state is far more limited in its options of ridding itself of its debts than a company run as a private enterprise. As was made clear - not least - by the debt crisis, a government cannot simply cast off the claims held against it by declaring bankruptcy, because its illiquidity would affect the credibility of an entire economy. Its credit rating depends somewhat less on the concrete projects it undertakes, which is why bad debts on its part must necessarily entail an enduring loss of confidence. This is closely associated with the fact that the state, as the monetary authority, can potentially issue money when it is in an emergency situation in its function as a debtor. As was mentioned above, this is inconsistent with a basic principle of credit economics. It is bound to weaken the acceptance of the national currency.

The case is similar when government seeks to substitute for the function of portfolio owners. The conventional objection that only a microeconomic unit can pursue a microeconomic profitability rationale can also be applied against the state as the mere owner of state enterprises with an independent and sanctionable management of their own. In this role, the state also tends to use its finances to expand production processes to such an extent that in the end the interest due is no longer guaranteed. This leads to the problem, more fundamental in the view of this study, that the state has no rationale of liquidity preference that would reflect the threat of potential illiquidity. On the one hand, the state cannot be sanctioned in the way in which the private sector can - which, it is true, can cause this sector to react all the more sensitively to abuses of state power. On the other hand, the state has the formal option to supply itself with liquidity by helping itself to the money it issues.

So what, in functional terms, is left to macropolicy is the unsure means of seeking to influence expectations, but not of replacing the private sector with its higher liquidity preference or higher claims to profit so as in this way to force income generation.

3.3   The Financial Sector in Monetary Development

The conclusions on the role of the financial sector in the process of monetary development and how this role might be filled in terms of economic policy can be illustrated as a contrast with the approaches predominant in the literature. Yet it should be noted at the outset that the authors writing on this topic argue for the most part eclectically, thus making a certain measure of schematization unavoidable here.[74] They may be distinguished in terms of whether they see, owing to a neoclassical-liberal tinge, policy failure or, owing to a structuralist parti pris, market failure as the crucial cause of underdeveloped financial systems. They can also be distinguished accordingly with regard to their recommendations on how to redress this obstacle to development. It is all the more surprising that they generally agree in their ideas of what will constitute the end result of financial-sector development.

A structuralist diagnosis stating that imperfect markets give rise to a weak financial sector results in the recommendation that this condition should be remedied above all by means of "institution building" and a selective credit policy. What is meant be "institution building" is the development of subsidiary institutions such as a deposit insurance system, but also the creation of financial institutions, in particular development banks, that could lend on a long-term basis. The selective credit policy refers to interest regulations and quantitative targets concerning the allocation of credit. The addressees of a selective credit policy would be the customers of the banks. The "market imperfections" are seen in this case as an exaggerated risk-aversion or in the exploitation of market positions vis-à-vis small borrowers and depositors.

If, in contrast to this view, the neoclassical-liberal diagnosis sees financial repression as causing a weak financial system and hence an inefficient temporal allocation of consumption, then what it sees as necessary to cure the situation is liberalization, in particular by deregulating interest rates. Government intervention would then be restricted to regulatory policy and supervision.

Despite these differing diagnoses and the divergent views attendant upon them about ways in which the development of the financial sector might be encouraged, both camps tend to favor a *supply-side approach* (Patrick 1966, pp. 174ff.): in the structuralist view, there is a lack, both quantitative and qualitative, of sufficient financial services that mediate between surplus and deficit units, households and enterprises. In the neoclassical-liberal view, deregulated - and in a financially repressed economy that means: higher - interest rates would increase the volume of savings and hence the possibility of broadened financial intermediation.

The supply-side orientation common to these two positions in the end implies that the profitability of investment projects and the propensity to defer consumption are determined in real economic terms. Here, the task of the financial sector is merely to broker between the demand for and the supply of deferred consumption, or to heighten the attractiveness of deferred consumption. The broader-based this intermediary infrastructure is, the more efficient, the more in line with the underlying real economic circumstances the intertemporal allocation of resources will be.

Objections to these approaches and the conclusions drawn by this study can relate to three arguments advanced in the discussion conducted thus far: the problem of *uncertainty about investment returns* in the first place implies a profitability defined in monetary terms. In a state of equilibrium, when expectations are fulfilled, the liquidity preference and the marginal efficiency of capital determine the interest rate and the profit rate, and, given nominal wages, the current price level. The interest rate demanded here represents the barrier for investors that forces them to undertake adjustments as regards output levels, choice of technologies, product differentiation, etc. This is crucial to assessing the relationship between encouragement of the financial sector and "classical" development-policy measures and the shape this encouragement is to be given.

In the second place, the problem of uncertainty about investment returns can be reformulated in such a way as to make visible the contribution that can be made by a developed banking system. If suitable financing instruments and investments diminish this uncertainty, longer-term creditor-debtor relationships will come about, thus making possible a concentrated accumulation of tangible assets. This reformulation provides a criterion for the design of adequate financial-sector policies.

The division of labor that is made possible by long-term financial relationships and separates the formation of tangible assets and net worth can give rise to a *specific structural effect of development under monetary conditions*. Monetary production, i.e. production based on creditor-debtor relationships, starts with the presumption that the value of the money to be advanced will be increased. Production at subsistence level contains no such specification on increasing value. Maximization of expected returns is dominated by the endeavor to stabilize the expected return above the subsistence level (Timmer 1988, pp. 297ff.). As a result of their being relatively less dynamic, the economic units referred to here as productive households are therefore pushed into "backwardness". And the regions in which they are primarily located also tend to be peripherized. This shows, among other things, that the financial system, even assuming perfect markets, is not neutral with regard to real economic development and cannot be reduced to a mere intermediary function. Encouragement of the financial sector is thus at the same time faced with the task of taking this structural effect into account and, if need be, taking measures to counter it.[75]

The development of a dualistic economic structure in connection with monetary development - which, as was discussed in chapter 2, can also result from erosion - once again shows the *dominance of the macroeconomic context* that has been referred to repeatedly in the course of this study. During transition from the money-using economy to the monetary economy, the development options available to certain economic units will be altered by the simple fact that income generation is now controlled by advances of money based on investment rationales. Portfolio holders, as the banks and financial institutions have been termed, take up the crucial position between monetary and commodity sphere, between public and private sector. Banks were introduced less as carriers of an intermediary infrastructure than as fundamental instances of monetary control. The goal of financial-sector development is thus not primarily to build up an "efficient" in-frastructure. A traditional financial system can be just as efficient or even more efficient in the sense of being adapted to real economic conditions. Instead, its goal should be to foster the emergence of a two-tier system of liquidity supply which is, among other things, a prerequisite for any effective monetary policy.

To sum up: three arguments have been advances, namely, that the un-certainty over investment returns is generally the decisive obstacle to financial contracts, the growth of credit relationships tends to form structures, the macroeconomic function of the financial system is the crucial factor involved. Several general propositions regarding the relative importance and the organization of financial-sector encou-ragement can be made on the basis of these key points.

Once uncertainty over investment returns has been identified as the basic problem, a marked supply-side orientation of financial-sector encouragement appears inappropriate. This uncertainty is aggravated under the conditions typical for a developing country; it can stem from market imperfections, unpredictable interventions on the part of government, or from events exogenous to the economic process. A forced expansion of a branch network or a concessionary loan may only imply that additional financial contracts are concluded not be-cause of a decrease in the imponderables, but in spite of their exis-tence. And an increase in saving deposits may make sense in terms of stability, although, on its own, it will not create development.

This reveals plainly and simply that financial-sector encouragement must be guided by the principle of diminishing the uncertainty inher-ent in financial relationships. That implies above all that projects less creditworthy in terms of commercial standards should not be financed all the same, but that they should be either directly subsidized or made creditworthy from the very start. It might, in this sense, be pos-sible to speak of a priority of the "classical" development policies such as industrial and agricultural modernization as opposed to en-couragement of the financial sector. Even the struggle against poverty can be seen as an indirect financial development measure to the extent that it helps to prevent distress lending at unrealizable terms.

Traditional development-policy measures can support producers in overcoming the "interest barrier" by promoting the implementation of suitable technologies, development of market niches, diversification of product lines, and the like. This may, at least for promising economic units, help to limit the adjustment impacts stemming from output level variation. - As far as the deposit side is concerned, the supply-side approach appears fairly reasonable. The willingness to invest savings in the financial sector can be heightened by confidence-building institutions such as banking supervision and deposit insurance. As uncertain as this effect is both quantitatively and in terms of its duration, since it aims at altering (saving) behavior and thus constitutes only one influencing variable among others, it could nonetheless make possible growth in income generation accompanied by monetary stability.

These thoughts on the general import of financial-sector encouragement therefore imply that its role is more one involved in supporting other development policies. It is itself strengthened by economic development of the borrower side. A direct approach oriented toward the supply side always presents a risk of generating credit losses among the banks, giving rise to a widely ramified but unprofitable financial system, and promoting an excessive build-up of capacities that tend to erode profitability.

As far as individual measures are concerned, what has been said implies that it is important to encourage *institutions and financial instruments* that are suited to diminish uncertainty and do not per se increase the volume of deposits and loans provided. For what is known as "institution building", this means supporting subsidiary institutions such as credit information agencies, indemnity funds set up within the framework of group credit plans, adjusted forms of insurance plans for borrowers and savers, etc. No one will dispute that it is essential to implement effective measures governing supervision and contract law, yet this is a desideratum that is nearly as difficult to achieve as an effective system of taxation.

Financial instruments that include non-institutional insurance elements already exist in a variety of forms: the group credit plans just mentioned safeguard creditors directly, via their modalities covering liability, and indirectly, via the social pressure generated among the debtors, which increases repayment probability. When such loans are prolonged, only short terms are granted at the formal level, although these can be extended routinely in keeping with a standardized procedure. It is, in other words, possible to motivate creditors to hold a de facto longer-term claim by providing them with the opportunity to revise their decisions within reasonable periods of time. Another approach, known as graduated credit, is to grant a debtor at first only small loans; once he has "proven" himself, however, he - or in rare cases, she - is qualified to apply for larger loans (World Bank 1989, pp. 146f.). Such arrangements can be more appropriate, particularly for productive households, than direct loans at concessionary terms. This prevents overindebtedness and is thus in the interest of both debtor and creditor.

Investment financing via capital markets can have an insurance effect comparable to that of prolongation in that the investment return is not tied solely to the liquidity of one or more specific debtors, although for the debtors this means that their creditworthiness and profit-earning capacity is daily exposed to a market rating. This rating can accelerate a business crisis expressing itself in declining share prices in that it becomes unlikely that a company in this situation will obtain sufficient additional long-term orders or short-term commercial loans. Capital markets are extremely volatile in developing countries, not least as a result of these cumulative processes, which can arise rapidly in comparatively thin markets (World Bank 1989, p. 135). Financing via the capital market as an alternative to borrowing would thus for the most part appear relevant only in a relatively late stage of financial development, where it might prove beneficial to a larger number of enterprises. But this form of financing assumes significance in providing a more adequate means of financing government deficits than central bank loans.

Finally, development banks can play a major role in providing long-term financing for target groups of development policy. Seen as a subsidiary institution, a development bank can above all offer integrated loans linked with special consultation services and employment programs. This is not possible for commercial financial institutions, although it would, if it succeeded, enhance the creditworthiness of their future debtors.

But a development bank should not, as has been customary till now, restrict its activity to lending and seek refinancing primarily with bilateral and multilateral donors or the national central bank. As was discussed at length, this has a destabilizing effect in macroeconomic terms, since an increase of the volume of money does not automatically entail investment opportunities. Such credit outlays disturb the balance between holdings of claims and liabilities, which gives rise to attendant shifts in the price level or the exchange rate.

Apart from the central bank, development banks are often the agents of a *selective credit policy*. In essence, this policy consists of regulations on lending to banks, lending at preferential interest rates, a refinancing system adequate to the ends for which credit is provided, and credit guaranties and credit programs offered by the development banks (World Bank 1989, p. 68). Credit policy can - and should, as seen from the perspective of this study - be used to discriminate in favor of financing the formation of productive tangible assets and to provide the above-mentioned structural effect with the direction desired.

It should be clear that both goals cannot be achieved through a policy of cheap credit. This would, in particular, impede global control of the money supply. Discrimination in favor of investment lending can thus be achieved primarily through penal interest charges on loans taken out for consumption purposes. Nor are concessionary measures necessarily a boon to the productive households disadvantaged by development under monetary conditions. As a rule, these measures lead only to overindebtedness of these households, if the funds intended for them reach them at all. A "structural adjustment" of these households can probably only be encouraged with the aid of credit programs that provide for more comprehensive development-policy measures. They will be able to free themselves from the exploitive practices of informal money-lenders only when their economic position has been strengthened.

To this extent, the dualism of the economic structure must be seen as one factor that, independently of macroeconomic instability and any regulation of formal credit markets, is capable of keeping an informal financial system alive. Neither regulatory measures such as a ban on loan sharking nor a liberalization of the formal financial sector is of itself likely to prove sufficient to eliminate the dualism in the financial sector. Not substitutions but integration of informal savings and credit institutions should thus be the strategy of financial sector development - which seems in the interim to have become the prevailing opinion.[76]

Monetary development theory in general and financial sector development in particular have concentrated on the issue of *liberalization*. As noted briefly in part I, the experience made in the interim has led to a clear-cut shift of emphasis:

"*Raising real deposit rates of interest and proliferating bank branches in rural areas do not in themselves constitute a general program of financial development*" (Fry 1988, p. 412). An effective system of supervision and in particular macroeconomic stabilization, which requires above all a solution of the fiscal problem, are now regarded as the conditions that would permit an opening of the financial markets in the first place. What is furthermore recommended is a specific sequencing of liberalization steps and a gradual approach (World Bank 1989, Chapter 9, esp. pp. 155f.). That accords with the thoughts presented here to the extent that the central importance of the acceptance issue and decisions on financial holdings can explain why shock therapies give rise to the opposite of what they were aiming at. Given an already fragile status of acceptance, the ensuing crisis of confidence is bound more to encourage than to prevent an exodus from the currency concerned. Such an abrupt change in the basis on which intertemporal creditor-debtor relationships are decided therefore threatens to cause current income generation to collapse and to impair the future accumulation of financial assets.

It is not possible to discuss even approximately the aspects of an adequate liberalization policy that have been addressed in the literature. Here again, however, the thoughts presented on the development of a monetary economy make it possible to indicate a criterion that should provide orientation for any opening of financial markets. This criterion would test the measures taken to determine whether they contribute to establishing a two-tier system of liquidity supply. The three most important elements of such a system are a central bank capable of pursuing a stability-oriented monetary policy, an independent banking system which controls the money supply, and the establishment of a money market in which short-term claims to central bank reserves are traded. The latter would allow banks and financial intermediaries to equalize their liquidity and thus to ensure their liquidity at any given time. Selective interventions would be consistent with this as long as they do not prevent the liquidity preference of the portfolio holders from determining the global level of interest on borrowed money.

This criterion also provides a clue as to who might function as the agent of *financial-sector development*. It would not be consistent with a two-tier supply of liquidity if the central bank were mainly responsible for implementing this support. That would require it to hold long-term claims and possibly also to subordinate global control of the money supply to sectoral credit allocation. Both would undermine its responsibilities in the two-tier system, i.e. its ability to implement a tight-money policy and to further tighten the money supply. Financial-sector development should therefore be entrusted to one or more development banks. These would be responsible for allocating, in keeping with development-policy criteria, volumes of credit attuned to credit policy, furnishing longer-term refinancing for formal and informal institutions, and/or holding long-term shares of institutions of the credit and financial markets.

This classification stands in contradiction to the line current in the literature on development policy since Sayers' claim (1957) that the central bank of a developing country has a development function no less important than its task of providing for stability. The welfare-economic "trade-off" (Chandavarkar 1987, p. 36) between stability and development fails, for reasons discussed above, to do justice to either goal, because development implies not merely microeconomic efficiency and macroeconomic income generation. The crucial monetary condition for both is that the constitutive monetary context remain intact. That is the reason why the relationship between macroeconomic stabilization and the goals of development is neither competitive nor harmonious; instead, the former imposes restringent conditions on the latter.

This closes the circle entered when it was stated that development is always development located historically, systematically, socioculturally. In what follows, selected development problems facing India will be interpreted along the lines of these discussions. Owing to its numerous special features, India by no means represents the average of the developing countries, if there is any such country. Rather, India's monetary economy stands for the marked constellation of a development comparatively stagnant, yet stable, one that was encouraged with considerable government involvement. It might appear that the dilemma of stagnation and erosion had been solved here to the extent that at least erosion has been prevented. It will, however, become evident that monetary stabilization has been alternately replaced with, supplemented by, and overlaid with regulations applied at the microeconomic level that were intended to neutralize the macroeconomic constraint on contrived development. The welfare-economic orientation of Indian policy makes it impossible, understandably, to recognize a functional hierarchy of the conditions of development under the conditions of a monetary economy. The corresponding deformations have taken on an alarming shape in the early 1990s.

Part II   India's Monetary Economy since Independence

4   The Development of the System of Economic Policy

India's system of government and economy displays features so singular that it hardly seems possible to classify it among the categories in current usage. In the political economy of developing countries, India has given occasion to coin new terms characterizing systems of this type. What terms like "mixed economy", "intermediate regime" (Kalecki), or "soft state" (Myrdal) have in common is that they raise their hybrid character to the level of a defining characteristic. In India, the following constellations are likely to have been responsible for this impression:

- India's independence in 1947 meant the emergence of the world's most populous *democracy*. This form of government presupposes theoretically a certain degree of homogeneity of the population forming the state, and this population should feel bound through certain fundamental inalienable values. Yet India's populace, strongly segmented across linguistic and cultural lines, by no means meets this requirement.[77] Its federalist organization into 23 states and 8 union territories, basically in keeping with linguistic criteria, may do justice to these disparities. The federal element of India's constitution is, however, largely counteracted by a strongly centralist administration.

- The *declared intentions as regards social and economic policy*, shared by the prominent elites, but also by broader segments of the population, can be summed up in the formula "equity cum growth" (Krishnaswamy/Krishnamurty/Sharma 1987, p. 7). The dual objective reflects the range of social and economic problems facing India. Even today, the two components of this formula can be identified with the names of India's legendary founding fathers: the name Mahatma Gandhi stands for the component of an equity to be achieved through promotion of labor-intensive activities, i.e. one that required a concentration on agriculture, the skilled crafts and small trades. The name Jawaharlal Nehru stands for the growth component that was to be achieved via an industrialization largely induced by government. The latter component has for the most part dominated the practice of Indian development planning (Wiemann 1988, pp. 40ff.), although the element of equity has in part been realized by means of government redistribution measures.

- Thus far, this two-track development strategy has followed a parallel and sequential path along Gandhian and Nehruvian lines, a path entailing preservation and revolution of existing forms of life and production rather than representing the cooperative effort originally envisaged. It thus has more the function of a unifying ideology than that of a directive guiding economic policy. In the course of time, however, it has been used to create a variety of claims against government. The *relationship between state and society* has consequently been marked by the unremitting attempt to forge a precarious compromise between an extremely wide range of interests: the interests of the agricultural and industrial sectors, management and wage-labor, small- and large-scale farmers, the landless and the landed, the socially declassed and the established, to name only the most important among them.

- India's economic system can, as far as its regulatory policy is concerned, be referred to as capitalism with extensive government intervention. The *relationship between state and economy* simultaneously displays complementary, substitutive, and antagonistic traits: the state supplements private-sector activity with numerous protective and promotional measures, in particular with subsidies, development of infrastructure, and measures aimed at safeguarding market shares against domestic and foreign competitors. The right of private property was respected even when the state was seeking to substitute for private economic activity. The indemnities paid, e.g. for the nationalization of key industries, were calculated in such a way that it made little sense to speak of expropriation. Conversely, however, Indian governments have always expected private-sector interests to submit to the priorities set by economic and social policy. If it proved impossible to achieve this by consensus, they have not hesitated to take far-reaching legal and administrative measures restricting the disposition over private property.

Each of the constellations indicated - the connection between democratic government and an electorate differing with respect to fundamental issues, a development program appealing at the same time to the underprivileged and the elites, and controversial distributions of rights and competences between government on the one hand and social groups and economic interests on the other - contains considerable potential for conflict. The discussion that follows centers on the last-addressed point, the relationship between state and economy, although it is not possible to abstract fully from the other characteristics of India's social system in doing so.

Proceeding from Part I, Part II will investigate the relationship between state and economy in India with the aim of establishing whether regarding India as a redistributive regime would further any understanding of it. On the one hand, gaining a systematic picture of the confusing diversity of policy measures would constitute an increase of knowledge, if these measures were interpreted as elements of a policy regime of this type. On the other hand, the concrete form it has taken on could then be judged in terms of whether it, as a regime of a monetary economy, is in keeping with the functional requirements of such an economy.

4.1   Phases of Development since Independence

Before the questions posed in the last section can be answered, it will prove necessary to outline step by step the basic features of the development of India's economic system. This will be based on a phasing scheme current in recent studies on India's economic history (da Costa 1985), although this scheme will be substantiated specifically: the study will identify the problem defining each subsequent phase in the development of India's monetary economy. This will then be followed by a study of whether what emerged in connection with the manner in which these problems were dealt with might be termed a redistributive regime and whether, as such, it has done justice to the demands set by development under the conditions of a monetary economy.

1947-55: Transition to sovereignty

Under the pressure of strong efforts running in the direction of independence, India had long been prepared for its transition to the status of an independent state. Not least, the foundation, in 1935, of India's central bank, the Reserve Bank of India (RBI) served this end. But Britain's first postwar government was unexpectedly quick to part with India. The first sovereign government under prime minister Nehru was therefore suddenly faced with a highly diverse set of problems, of which the integration of a highly heterogeneous population, the separation from Pakistan, accompanied by bloody conflict, and the definition of its territorial boundaries were only the most evident ones.

The transition from a colonial war economy to a formally independent monetary economy represented the crucial problem facing the country in this period. For India's central bank, this meant first and foremost combatting inflation. During the war, the volume of rupees in circulation had risen sharply, since in this period the British government on several occasions borrowed from the RBI in order to procure war material in India. In return, the Reserve Bank acquired obligations in sterling that were credited to its account with the Bank of England. When India achieved its independence, it had become a creditor of its former colonial power - a comfortable position, which, however, must be qualified to the extent that the pound sterling had lost its status as the world's key currency.

In other words, the monetary situation from which India started was marked by a high inflation potential and a comparatively favorable reserve position. The latter could only heighten the acceptability of the rupee, for it did not yet have the character of an independent currency. During the war, the English government had prevented the evolution of a free rupee market in New York (RBI Bulletin 1950, pp. 297f.) Thus the rupee was related only indirectly, via the pound, to other currencies and had to achieve its quality as a full-fledged currency in a period of postwar inflation and stagnation.

The phenomenon of persistent stagflation went on until the period of India's First Plan (1951/52-1955/56),[78] i.e. the situation confronting India was one of stagnant growth of the national product until 1950 and relatively high price rises continuing until 1951. The newly independent country's dependency became drastically evident when the pound was devalued, taking the entire sterling currency area with it. This called for a massive devaluation of the rupee in the autumn of 1949 in order to come to terms with a foreseeable foreign trade imbalance. Even while India's economy was adjusting to these price rises resulting from the devaluations against the non-sterling areas, the Korean War broke out in the middle of 1950. Worldwide inflation again forced the Reserve Bank to take defensive steps in the form of anti-inflation measures.[79] India was limited in its ability to participate in the ensuing demand boom, because it was lacking in productive capacities.

When in 1950 the first planning period began, industrial and agricultural production rose to surprising levels, increasing real income by some 20 %. In view of war-related supply bottlenecks, the obvious measure required was to step up support for agriculture - a policy that was reinforced by extraordinarily positive weather conditions. Yet the rise in real income was nevertheless surprising in that it was achieved at a moderate rate of price deflation.

Monetary policy was restrictive in the first years of planning. The money supply was even reduced and then expanded only moderately. Only in the 1955 planning year was recourse had to a "reflationary" monetary policy, since grain prices were collapsing under the weight of two successive years of production surpluses. As expected, this was unable to prevent sizable losses of income for agricultural producers.

The balance-of-payments situation was very favorable for two years following the 1949 devaluation. Even following this period, only a moderate foreign-exchange outflow was necessary to finance the balance-of-trade deficit.

In the literature on India's economic history, the first planning period has subsequently been referred to as the "Golden Age in the management of the Indian economy" (Costa 1985, p. 57). This was the first and last time that the planned growth rate was surpassed by the growth rate actually achieved. Essentially, this was due to a low initial national income level, favorable external conditions for agriculture, and a macropolicy thinking in terms of consolidation. The good results of the first planning period made it appear justifiable to pursue more ambitious goals in the future.

1956-66: Contrived expansion and impending crisis

Borne on the wings of a technocratically conceived modernization theory, India's development planning set itself the goal of accelerating the process of its late industrialization. The model was the Soviet economic planning of the 1930s which had transformed the formerly agrarian country, with breathtaking speed, into a state with a remark-

able industrial base. The specific link of state and economy represented by the Soviet Union was bound to appear highly attractive to
the political elites in India - as in other developing countries: on the
one hand, the state apparatus explicitly placed itself in the service of
economic development, thus raising the means of the nineteenth century national state to the level of an end in itself. On the other hand,
it occupied the "commanding heights" of the economy, as is noted in
India's first Five-Year Plan - thus extending these heights far into the
level plains of the production process. This appeared to be the ideal
model for a developing country that exhibited no more than a tiny
middle class and was unwilling or unable to imitate the development
courses of the dominant industrial nations. The "socialist pattern of
society", which the Congress Party raised to the level of a platform
under Nehru and now sought to implement, was the stand-in concept
for a system beyond the capitalism practiced in the West and the
communism aspired for in the East.

The late development of India's monetary economy, which can be
seen as the central task of this period, was accordingly geared to a
model that provided for planning of the physical structure of the
economy. The basic model, named after chief planner Mahalanobis,
represented a system of equations for two sectors, investment and
consumer goods, in the tradition of the Harrod-Domar growth theory.[80] Increased quantitative output in the investment-goods sector
was to create the conditions for a long-term expansion of income.
This proposition can obviously be made only under the assumption of
constant prices, as was common in the then-current understanding of
Keynesian theory.

The legislative foundations were laid for a comprehensive program of
investment direction aimed at implementing the physical targets. By
introducing a licensing procedure, the "Industries (Development and
Regulations) Act" of 1951, regulated entrepreneurial decision-making
on siting, capacities, and product lines.[81] The "Industrial Policy Resolution" of 1956 reserved exclusively for state-owned enterprises a

number of industries and infrastructural sectors or assigned them initiator role there (Rangnekar 1984, pp. 295f.).

The financial requirements were defined, as it were, more or less along the lines of the planning of machine or energy units, as residuals. The volumes of expenditure of the two plans were either more than doubled (2nd plan) or nearly doubled (3rd plan); only around one third was financed from government revenues, while foreign assistance and deficit financing made up a sizable share. The potential for crisis accumulated in this expansionary course erupted when events exogenous to economic planning intervened, viz. border conflicts with China (1962) and Pakistan (1965), weakened government following Nehru's death (1964), and two disastrous drought years (1965/66). Finally, there was no longer a base to finance the Fourth Plan, when, following the war that had been started by Pakistan, the Western donor countries discontinued their development assistance (Weiss 1967, pp. 210f.; Rothermund 1985, p. 163). It became only too apparent that, contrary to its declared intent, India's dependency had widened.

During the course of the second planning period, national income grew in real terms by over 20 %, a level below the target set, though higher than in the first period. Owing to the exogenous factor named, the growth in the third period fell to around 15 %.[82] From 1964 on, the price level increased at two-digit rates (Annex A). The output of the agricultural sector shrank even in absolute terms during the first half of the 1960s, while industrial production grew by over 40 % in the course of the two planning periods, but then stagnated at the level it had reached.

Monetary policy is closely linked to the financing of the current-account deficit. It was first managed via drawings with the IMF and by lowering foreign-exchange reserves. At the end of the Second Plan, this last source of finance, which in itself had a contractionary effect on domestic money supply, was exhausted. What was now introduced, supported by persistent capital imports, was an easy-money policy. The ensuing crisis announced itself in a shift into bank deposits of short-term maturity.[83] These depositor reactions may be interpreted as expressing expectations of further price increases. This caused the velocity of circulation to accelerate, exercising a cumulative effect on the inflation rate.

Inflation rates distinctly higher from 1964 on caused the current-account balance to deteriorate rapidly. The deficits finally prompted IMF and World Bank to link the grant of further loans to the implementation of an adjustment program. In 1966 the rupee was devalued by 36.5 % against the US-dollar, and foreign trade was liberalized (Bhagwati/Srinivasan 1975, Chapter 6). But these measures failed to lead to any improvements in the balance-of-payments situation, and in 1968 India consequently rescinded its attempts at liberalization.

The attempt to force development, and in so doing to pay little heed to the implications of dynamic income generation, had reached its limits. As will be discussed at greater length in the following section, India's economic policy responded above all with two new sectoral programs: first, with a modernization of the agricultural sector aimed at diminishing, among other things, the "cost-push" factor of inflation; second, with an expansion of the financial sector aimed at raising the share of domestic financing in development expenditures. The sectoral policies may be interpreted as a tribute paid to the restrictions imposed by development under monetary conditions, although this statement contains no implications on how worthwhile this tribute proved to be.

1967-80: Persistent crisis management[84]

It is presumably not an exaggeration to term this period the greatest challenge thus far to India's economic policy of the postwar era. In adjusting to recurrent crises, a package of highly diverse measures was implemented in the agricultural, industrial, and financial sectors. An outline of these measures against the background of the macroeconomic problem involved may prove informative for the discussion of the regime of the Indian monetary economy that follows it. This period will therefore be given detailed consideration.

The economic situation, again and again heading into crisis, implied at the political level that India's government, which had subscribed to the goal of contrived development, was exposed to constant legitimacy pressure. As a rule, it sought to encounter this pressure by intensifying government influence on the economy.

The problem of legitimacy was posed at the very outset of this phase, when, between 1966 and 1969, medium-term development planning had to be suspended. Nehru's daughter Indira Gandhi, appointed prime minister in 1966 as a compromise candidate, was backed only by a weak majority of her Congress Party following parliamentary elections in 1967 (Frankel 1978, pp. 232f.). Domestically, the situation was very tense, making itself felt, among other things, in determined strikes that indicated severe losses of income among wide segments of the population. When the Congress Party split in 1969, Indira Gandhi pursued a left-wing populist course in which fighting poverty ("*gharabi hatao*") and self-reliance in development became much-touted catch-words. But the declarations of intent they implied remained rhetorical, be it because they in any case sprang merely from electioneering (Rothermund 1985, pp. 168-170), be it because they were unfeasible under the pressure of events.

A rise in smuggling and other black-market transactions indicated that income earned in domestic currency was successively being replaced by barter and foreign-exchange dealings, that, in other words, an erosion of the monetary system was immanent (RBI Bulletin 1966, p. 129; ibid 1977, p. 772). In 1975 Prime Minister Gandhi declared a state of emergency, but then, in the spring of 1977, lost the first elections called after this suspension of fundamental democratic rights. The emergency regime had backed a restrictive monetary policy and begun to prosecute illegal transactions. This austerity course was suspended under the new Janata government in favor of a stepped-up promotion of the agricultural sector and economic liberalization. But the critical situation that ensued from the second oil-price hike again favored strong leadership and brought Indira back to power as prime minister in 1980.

The changeable fate of Indian governments during these years can be understood as an expression of crises of political legitimacy, a political pendant, as it were, to economic crises. Beginning with the middle of the 1960s, economic policy responded to them with a large-scale program of agricultural modernization, a far-reaching nationalization of the banking sector, and laws on industrial regulation. All these measures can be interpreted as attempts to solve the dilemma of an underdeveloped monetary economy: although the prevailing level of development appears to call for an expansionary strategy aimed at rapidly overcoming the most pressing problems, development under monetary conditions nonetheless imposes certain constraints on an expansionary strategy. At the end of the last phase (1966), the foreign-trade constraint had made itself felt in an acute balance-of-payments crisis. The rise of a parallel economy in this phase indicates that there were also domestic constraints and that evasive reactions of the private sector could force government to undertake stabilization-oriented interventions.

As was mentioned above, there are signs indicating that the "Green Revolution" was first and foremost used as a measure for combatting inflation by structuralist means. The official justification for a strategy of agricultural modernization are entirely in harmony with the economic canon of that age, which saw inflation not as a process but as a reaction to cost push or demand pull. The cultivation of high-yield varieties, later proclaimed the crucial element of the "Green Revolution," plays no part in the initial planning documents.[85]

Finally, part of this program involved the introduction of an agricultural-price policy aimed, among other things, at moderating price rises for basic foodstuffs. This policy, it is true, did not merely pursue a stability-oriented goal: in guaranteeing prices it sought to provide productive incentives for farmers. The government bought up agricultural produce at these prices with the intention of building up buffer stocks.[86] The instrument of fixed prices ("procurement prices" or "issue prices") was used to pursue regional and sociopolitical goals on the demand side. These prices were to form the basis of exchanges of produce between the federal states or the sale of basic foodstuffs to poor segments of the population in so-called "fair price shops". In the concrete situation in which it was initiated, this poverty-alleviation measure served, from a macroeconomic perspective, to attenuate the adverse distributive effects of inflation.

Another sectoral policy was associated with the macroeconomic situation, i.e. with financing of increased government spending and with the withdrawal of foreign assistance following the war against Pakistan in 1965: toward the middle of 1969, the 14 major banks were nationalized, transferring some 80 % of banking-sector assets to state ownership. Another six commercial banks were nationalized in 1980, and India's private banks today have a share of only some 4 % in all deposits and/or lending (Breuer 1990).

The previous policy of social control, which had set its hopes on moral suasion and representation of social groups in the banks' supervisory boards, was thus declared a failure. What now began was a massive, state-decreed expansion of the banking network. The main intention was in this way to mobilize savings in regions that had until now been neglected so as to achieve ex ante a domestic means of financing investment. Further developments in the financial sector will be discussed in chapter 5.

Industrial policy displayed a tendency toward more intensive regulation that found expression, for instance, in the passage of a cartel act ("Monopolies and Restrictive Trade Practices Act" = MRPT) which imposes on enterprises above a certain size incisive restrictions as regards expansions of their capacities and choice of product lines. The licensing system was tightened up and new restrictions were imposed on foreign investors wishing to invest directly in Indian enterprises.

From 1968 on, the system of foreign trade had again reached a high level of protectionism. - It was the Janata government that undertook the first steps in the direction of promoting, through liberalization, private-sector activity, in particular on the part of foreign firms. This was also continued after 1980.

Macroeconomic development in these years does, however, indicate that the sectoral policies mentioned are unable to replace stability-oriented monetary and fiscal policies. At least temporarily, the economic-policy imperative of dynamic industrialization had to be abandoned, sacrificed as it were to the exigencies of stability.

Enormous fluctuations in the growth rates of the most important macroeconomic variables are the signature of this period (Annex A). Whereas in the first three years of this period (1967-69) real income rose by an average of 5.8 %, this rate fell in the following decade (1970-79) to an average of 3.2 %. The increases in price levels were moderate until 1972, rose exorbitantly in 1973/74, and were subsequently subject to sharp fluctuations. This development resulted from the coincidence of a high domestic liquidity potential and exogenous disruptions that triggered price rises and made ad hoc monetary policy measures inevitable.

Following a drought disaster in 1965/66, agriculture showed clear-cut signs of recovery. Observers at first regarded them as initial successes of agricultural modernization. It has, however, become evident in the meantime that the "Green Revolution" resulted in essence only in a noteworthy increase of the wheat yields per unit cultivated, which has led to a far-reaching regional differentiation of the Indian countryside into wheat-growing areas and other farming areas. While average farm incomes scarcely rose in real terms, and even fell in comparison to nonagricultural incomes, modernization led to a stronger concentration of incomes stemming from agricultural activity.[87]

Industrial production stagnated in this period, in comparison with both the previous decade and the decade following: the growth rate fell by one half from some 8 % (1955-65) to 4 % (1965-76), although it rose slightly again in the last years of this period.[88] It is instructive to note here the industries mainly responsible for the decline of the industrial growth rate: the period between 1966 and 1970 saw a sharp drop in the investment-goods sector that clearly reflects business expectations, since these shifts are not recognizable when referred to the changes taking place at the same time in the area of import policy (Bhagwati/Srinivasan 1975, pp. 159ff.). The period from 1971-75, on the other hand, showed a sharp decline in the consumer-goods sector, which points to a drought-related contraction of incomes, the first jump in oil prices, and anti-inflation measures. Both investment expectations and income generation were surely impaired by the decline in public investment. The recovery in the second half of the 1970s at any rate coincided with a rise in government investment activity.[89] The utilization of capacities in the individual industries serves to underline the picture that results from consideration of the growth rate.

As early as the beginning of the 1970s, it became clear that the sectoral-policy measures had succeeded only in preventing the crisis from erupting. The war against Pakistan (1971), two successive drought years (1972/73), and the first oil price hike again gave rise to an acute need for adjustment. One attempt to address the problem was that the Reserve Bank for the first time practiced a monetary anti-inflation strategy. The growth of the money supply was reduced from close to 20 % (1973) to some 2 % (1975). This was made possible by a restrictive fiscal course that led to a clear-cut decrease of the government's demand for money with the RBI. Only toward the end of the 1970s did the volume of claims held by the RBI again begin to increase rapidly, which is due to heavy government borrowing (Annex B).

The basic tendency of monetary policy - restrictive since around the end of 1973, expansive from 1977 on - is likely to have been an important reason for the differences in the way the two oil-price shocks were absorbed by adjustment measures. The balance-of-payments problem resulting from the first increase in oil prices was mastered unexpectedly well as a result of major transfers of foreign exchange. The transfers stemmed for the most part from Indian workers employed in large part as technicians in the Gulf States. Special foreign-exchange accounts ("non-resident external rupees (NRER) deposits" and "foreign currency non-resident (FCNR) accounts" were set up to encourage them to remit their dollar earnings, in subsequent years other foreign-exchange earnings as well. The 1974 and 1976-78 current-account balance therefore showed major surpluses, which were in part backed by the balance of trade as well. - The adjustment to the second oil-price shock, which saw the Janata government abandon the macroeconomic austerity course, shows exactly the opposite picture. The period after 1979 saw persistently high - though not exorbitant - price rises, and the balance of trade deteriorated dramatically. Since the adjustment to the first shock had meant sharp drops in income for many segments of the population, a similarly drastic restrictive policy would scarcely have been implementable. The worldwide recession in the wake of the second oil price hike presented an additional aggravating factor (Ahluwalia 1986).

So this phase, which began with adjustment to a balance-of-payments crisis, ended with an attempt to adjust to another one. The foreign-trade side has until today remained the Achilles heel of India's development.

1981-90: Attempts at reform

In Indian expert circles, the stagnation of industry displayed in the last phase and the deteriorating balance-of-payments situation are the subject of persistent discussion. Even in the 1980s - against the background of distinctly higher growth rates in industrial production and exports - this discussion has lost none of its intensity.[90] This may be seen as an indication that the development of industry and exports has become an issue of legitimacy for the Indian interventionist state. Not only has the scope for domestic redistribution narrowed, making it more and more difficult to fulfill the numerous demands bound up with the regulatory system (Dhar 1987, p. 15). India's economic successes, small when compared to those of other Asian countries, also entailed a decline in its significance in the theater of world politics. Its claims to regional hegemony can in part be realized only through threats of military force - an instrument of power politics that represents a severe budget strain.

This legitimacy pressure, stemming from both domestic and foreign problems, may be the reason why the course embarked upon by the Janata government was retained by the governments succeeding it. Indira Gandhi performed an about-face fraught with consequences, when seen from today's perspective, by switching from a policy geared to the terms of socialism and secularism to an economic policy expressly conducive to Hinduist fundamentalism and business interests. According to Kohli (1989, pp. 308f.), these links - socialism and secularism or, alternatively, Hinduism and pro-business policy - are those most likely to mobilize sufficient political and economic support in India's democracy.[91] Carried by an electorate addressed via the latter link, the Janata government had undertaken initial attempts at liberalization, which were continued by Indira Gandhi. Rajiv Gandhi, coming to power upon his mother's assassination in 1984, considerably stepped up the pace of reforms.

In view of growing resistance against his policies, which altered the redistribution of incomes in favor of the urban middle classes, he was forced to modify both this pace and the direction of liberalization. Even the business world, which generally supported his policies, was split on concrete measures: the representatives of import-substituting enterprises spoke out against a rapid liberalization of foreign trade and pushed corresponding restrictions through. Kohli (1989, p. 318), although he sympathizes with Gandhi's policies, nevertheless concedes to his opponents that his political agenda was first of all "pro-business" and only in the second place "pro-market" and "pro-competition". This proposition leads to the conclusion that Gandhi's liberalization policy involved significant mercantilistic features, integration into the world market along liberal lines was not its uppermost goal.

Later, however, it became evident how fragile and risky it was to seek, in a democracy marked by poverty, to win majorities for a pro-business policy by appealing to religious chauvinism. Even toward the end of Gandhi's term in office, it became apparent that fundamentalist Hinduist currents were beginning to develop coalitions with big farming interests. During the Singh government's brief term in office, it was primarily the - fiscally costly - fulfillment of disparate demands that permitted a continuation of deregulation efforts. Hinduist fundamentalism, which had made of economic liberalization a policy capable of mobilizing majorities, was in the end responsible for toppling the Singh government.

This lengthy discussion of the political background is justified in that it casts light on the complexities and difficulties - heightened in a formal democracy - involved in reforming a highly regulated monetary economy. Toward the end of the 1960s, the establishment of a sophisticated regulatory system was seen as a suitable means to stabilize an economy prone to development-related disruptions. This led to the creation of more and more competences and responsibilities for government bureaucracy. But a world economy in the process of change restricts the organizational and regulatory latitude open to internal economic control, thus requiring budgets to be expanded constantly so as to contain the inconsistencies between world economic evolution and domestic economic planning.

If this discussion has pointed to the mercantilistic aspect of India's liberalization policy, its defensive aspect will now become apparent: it consists of relieving government and its economic policy of tasks and requirements with which it has shown itself less and less able to come to grips - as is shown by the factional splits along domestic policy lines and the macroeconomic situation described below.

The problem as stated here also becomes visible in sector-to-sector policy measures. No apparent attempts at liberalization were undertaken in agricultural policy. Instead, the measures seemed intended to satisfy highly diverse interests of a rural population sharply differentiated in the course of modernization. In May of 1990, for instance, an "Agricultural and Rural Debt Relief Scheme" came into effect that, under certain conditions, permitted cancellation of rural borrower debts of up to 10,000 iR, i.e. these debts were taken over by the federal government (RBI Annual Report 1990, pp. 160f.). Since 1980 the prices regulated under the terms of India's agricultural price policy have been fixed on the basis of cost considerations, while the previous policy was to perpetuate historical market prices. In the meantime the recommendation of an expert commission has even given rise to a discussion as to whether it might not also be possible to include in these costs a managerial salary indexed for inflation.

In the industrial sector, on the other hand, a great number of liberalization measures were introduced. Several industries were granted exceptions to the licensing regulations, while certain restrictions on license-free investment were raised for others (these limits vary from site to site).[92] The cutoff point set by antitrust legislation was likewise raised. Some industries were wholly excepted from the stipulations of this law. Finally, one important measure was the release of cement and aluminium prices, although administrative prices have continued in effect for a considerable number of products.

Foreign trade has also been reformed, this finding expression above all in advance notice of the measures planned for a three-year period. A constantly updated positive list of imports was also introduced; these goods are covered by the so-called "Open General License", may, in other words, be imported without any further permits. The structures of tariffs has been unified, although the average nominal protection level appears to have risen. The most important change in foreign-trade policy is, however, a resolute support of exports.[93] This consists chiefly in subsidized loans and a liberal import policy for goods that benefit export production.

The financial sector has, finally, also developed a variety of reform-directed efforts (RBI Annual Report 1990, pp. 148ff.). The most important changes concern the promotion of an extended money market and the "price policy" for lending (cf. chapter 5). Yet the signs point more in the direction of consolidation than liberalization, because the credit status of the banks has deteriorated dramatically. This context thus includes measures aimed at tightening up banking supervision and the above-mentioned "Debt Relief Scheme" for rural debtors.

In comparison with the preceding phase, the macroeconomic variables indicate continuous growth. Adjusted for price, the gross national product grew by an average of 5.5 % (Economic Survey 1990, p. 1), although the agricultural sector remains very susceptible to weather factors and is suffering more and more from the ecological strains attendant on modernization. Industrial output, on the other hand, has risen distinctly, namely, adjusted for price, by over 7 % (ibid). This positive development was, to be sure, accompanied by higher price rises that failed to decline toward the end of the 1980s despite good harvests and a slow-down in the expansion of credit. The Reserve Bank attributes the responsibility for this to various factors such as supply bottlenecks for individual basic foodstuffs and higher import prices caused by devaluation, though it emphasizes the exorbitant rises in the budget deficit, which is largely monetized (RBI Annual Report 1990, p. 70; Chapter 6 of this study). Not the least reason for the increase in government spending is high interest payments on chiefly domestic public debt instruments. This budget item is already devouring close to one third of the current expenditures for the 1989/90 fiscal year.

In view of the huge amount of resources required to finance the deficit, the central bank is no longer able to control the money supply. In the 1980s, the volume of money and credit reached two-digit growth rates; the obvious reason for this is the rising government share in the volume of domestic credit and the claims held by the RBI (see Graph 4, Annex B). In view of an easy-money policy of this sort, the industrial expansion of the 1980s is not surprising, even if other favorable factors may have supported it.

As might be expected, the comparatively flourishing generation of income has been accompanied by high deficits in the balances of trade and current account, especially since liberalization policy has eliminated certain administrative obstacles. Persistent devaluations of the rupee have been unable to contain the high deficits even in the midterm, even though a good part of the striking rise in exports is apt to be attributable to this measure.

The persistent budget deficits, an excessive expansion of the money supply, and the external debt resulting from the balance-of-payments situation have created an highly explosive macroeconomic situation. In view of the strains stemming from the Gulf crisis, which were further deepening the foreign-trade deficit and reducing the foreign-exchange transfers from the Arab states, the situation had taken a rapid turn for the worse. The trek to the IMF had become unavoidable at the end of this phase(cf. chapter 6).

4.2   The Regime of India's Monetary Economy

The nations granted their independence since the Second World War saw themselves faced with tasks of a twofold nature as regards economic policy: they were forced to develop their economies in a world dominated by established monetary and planned economies, and they were forced to develop as monetary or as planned economies. Developing as a monetary economy implies setting in motion a monetization process and controlling it with an eye to world market competition; developing as a planned economy implies steering the national production process by means of quantitative targets and price administration.

As is shown by India's transition to sovereignty, the difficulties involved in developing under monetary conditions entail a specific problem complex related to legitimacy: the establishment of social coherence via creditor-debtor relationships, the constitution of a national monetary economy, requires an accepted currency to which the rationale of the contracting parties is referred and by means of which the parties can terminate a given contract. In India's case this required in the postwar period first and foremost an antiinflationary strategy, because it is only a scarce currency of relatively stable value that can guarantee this acceptance in the long run. The antiinflationary strategy is, however, bound to impair a second element of development that, understandably, had foremost priority following liberation from the fetters of colonialism. Increased generation of income and the buildup of an industrial base independent of conditions imposed by nature were impeded by depression in demand and a heightened interest-rate barrier.

Thus, for instance, the rise in the traditional indicators of income and agricultural and industrial output also caused disappointment among the makers of India's economic policy (Sen 1982, p. 100), even though the growth rates in the First Plan looked reasonable. In view of widespread poverty, the welfare and employment picture, such growth rates - which proceeded from an extremely low base - did not in the least indicate how and in what period of time the means were to come about that might provide tangible relief for these problems. The obvious conclusion is that a forward-looking economic policy would have to stage the "big push," as long as market conditions were unfavorable to private-sector income generation. As in most developing countries, the Indian government was thus assigned a major economic role that implied a deployment of state interventionist instruments.

The formula cited above, "equity cum growth," lends programmatic expression to the view that this economic role of government should not consist merely in replacing or supplementing private-sector activity for the purpose of stimulating growth. This, instead, also implied an obligation on the part of government to make use of its sovereign function in redistribution. To emphasize even further this redistributive aspect of state economic activity, one might paraphrase this formula as postulating: both to redistribute, according to political criteria, what is available and to increase latitudes for redistribution. This paraphrase makes it plain that in pursuing this goal the Indian government had to seek to centralize sizable shares of the means of production and the yield of national economic production. In this it shares one of the features typical of the redistributive regime qua nation state; the concept was elaborated by Polanyi and others from studies in the fields of social anthropology and economic history.

But to avoid the impression that India's economic-policy system is here to be put up as an ahistorical "ideal type," it will, to identify further features, be necessary to describe briefly how this system has changed since independence. This *process of change* affected not only points of emphasis in economic policy, but structural aspects of it as well. This can be illustrated vividly with the example of the shifting relative position of the planning commission. This exemplary description may at the same time illustrate that India, despite the existence of this institution that originally found its orientation in the Soviet model, does not constitute a planned economy.

Directly following independence, the switches were set for the two-track approach that appeared appropriate to a "mixed economy", i.e. capitalism with extensive government intervention: on the one hand, war-related price controls were rescinded and direct taxes lowered in an attempt to create an investment climate conducive to private enterprise. On the other hand, a law on industrial regulation was passed that granted the government certain monopolies and the exclusive right to found enterprises in individual sectors (Frankel 1978, pp. 76f.). Initially, the planning commission's only function was, in its (first) Five-Year Plan, to provide orientation for the allocation of budgeted funds and the goals specified, which proved subsequently to be realistic targets.

That changed with the Second Plan, in 1955, when Nehru raised the planning commission to the level of an executive organ for economic policy, transformed it, as it were, into a staff department of his cabinet. It was above all the interlinkage of personnel in commission and government that was intended to ensure this. The ministers of finance and defense sat on the five-man commission; conversely, one of its members was given cabinet rank, the job of minister of planning. This led to a strong concentration in the design and development of economic planning. Thus, for instance, the commission decided on the level and uses of centralized financial allocations to the federal states. The most influential and longest-serving members - from 1964 on, their terms of office were not subject to limits - had no formal economic training. Professor Mahalanobis, who became known for his planning model, was a physicist and the honorary chairmen of the "Indian Statistical Institute" (Frankel 1978, pp. 113-116).

The upgrading of the planning commission was closely linked to the attempt to give rise to "a socialist pattern of society". This orientation implied not eliminating proprietary rights to the means of production, but easing them out through a sort of "top-down evolution", as Nehru's words suggest:

> "Obviously, most persons who believe in a socialist pattern must believe in the public sector growing all the time. But it does not necessarily mean that the private sector is eliminated, even at a much later stage. In regard to the private sector and the public sector, I think the criteria should be basically two. One is to have as much production as possible through all the means at our disposal, and the second is prevention of accumulation of wealth and economic power in individual hands."[94]

The government was, as it were, to become the custodian, not necessarily the owner, of economic wealth and to control its uses in keeping with social and political points of view.

When Nehru's authority began to decline as a result of misjudgments in foreign policy and a tense domestic economic situation, it turned out that the planning commission was an institution based on the grace of the Prime Minister. Members of the government complied only formally with the commission's directives, or simply ignored them (Frankel 1978, p. 225). This passive resistance revealed the political will of some cabinet members to implement economic regulation less via planning directives than via the creation of economic incentives. When, after Nehru's death in 1964, prime minister Shastri came to power, this will found expression in practical terms: among other things, in the attempt to introduce an agricultural price policy oriented in terms of market realities instead of being geared to the exigencies of redistribution and to accord greater weight to private investment.

Even though these moves toward liberalization proved ineffective, or, indeed, even had to be rescinded in the face of a precarious budget situation and high price rises, the shift in emphasis all the same implied an incisive decline in the planning commission's status. The linkages between membership in cabinet and commission were for the most part severed and a limit was imposed on the terms of office of commission members. This restricted the planning commission's functions to the advisory role of an expert commission.

This process of neutralization was continued under Indira Gandhi when she acceded to power following Shastri's sudden and unexpected death in 1966. The commission was soon restaffed with liberal ministers and party members, spelling the end of the sway held by those who had opposed Shastri's liberalization policies. The commission presented a draft plan for the reorganization of federal finance policy that was later implemented; it provided for replacing the system of specifically earmarked allocations to the states with claims calculated in a standardized procedure.[95] The federal government had thus moved away from the idea of any all-encompassing national planning. This planning from now on related only to expenditures made by the central government, and the focal point of these expenditures was shifted in favor of infrastructure and away from financing industrial capacities (Frankel 1978, p. 313).

The economic crisis in the second half of the 1960s further aggravated existing inequities in the population's standard of living. In view of the tense budget situation, the government found itself unable to continue to pursue the dual objective of "equity" and "growth", and instead fostered the latter by promoting private-sector initiative. But when communalist struggles, strikes, and foreign-policy conflicts began to assume ever more threatening forms, a return, at least rhetorically, to Nehru's program of socializing India's society was the result. That nevertheless did not imply an upgrading of the planning commission. This can be seen in exemplary fashion in the nationalization of the banks, under discussion since 1963: less then 48 hours before the parliament was to be convened because of the resignation of the finance minister, the prime minister, in an autocratic act, announced the nationalization of India's 14 largest banks. In this so-called "political blitzkrieg" (Frankel 1978, p. 419), she succeeded in striking the decisive blow: *"The decision to carry out bank nationalization by presidential ordinance had an additional political advantage. It identified a striking 'progressive' measure (...) exclusively with the prime minister."* (Ibid, p. 420)

Thus, with the bank nationalization, began the era of politics centered around the person of Indira Gandhi, an era in which crisis management was to be forced through by authoritarian means. This attempt led into the emergency regime of the 1970s, which ended up in recentralization. The implementation of socioeconomic goals was explicitly placed above the protection of constitutionally guaranteed rights, a state of affairs which, in extremis, permitted encroachments going as far as forced sterilization.[96]

In the late 1970s, first under the Janata government, but then also under the government of a reelected Indira Gandhi, first steps toward global control and microeconomic liberalization were undertaken. The planning commission continues to exercise the task for which it is formally responsible (Misra/Puri 1983, pp. 295f.), although, in a political context seeking to reform the existing regulatory system, it appears to have become a relic of the ancien régime. This is indicated by the fact that the new prime minister, Rajiv Gandhi, in forcing through his liberalization course, found backing among a staff of new advisors, most of whom had been trained in the USA (Kohli 1989, p. 312). Prime minister Singh, recently resigned, also appears to have sought expert advice more from the "Economic Advisory Council" than from the planning commission experts (Wadhva 1990, p. 447). Indications from his brief term in office point to a fresh change of roles for the commission:

Comparatively unorthodox social scientists were appointed to it, including, for the first time, a woman who had become known as an activist in the women's self-help movement. This gave the commission more the function of an important committee conducting hearings with the aim of providing a forum for socially disadvantaged groups in the executive and administrative branches.

This concludes the discussion of an important institution, exemplifying the metamorphoses which India's comparatively stable system of government and economy has undergone. As far as can be determined, planning has never influenced the process of economic production so profoundly as to neutralize its fundamental character as a monetary economy. The dysfunctionalities nonetheless possible will be discussed in various contexts below. The present task, however, is to look into further features that, taken together, justify speaking of a *redistributive regime of India's monetary economy*, bearing in mind that the specific shape of this economy is in constant flux.

Reference has already been made to the primary identifying feature, viz. the *centralization of finances* ensuing from the intended redistribution. The first part of this study noted that a commercial regime and a redistributive regime of a monetary economy can be distinguished according to the origin of the advances of money that constitute the macroeconomic budget constraint. In a commercial regime, these stem primarily from investments made by the business sector, while in a redistributive regime they come from budgeted government spending. Government spending can be financed from taxes and levies imposed on households and enterprises, which is comparable to the earnings retained by businesses. It can also be financed via borrowing in domestic and foreign financial markets and/or central-bank credits. The latter option constitutes the special position of a state as compared with private enterprises as agents of monetary income generation. This can be compatible with the manner in which a monetary economy functions if, in borrowing from the central bank, the government bears in mind the priority of stabilizing the value of money and the exchange rate, which necessarily implies limited and short-term indebtedness.

- In India, government spending, or, as its dual, the financing of the government budget, is the most important component of the macroeconomic budget constraint. Since the middle of the 1980s, expenditure of the central and state governments has accounted for a share making up roughly one third of the gross national product, whereas this share was 20 % at the beginning of the 1970s. Over 90 % of central-bank money supply now stems from government borrowing with the RBI. It is thus the monetization of the budget deficit that forms the basis of further lending, not refinancing of the commercial banks with the central bank. Some 50 % of the liquidity supply drawn by the banks goes back to the government's domestic borrowing (Annex B, Graph 5). All of these indicators - government spending, government's part in the creation of money and the volume of credit - speak in favor of the assumption that India is a redistributive regime to the extent that its public budget is crucial to the constitution of the macroeconomy.

- What follows directly from this is that macropolicy is dominated by the budget, while the money supply is determined residually. This is clearly demonstrated by the refinancing of the commercial banks by the RBI (see chapter 5). This allocation of priorities nevertheless does not imply that in an independent India fiscal policy and monetary policy have always been hierarchically related and appropriately attuned to one another. At the end of the 1960s, for example, the government embarked on a restrictive fiscal course, while the Reserve Bank, in part contrary to its stated intentions, satisfied the correspondingly high level of money demand. Following the first oil price rise, this relationship was then reversed. A committee set up at the beginning of the 1980s to work out proposals on reforming India's financial system (RBI Report 1985) recommended among other things a closer harmonization of monetary policy between finance ministry and central bank. This recommendation aimed at providing an institutional foundation for global control was accepted formally, but it appears that the priority of fiscal policy that would have been expected was in this way merely provided with an organizational framework, as is suggested by the expansionary and inflationary strategy practiced since then.

- Accordingly, India's monetary constitution is characterized by a dependent central bank. The reference to the contrary signals set by fiscal policy and central-bank policy draws attention to the circumstance that the RBI's legal status is only to a limited extent an indicator of the actual room for maneuver open to it and the constraints affecting its actions. Another question, difficult in itself and requiring different answers over time, is whether the financial system has a two-tier structure. From an economic point of view, questions of legal ownership, i.e. the existence of a nationalized banking system, cannot be the decisive criterion, because even a state-owned bank may be subject to a microeconomic budget constraint. It is just as unclear how the extensive and detailed regulations on selective lending should be evaluated. After all, these are general regulations specifying, for instance, that 40 % of the volume of credit go to borrowers rated as priority debtors, like small-scale industry, and not directives to be implemented without taking account of the microeconomic situation. While these two factors, ownership and credit regulations, point in the direction of a system of monobanking, it is at the same time possible to make out a tendency running in the direction of delinking Reserve Bank and commercial banks. This follows from the facts mentioned above that central-bank money essentially comes about as a result of the government's demand for credit and the commercial banks play no more than a minimal role in the expansion of the money supply. They are in large part refinanced via development banks with sectoral competence, the National Bank for Agricultural and Rural Development (NABARD) or the Industrial Development Bank of India (IDBI). This institutional structure, badly in need of interpretation, which determines the process of money supply, is discussed at length in chapter 5.3.

- The central significance of the budget and the dependent status of the central bank imply that monetary regulation is an even more complex task. The central bank need not, as would be the case in a commercial regime, be geared to safeguarding the monetary function in the sense that (private) creditors are protected from a depreciation of their property, as (private) debtors are protected from an appreciation of their liabilities. A further condition for these safeguards to work is the fulfillment of government budget requirements. Because government is as a rule prevented from ridding itself of its debts by declaring bankruptcy, an intertemporal budget equilibrium presents an additional criterion of direct monetary relevance to the activity of the central bank. Maintaining such a budget equilibrium is facilitated in particular by borrowing at low interest rates. Since it proved, for various reasons, unable to create the market conditions for this, the Reserve Bank attempts to meet this criterion by implementing a discriminatory interest-rate policy in connection with deposit regulations. Moreover, the make-up of a number of different institutions ensures that a sizable share of household savings go to the government.

- A further criterion that affects macropolicy and macroeconomy and indicates that India's monetary economy must be seen as a redistributive regime is the relationship between external and domestic economy. Adherence to economic-policy goals does not allow any unrestricted convertibility of the currency, because private claims to wealth have to be limited in scope if development-oriented redistribution is to take place at all. Thus, in India it is normally illegal to hold foreign exchange, and foreign exchange is rationed as a result of the tight reserve situation. This is consistent with the functional requirements of a monetary economy if the returns that can be achieved domestically are at least geared to the interest paid on foreign investments. This sets certain limits on the overvaluation of the domestic currency required in connection with an import substitution strategy. One indication that the restrictions on the convertibility of the rupee have been working is that special foreign-exchange accounts for Indian citizens working, for instance, in the Gulf states have led to a repatriation of sizable foreign-exchange accounts. The flight of capital appears to have been restrained, and black markets for foreign exchange have thus far, in comparison with the role they play in other developing countries, remained relatively insignificant.

- Finally, one factor that remains to be considered in defining a redistributive regime is the economic-policy role played by government in a monetary economy. It was noted above that a regime of this type differs from a commercial regime in one specific respect that makes it possible to emphasize that the budget is the pivotal point of any such regime. Attempts at redistribution obviously imply economic-policy intervention on both sides of the market. Thus, for instance, the agricultural policy pursued in India serves to set producer prices at levels that provide incentives to farmers and at the same time to establish selling prices for needy groups of the population. The difference must obviously be borne by the government budget. The repeated efforts to nationalize trade in essential goods are one factor to be considered in this context (Frankel 1978, Chapter 4). Intervention on both the supply side and the demand side will prove to be a characteristic feature of the overall regulatory system (see chapter 5.1). Other tasks of economic policy can be made out as well, although these are not restricted exclusively to one type of regime. For instance, far-reaching government interventions, in particular restrictions on domestic and foreign competition, may be interpreted as an attempt to lower the liquidity premium in an environment typical for a developing country which is not wholly favorable to private investment. This interpretation indicating that India's economic policy has aimed more at lowering interest rates than raising profits is suggested, e.g., by measures taken in the financial sector designed to bring about direct interest-rate reductions, at least for small and medium-size companies. The other function - stabilization of market processes that tend for endogenous reasons to become cumulative - can be seen as well in the diversity of measures designed to combat inflation. This issue will be discussed at greater length below, because one of the central theses of this section is that the most important sectoral regulations in India have their rationale not least in preventing inflationary processes.

This closes the circle whose beginning and end is the government budget. To the extent that this is the characteristic feature of a redistributive regime, India's regime may be seen as a redistributive one. Since this concept was developed in connection with Polanyi's anthropological writings and on the basis of theoretical considerations on development under monetary conditions, it is evident that all economic-policy measures must be judged as to whether they contribute to or prevent the establishment of an integrated national economy.

In a broader context including the debates in the literature on India's economic policy, the following chapter will discuss the problems facing such a regime. An attempt will be made to demonstrate that the monetary consequences of persistent budget deficits has necessitated the numerous interventions seeking to keep the threat of inflation under control. This, however, has not at all led to the desired results, and has entailed severe dysfunctionalities (see chapter 5). In particular, considerable deformations in the financial sector appear to have come about under the influence of a destabilizing policy of government spending and the simultaneous attempt by the RBI to limit this damage (see chapter 5). It will be argued on the basis of the problems discussed in Chapter 2 that the balance-of-payments crisis in connection with accumulated government indebtedness should compel the government to take an unusual measure, not only to restore the functional conditions under which India's economy can operate, but to keep open its development options at the same time (see chapter 6).

5 Problems of India's Development as a Monetary Economy

This chapter will investigate three complexes of related problems that have been accorded different degrees of attention in the literature on India's development and until now have been addressed in isolation from one another.

The first complex, the sluggish development of income, has been under intensive discussion for at least two decades now. What, in a bitter commonplace, is termed the "Hindu rate of growth," estimated at approximately 3.5 % and, in view of population growth of over 2 %, spells out prospects for a very low increase of per capita income, summarizes in precise terms the subject of this discussion. The basic issues relevant to development economics can be dealt with in this vein; these are the essential problems of this gigantic domestic market.

In contrast, monetary stability and the specific form in which it has been maintained since independence have not attracted any sustained attention. Although it is true that the problems surrounding inflation have on occasion been discussed in topical writings on India's development in the 1980s. The third complex, finally, the disintegration of India's financial system, is by and large still in the stage of empirical investigation.[97] This problem has as a rule been taken as an occasion to demand liberalization of India's banking sector, a demand first underpinned theoretically by McKinnon (1973).

In what follows, an attempt will be made to win some new insights from this broadly familiar topics by interpreting them within the context of an inquiry into the conditions and problems of development along the lines of a monetary economy. In keeping with the preliminary remarks on the method and intent of this study, no attempt will be made to establish quantitatively which factors have been the empirically decisive ones. The intention is, rather, to check, with reference to findings already available, the most important arguments that have been advanced as to their general validity, in order then to assess their significance for phenomena that can be observed in India. The intention is to employ this hermeneutic approach to render India's specific development transparent for problems faced today, in more or less severe forms, by every country of the Second and Third Worlds.

There is a connection between the three problem complexes named: that stagnant income generation has, at least since the middle of the 1960s, resulted from the anti-inflation strategies that have become necessary since then - anti-inflation strategies that, however, display features entirely characteristic of India's regime of a monetary economy. The disintegration of its financial system may be interpreted as a pathological symptom resulting from the attempt both to stimulate income generation and to control inflation.

5.1 Stagnant Income Generation

The most important attempts to explain in concrete terms the sluggish income generation in post-independence India in general and industrial stagnation since the mid-1970s in particular can be related to the economic sector to which they first direct their attention (Ahluwalia 1985). One line of argument looks for obstructive factors above all in the agricultural sector, another seeks them primarily in the industrial sector, while a third one points the finger chiefly at the public sector as the culprit responsible for low rates of income growth.

But highly divergent theoretical approaches are concealed even in attempts that localize the problem in one area, e.g. the agricultural sector. It would thus have been possible to identify, and to take as an underlying basis of discussion, a supply-side and a demand-side type of explanation. Characteristic of the former is that cost-raising factors constitute the central factor for explaining the phenomenon in that they negatively affect producer competitiveness, thus giving rise to stagnation. Characteristic of the latter is that insufficient purchasing power or a weakness of effective demand provides the basis for explaining stagnating accumulation. The point of casting a cursory glance at these modes of explanation was to clarify what the explanation attempted here adds to the pertinent interpretations and what it fades out. To come straight to the point, a critique of these two types of explanation may be summed up as contending that the supply-side argument takes too little consideration of macroeconomic conditions, while the demand-side explanation tends to suppress the constraints implied by development under monetary conditions. In other words, the specific objections to these lines of argument restate what was specified as deficits of development economics in general terms above. All the same, no attempt has been made here to systematize the problem in accordance with this theoretical distinction. That would have required an explicit discussion of the paradigms underlying it, which would lead away from the main issue in hand.

The issue addressed in this section is whether India's comparatively stagnant income generation results from the dilemma that dynamic income generation and monetary stability conflict latently with one another. Seen from this angle, it seems as though Indian economic policy was openly confronted with this dilemma in the middle of the 1960s. The thesis to be substantiated is thus that economic policy in these years sought to avoid the depressive effects of a restrictive macropolicy by practicing a mix of fiscal and monetary caution and sectoral policies aiming directly at moderating effects. For reasons that can be explained, however, this mix succeeded only in repressing inflation instead of eliminating the conditions that made it possible. Consequently, what occurred was precisely what was to be prevented: stagnant development of both industry and income.

These propositions modify a position frequently met with in the relevant literature: it at the same time praises India for practicing a macropolicy geared to financial solidity and makes it directly responsible for stagnation due to overregulation at the sector-policy level (Ahluwalia 1985, p. 108). Overregulation at the level of sector policy is here seen not as arbitrary intervention but as a response to the problem of implementing a consistently restrictive macropolicy in a developing country. Consequently, it is held to be a lack of global control that is causally responsible for the perceivable phenomenon of stagnation.

The Contribution of the Public Sector

A good number of studies on the stagnating development of industry and income concentrates on the - in the narrower sense - economic activity of government as a supplier and a demander of market activity (Ahluwalia 1985, Chapter 5). One line of argument developed along supply-side lines concentrates on the public sector as the producer of a broad spectrum of public goods or goods seen as essential. It contends that it is above all the *lack of supply of services in the infrastructure sector* that undercuts the competitiveness of domestic producers. This critique is directed at both the quality and the quantity of the services furnished. The poor quality, displayed in frequent power failures, unreliable transportation, delays in completing public projects, and so on, has, so the argument goes, led to severe increases on the cost side. On the other hand, the structure of government investment has shifted away from spending for infrastructure, which has entailed bottlenecks in the supply of electricity, coal and rail transport services.

The empirical relevance of such shortcomings cannot be disputed. In particular, they are likely - at a given exchange rate - to have impaired the chances of Indian products in the world market. All the same, it must be pointed out with an eye to the methodological underpinnings of such explanations attempted in the literature that their partial character allows no conclusions to be drawn on an economic phenomenon of this sort. They fail to answer the question as to what prevents the costs from being passed on macroeconomically, i.e. why profit-earning prices fail to materialize, leading to withdrawal or lack of commitment on the part of market suppliers. On the one hand, it is only in answering these questions that propositions could be advanced on the level as opposed to the structure of industrial value added. On the other hand, what is indicative of them is that these arguments became relevant only after the stabilization crisis of the late 1960s and thus point to the underlying dilemma that macroeconomic exigencies were no longer compatible with the goal of securing profit-taking prices.

One consideration - and a consideration leading from the supply-side to the demand-side type of explanation - is whether the above-mentioned structural shift of public investment represents merely the process in which budget expenditures have been reallocated. In case their level had changed, overall monetary demand, the macroeconomic constellation, would have been affected if the additional investments had not been funded entirely from higher taxes.

Various - though not directly comparable - data on the government share of domestic capital accumulation (Rao 1983, p. 156; Ahluwalia 1985, pp. 100f.; Nagaraj 1990, p. 2321) agree in their tendency to indicate that in the decade 1965-74 public-sector *investment activity clearly showed a more reticent trend*. The extensive buildup of capacity in the preceding years certainly undercut the productivity of the plants created, so that the downturn that followed it lent strength to the structural deficits, which consisted in neglect of the agricultural sector and foreign trade.

Under the impression of the stabilization required, the government share of investment fell to an average of 40 %, while from 1960-64, and again from 1975-79, it amounted to roughly 45 %. In the 1980s, on the other hand, it reached levels of over 50 %, which doubtless constituted a significant contribution to the upturn experienced in this decade (Nagaraj, ibid.). In the second half of the 1960s, the declining government share in investment was associated with a decrease in the overall economic investment rate to around 17 %. This then gradually recovered and since the late 1970s has shown a distinctly higher average level of some 25 % (see Annex C).

It is instructive to depict in parallel government spending for consumption and the budget deficits across time. It is surely due to the IMF adjustment program carried out in 1966 that budget deficits financed through borrowing or monetization declined in absolute terms (Frankel 1978, p. 295). In relation to revenues from taxes and levees, the deficits fell to around one third, although, in absolute terms and relative to national income, they again started rising in the 1970s. Only in the 1980s did the ratio of budget deficits to budget revenues again begin to deteriorate significantly (see Annex C). This largely accords with the development of the share of government demand in national income, which - excepting the war year of 1971/72 - displays a slight downward trend continuing into the middle of the 1970s. This share again rises distinctly in the 1980s, revealing a sharply expansionary effect of the public sector when government spending for investment, likewise rising, is taken into consideration.

The course of the indicators named suggests that India's government attempted in the second half of the 1960s to consolidate the budget. This attempt was, however, at first not accompanied by a restrictive monetary policy on the part of the central bank. Consequently, overall economic demand, in particular the investment component, was restricted, although the inflationary potential was by no means reduced. A policy of budgetary adjustment not linked with monetary austerity intensifies the in any case inconsistent character of fiscal consolidation and bears in itself the seeds of failure. Even for reasons of accounting identities, fiscal consolidation is bound to find expression in falling private savings and/or sinking (unredistributed) business earnings and/or falling imports (Spahn 1986, p. 237). The program of mobilizing savings initiated at the end of the 1960s basically prevented the first effect, although a declining investment rate and -

with the exception of the war year of 1971 - an improving foreign-trade performance are at least in part a passive reflex of the attempted consolidation of the budget.

While the comparatively restrictive fiscal policy thus produced the intended foreign-trade effect, the inconsistency inherent in it found domestic economic expression in low investment levels that cut income generation and sales of goods, thus undermining the tax base. In fact, earnings stagnated precisely in the years (1966-69) in which the budget deficit declined in absolute terms (see Annex C). This inconsistency, present in principle, is aggravated when the monetary effect of fiscal and monetary policy run counter to one another.

Persistent inflationary pressures lead to corresponding pressure on wage demands raised by those employed in the formal sector, in particular government employees.[98] They force the government to grant various subsidies aimed at softening the impacts of the price rises on income distribution. And, finally, the concomitant structuralist, viz. sector-policy, approach to combatting inflation entails fiscal costs. This will be discussed at greater length in the following sections. It must be borne in mind that under these circumstances higher government spending was bound to ensue.[99]

An exogenous event, the rise in oil prices, then triggered high price rises and sped up the failure of this combination of policies. In view of the existing liquidity potential, offering no resistance to further prices rises, the Reserve Bank for the first time found itself compelled to sharply restrict the growth of the money supply. But even this monetary policy, which was practiced only for a limited period and helped in the nick of time to prevent the threat of a flight from the rupee, appears to have been enforceable only with the support of the state of emergency proclaimed in 1975. If wage-earners and the poor, with their inelastic demand for certain goods, were the losers of inflation, they were certainly not the winners of anti-inflation efforts. After all, a restrictive monetary policy blocks efforts to raise prices, thus hitting business with unexpected losses that in the end force them to lay off workers. The increase of unemployment, tantamount to a reduction of overall wages, is then expected to prevent any further increase in monetary wages. In India this market mechanism worked only in part, because some companies were required by law to keep on their workforce (Misra/Puri 1984, pp. 205-207). It is no coincidence that the problem of the "sickness" of enterprises, discussed at more length below, became virulent at this juncture.

In a redistributive regime like India's, a restrictive monetary policy will aggravate any existing fiscal imbalance. Spending will grow more rapidly as a result of the factors mentioned, even when efforts are made to increase tax revenues. An additional factor is the cumulative effects of government indebtedness, which result among other things from the fact that new public debt becomes more expensive due to the attendant rise in market interest rates (Bhattacharya/Guha 1990, pp. 782/785). To limit this effect, the nationalized banking system were induced to take into their portfolios a rising share of low-interest government debt instruments. As will be discussed below, a debt trap began to open up owing to the rising interest burden (see chapter 5.2), the reactive measure appears to have rendered a restrictive monetary policy impossible, if the liquidity of the entire financial system was not to be put at risk (see chapter 5.3).

This vicious circle is characteristic for the appearance taken on in India's regime by the dilemma of development under monetary conditions: owing to the sheer weight of budget expenditures, even moderate restrictions can give rise to quantitative effects so strong that willingness to invest inclines toward persistent attentism and the economy is trapped in stagnation. On the other hand, government's important economic role places it in a position to initiate a more dynamic generation of income, at least in the short or medium term - a circumstance making it appear close to irresponsible not to make use of this instrument.

At the end of the 1980s, however, it became clear that an extensive utilization of this instrument can in the end lead to a blockade: "The

Government budget is no longer a source of finance for investment. Current revenues are less then current expenditure because of sharp increases on account of defence, subsidies and interest payments." (Dhar 1988, p. 14) The looming vicious circle might be the explanation why Indian governments never practice a restrictive macropolicy for long, even though they have shown the political will to do so and have done so in acute crises. The sectoral policies implemented since the late 1960s will now be considered against this background - of incapability to practice a restrictive macropolicy.

The Contribution of the Agricultural Sector

One thing common to the tentative explanations subsumed under this heading is that they regard the low growth of incomes and agricultural production as the cause of the overall stagnation observed. On the one hand, this can be causality in the statistical sense, i.e. the low growth in the agricultural sector itself depresses average growth figures. On the other hand, sluggish growth can also exercise a retarding influence on the rest of the economy, in particular on the industrial sector.

A glance at sectoral growth rates confirms the dampening effect of agricultural development in the statistical sense in that the agricultural sector has in fact remained far behind the average growth rates of the other two sectors.

Macroeconomic and sectoral growth rates

	1965-80	1980-88
GDP	3.6 %	5.2 %
Agriculture	2.5 %	2.3 %
Industry	4.2 %	7.6 %
Services in the broader sense	4.4 %	6.1 %

(Source: World Bank, World Development Report 1990, pp. 180f.)

The agricultural sector's contribution to national income thus constantly fell, reaching roughly 32 % in 1988, with over 60 % of the population still employed there. A great number of structural problems are obstructing a more dynamic generation of income in agriculture. The more important ones are:

-   failure to carry out an effective land reform that would have brought about an allocation of land more conducive to increasing yields (Frankel 1978, pp. 87 and 506f.);

-   increasing parcelling of land into units unproductive in view of agricultural modernization and the low level of growth of employment in other sectors, a development all the more serious as new technology seems to exhibit increasing economies of scale with respect to yields per unit of area under cultivation (Dasgupta 1977, Chapter 4);

-   changing yet persistent semifeudal conditions of dependence (Frankel 1978, pp. 548f.);

-   in part extreme climatic conditions and a deteriorating ecological situation in particular with regard to soil quality and the supply of water as a result of modernization and population pressures.

In view of this diagnosis, simple solutions to the problem of stepping up income generation in Indian agriculture are not to be expected, and this study is not in a position to discuss them adequately.

It is, however, of interest for the issue under discussion here that the Green Revolution has had no sustained impact on agricultural growth rates. It was of course carried out in a period *marked by crisis management*. This was not the least of the reasons that robbed it of any convincing success: in macroeconomic surroundings such as these, neither advance nor follow-up industrialization will take place on any large scale, and the drop in overall income offers little incentive to diversify or, indeed, to expand agricultural production. The successes achieved thus appear basically to be due to government initiative, i.e. initiative not geared directly to commercial criteria. To this extent it would be possible to advance the thesis - difficult to prove empirically - that the Green Revolution may have fallen victim to the very situation to which it owes its existence.

The latter formulation is meant to indicate that the Green Revolution was not only conducted under the influence of a need to combat inflation, but that it was at the same time conceived as an instrument of anti-inflation policy. Quantitatively higher output was intended to lower cost pressures in the economy which acted via real wages and prices for primary products used in other manufacturing processes. These and related measures aimed at increasing physical productivity were accompanied by an agricultural price policy intended to subsidize low-income demand and at the same time create production incentives (see chapter 4.1 above).

This policy of moderated prices, seemingly geared only to achieving social and development goals, is comparatively easy to recognize as a component of an anti-inflation strategy. It was not by chance that thoughts were developed on an adequate price policy when the development of market prices began to pose an acute inflation problem (Wadia 1984, pp. 218-221; Misra/Puri 1983, pp. 495ff.).

Seen from this angle, it does then seem plausible to assume that agricultural modernization might have failed in consequence of its being used for purposes other than those originally intended. Deploying it as a structuralist anti-inflation measure aimed at restraining price increases while at the same time dodging a depression might have been precisely what lowered production incentives. And there are signs (Misra/Puri 1983, p. 504) indicating that guaranteed purchase prices fixed on a historical basis lead to attentism, in particular on the part of large agricultural producers, and speculative activities in the commercial sector as long as there is no effective control of the money supply.[100]

The following section seeks to explain why a policy that is able more to repress inflation than to stop it can only fail in terms of the targets set by it. Empirically, however, it is not possibly to say here whether it was the influence of crisis management or a (failed) contribution to combatting inflation that was more instrumental in preventing the Green Revolution from setting in motion any dynamic development in the agricultural sector.

As regards the specific issue of the extent to which the agricultural sector is impairing income generation in the rest of the economy, i.e. may above all have contributed to industrial stagnation, there are at least three explanations. They are in keeping with the possibilities of establishing an economic link between agriculture and industry (Ahluwalia 1985, p. 33), namely

- via the agricultural production of basic foodstuffs that make up the greater part of the so-called wage goods;

- via production of intermediate inputs for farm-like industries;

- finally, via the agricultural demand for industrial goods.

The first explanation of how the agricultural sector might have become a factor contributing to industrial stagnation since the middle of the 1960s concerns its *low productivity in the manufacture of wage goods*. Added up, the prices of these goods are an important factor influencing the level of real wages. In the argument put forward by Ahluwalia (ibid.), this linkage provides a supply-side theoretical explanation for the at times low growth of the industrial sector:

"(The idea of a wage goods constraint) requires the crucial assumption that the wage rate in terms of wage goods is rigid downwards at least in the industrial sector, even though there may be surplus labour in the agricultural sector (...). Scarcity of wage goods can exercise upward pressure on the wage rate relative to the price of manufactured product and this squeezes the profitability of the industrial sector and retards growth."

As was discussed in the last section, the theoretical supply-side explanation in itself is not sufficient. It fails to indicate the macroeconomic conditions under which it proves impossible to pass on the (nominal) wage costs - or the costs of intermediate goods, which will be discussed presently. In this period, it is apt to be anti-inflation measures that prevented aggregate costs from being passed on.

Yet even if this reservation is conceded, it remains necessary at least to explain how the profitability of industrial production is to be inferred from exchange relations said to have shifted in favor of agricultural supply (Misra/Puri 1983, pp. 504-509): after all, it is as a rule possible to import foodstuffs and other wage goods and to avoid domestic pressure on prices through exports.

The first objection points in the direction of the import restriction resulting from the balance-of-payments situation, which precisely in this period led to (moderate) domestic austerity, in this way adversely affecting a development of prices conducive to profit-taking. The balance-of-payments situation itself had reached acute proportions due to a cooling of India's relations with the USA, leading to major cuts in food assistance. The second external argument, i.e. the reference to export options, brings to mind the on average inadequate competitive position of Indian industry in the world market. Macroeconomically, this factor is determined by the exchange rate and the development of price levels relative to those abroad.

What is nonetheless instructive as regards the overriding issues concerning the redistributive regime of India's monetary economy is the extent to which this connection between agricultural wage-goods production and industrial stagnation might turn out to have a certain cogency. The theoretical discussion of producer rationale in a monetary economy prove useful here in that they make it possible to formulate this context more precisely as a market phenomenon and to gain a systematic understanding of dysfunctional economic-policy intervention. This is to indicate specifically where intervention might produce undesirable results, instead of having, in abstractly liberal fashion, to reject any intervention whatever. The following excursus seems justified in view of this tendency in development economics visible since the 1970s.[101]

Excursus: Labor Productivity and Profitability of Production in India

Low productivity in the production of basic foodstuffs can - disregarding for the moment any economic-policy regulations - only imply that real wages are low at a certain required profit rate, but not, as is often assumed, that enterprises would have to pay high real wages. True, it must be assumed that the trade unions, quite effectively organized in the formal sector of Indian industry, strive to safeguard real wages at a given level. But what, in the end, is negotiated is a nominal wage, and it is mark-up pricing on the part of the enterprises - which, as will be discussed presently, can succeed only in part - that decides on the level of real wages.[102]

If, at a given nominal wage rate, prices ensuring normal profits fail to materialize, i.e. if the resulting wage level is too high, enterprises would restrict production, and with it employment. The low rate of job growth in industry (RBI Annual Report 1990, pp. 142f.) points in this direction, but other reasons - above all the use of capital-intensive technology favored by the foreign-trade regime and a selective credit policy - may be responsible for it as well. It must at any rate be noted that enterprises cannot, with means of the market, be forced to pay real wages that are "too high".[103]

Under the conditions governing India's regulatory system, this decision-making rationale of enterprises must, however, be modified. As will be discussed at more length in the next section, administered prices can prevent mark-up pricing that ensures normal profits for a number of industrial goods. A quantitative adjustment via a restriction of production processes is likewise sometimes prevented by economic-policy directives. In this case, the market process must be replaced either with budget allocations or a guarantee of profit earnings via protectionist measures. The first method is most clearly expressed in the widespread phenomenon of "sick industries", the second goes in the direction of the system of industrial licensing practiced in India. The practice of insulating markets at administratively set prices will, over short or long, lead suppliers to lower quality, in formal terms: to shift the cost function downward (to the right), which entails a rise in earnings.

The contrast between business decisions in a commercial regime and in India's redistributive regime is thus that, in the former case, variation of unemployment and its limiting effects on wage rises is used to push through a price level consistent with market interest rates. In the latter case, the intention is to compensate, by fiscal means or by precluding competition, for a wage level inconsistent with the returns required. This results in a sizable strain on the national budget and/or disadvantages as regards competitiveness in world markets.

Given such a situation, raising productivity in the production of agricultural wage goods would have the function of permitting stabilization of the nominal wage rate at a level acceptable to wage earners, because sinking prices for goods would at the same time raise real wages. A one-time devaluation at given and sustainable nominal wages might then improve the chances of products hitherto geared to domestic markets to compete in the world market.[104] In other words: agricultural modernization is not an instrument that can be used to prevent an inflation process, it describes a program of nominal wage stabilization targeted to gain absolute advantages. A program of this sort is potentially suited to balance the divergent demands on wage levels that follow on the one hand from considerations of economic development and from considerations of social policy on the other hand. While the former, with an eye to the world market, calls for relatively low wage rates at a given exchange rate, social-policy considerations in the broadest sense can simply prohibit them from being lowered any further, since they have already reached the subsistence level.

Only this complete line of argumentation as presented in the last paragraph may concede a certain right to the wage-goods argument. Real wages result from the interaction between goods and credit market and are thus, once certain regulations have been cancelled, themselves a policy parameter not accessible to direct control, as many proponents of this argument suggest. At the same time, the proposed strategy of raising the nominal wage level with a view to exports, in that they are restrained by increasing agricultural productivity, does some justice to the problems linked till now with regulation: intervening on the demand and supply side of the labor and goods market, India's government seeks among other things to prevent a cumulative buildup of claims to profit and wage demands. It would, however, achieve this goal with fewer adverse implications if it were to enable suppliers of labor to accept a certain - possibly legally defined - minimum wage level. The agricultural sector here assumes a key strategic significance for development. On the other hand, it would have to enable the enterprises, the demanders of labor, to set adequate prices. It can in any case not dispute the claim of market-oriented enterprises to returns on the money they advance for production: in the extreme case, subsidies would otherwise have to be used to compensate for relatively high wage costs when prices are set administratively, if any production is to take place at all.

Ahluwalia's empirical study (1985, p. 48) in any case fails to find confirmation for the thesis of a "wage goods constraint". The study looks into this on the basis of the quantitative availability of wage goods, the exchange relations between industrial and agricultural goods, and the relative growth rates of labor-intensive versus capital-intensive industries. Its negative conclusion may on the one hand be due to the fact that these indicators are unsuited to verify this thesis. On the other hand, additional factors may have masked or compensated for the weight of wage-goods costs. Although, in other words, a connection between industrial and agricultural stagnation could be explained via this track, its factual significance is uncertain.

A second explanation argues via a link due to the *supply of interme-diate products to agricultural industries*, for instance in the case of cotton and the textile industry. If high prices for such agricultural produce prevent industries close to the consumption sphere from ex-panding, this would entail effects for industrial growth as a whole, for it makes up around one third of all industrial value-added.

The reservation expressed above also holds for this supply-side ex-planation. It might be added that even if it were advanced with refer-ence to the at times restrictive policy practiced since 1967, it would remain as difficult to verify empirically as the thesis just mentioned. After all, other industries were also affected by the macroeconomic austerity course, so that a general level effect would superimpose the structural effect working against the industries close to agriculture, as assumed in this thesis. Shifts in the industrial sector might, however, also have come about in connection with adjustment to weaker overall demand. This depends above all on the elasticity of the demand rele-vant to the industry in question, i.e. on a variable that can be deter-mined only empirically. So it is not surprising that Ahluwalia finds no evidence speaking for or against the thesis of an "agricultural raw materials constraint".

Finally, the third version argues for creating a link between the two sectors via the *purchasing power of agricultural earnings*, since they potentially represent demand for industrial products. The low rate of income growth in agriculture, it is claimed, has therefore obstructed industrial expansion.

A modified explanation of this type sees the reason for the same state of affairs in a distribution of income that has deteriorated as a conse-quence of the restrained development of the agricultural sector, lead-ing above all to a demand-side constraint on the production of simple mass-consumption goods. A glance at the development of income in the 1980s proves illuminating for this hypothesis. Concentration of agricultural incomes and an associated demand shift led to a restruc-turing process in the consumption-goods industry that chiefly favored the manufacturers of durable consumption goods such as washing machines, television sets, etc. According to Kelkar/Kumar (1990, p. 213), this involved more than a mere reallocation process; rather, the development of the 1980s proceeded along the lines of "consumption-led growth". This distribution-related theoretical variant can thus not be denied a certain cogency. It can, however, at best claim validity for a limited period of time in which a restrictive macropolicy is temporarily in effect, when restructuring processes and the opening up of new markets within a stagnating overall market faced with stagnation entail high risks.

The reference to an on average lower purchasing power from agricultural incomes also appears to be an important explanatory factor for the industrial stagnation lasting up to the beginning of the 1980s (Ahluwalia 1985, pp. 50ff.; Dhar 1988, p. 12). The low level of income generation in agriculture points to insufficient development of the domestic market that not only hampers India's development but also increases this economy's susceptibility to inflation. In contrast to a purely demand-side explanatory model, however, this study has pointed out that generation of purchasing power is strategically important not primarily because it constitutes a source of consumption. Rather, it has been addressed as a source of potential wealth formation. Other things being equal, the use of income in this way has a moderating influence on price levels, thus increasing the chances of domestic industrial production in world markets.

It is simply not sufficient to point to the weakness of domestic demand, in this case stemming from low agricultural incomes. A low level of domestic demand could be compensated for by improving export performance; or, if the level of demand were the only problem, the government could raise it by increasing spending. Approaches arguing along demand-side lines consistently plead for the latter solution. But here again, consideration of the 1980s, when India overcame the stagnation it was faced with, demonstrates that an accumulation driven by high domestic demand leads to an ominous foreign-trade and fiscal imbalance. The next stabilization crisis, again entailing a depression of domestic income generation, was therefore no more than a matter of time.

The Contribution of the Industrial Sector

Various aspects of the influence of industrial development on the incomes generated by the Indian economy were discussed in the last two sections. The economy accordingly entered into a stagnative phase when, in the decade following 1967, the government pursued a more cautious spending policy and redirected its investment expenditures toward the agricultural sector. Yet agricultural modernization did not materialize in the form of higher growth rates and an accordingly heightened demand for industrial goods, in particular in view of the fact that initially the better part of the seed, fertilizer, pesticides, and agricultural equipment required had to be imported (Frankel 1978, pp. 278ff.). The anti-inflation measures that followed then perpetuated the depressive effects on industry. Given the more narrowly drawn macroeconomic budget constraint, the cost-side disadvantages of domestic production assumed central significance in explaining the stagnation phenomenon.

The demand-side explanation type is therefore not in need of any more detailed discussion. Both the direct demand effect and the indirect income effects of monetary and budget policy speak in favor of the assumption that the profit expectations of potential investors were deteriorating in this period. That in itself might suffice to explain a stable state of depression that was counteracted only by fiscal stimulation in the 1980s. In view of the restrictive course, adhered to only temporarily, and the parallel development of a contrived system of sector-policy measures, it does, however, seem justified to look for factors other than macroeconomic that might have obstructed accumulation.

For that reason, what follows will chiefly investigate the arguments advanced by the supply-side view. They trace the restrained income generation back to the industrial sector, or more exactly: to the regulatory framework of the industrial sector. As opposed to these tentative explanations, the rationale of the regulatory system is here seen in the macroeconomic problem for which solutions were sought with the aid of instruments applied on the microeconomic level. This requires a detailed presentation of the diverse array of measures and their no less diverse objectives. The discrepancy between intended and observed effects can then be understood as an indication of possible dysfunctionalities of the policy pursued.

The numerous industrial- and trade-policy measures intervene in the *decision-making process of Indian investors and producers* on virtually all levels. Here, they will tentatively be referred back to the producer rationale in a monetary economy, as presented in Part I. That is not to suggest that rationales formulated by economic theory could be modelled on decision-making behavior observed seemingly without theoretical inferences. The reason for pursuing this approach is not any positivist inclination but an attempt to grasp systematically the effect of regulatory interventions. The decision-making parameters of profit-maximizing enterprises will provide the schema to be deployed to that end. In order to provide an orientation for the discussions that follow, the underlying decision-making process will again be sketched briefly.

From the perspective of an individual enterprise, the required returns on the capital advanced for production and the nominal wage rate are data determined by the credit market and/or the labor market. These two prices, which of course vary with the credit status of the enterprise concerned or the quality and scarcity of the manpower demanded, essentially provide the basis for calculating the sales prices the enterprise must achieve. In addition, localization is likely to alter wage costs per unit of labor, but lower labor costs must typically be weighed against agglomeration advantages.

Profits are realized by keeping production processes in individual industries so tight that profit-taking prices can be realized. That may explain why the typical enterprise in a monetary economy strives to produce for a finite market with a limited number of suppliers. In formal terms, this means that every supplier of a goods market has an incentive to differentiate his product in order to see himself "faced with" a falling revenue curve. Monopolistic competition thus permits him to influence sales prices to one extent or another by varying the quantities he offers. Any striving for an optimally profitable utilization of capital also involves the deployment of a profit-maximizing technology chosen from the array of technologies available.[105] This choice, on which the manpower requirements of the production process depend, is, as far as these considerations are concerned, geared to the relative prices of capital and labor, as well as the activity level in cases of nonconstant returns to scale. Finally, the structure of the final demand also influences the choice of technology to the extent that as a rule technologies with continuously variable labor-intensity are unlikely to be available for the manufacture of all goods. It is thus not possible to proceed on the assumption of completely homogeneous production technologies.

The industrial- and trade-policy measures increasingly implemented in India after 1966 seek to gain influence on all these decision-making parameters: on the choice of industrial sites, the sectoral orientation of manufactures in a broader sense, the activity level, and the choice of technologies. Additional economic-policy regulations, in particular selective credit policy and industrial-safety legislation, can change the prices relevant to an individual enterprise for its capital utilization and the manpower it deploys. With the exception of selective credit policy, which will be discussed at more length in chapter 5, an attempt will now be made to define qualitatively what effects the most important policies have had and what problems are associated with them.

Since independence, *foreign-trade policy* has represented an important instrument of India's development strategy.[106] A differentiated system of tariffs and quotas and a conscious program of indigenization stipulating a phased increase of the domestic share of selected industrial manufactures ("Phased Manufacturing Program") are the expression of a continuously pursued strategy of import substitution. Since the end of the 1960s, measures aimed at encouraging exports have, however, gained more and more in significance. The proceeds achieved through exports are exempt from income taxation, low-interest credits are available for exports, support is provided to expand export capacities, and exporters are granted easier access to imports. In addition, the Indian currency has been steadily devalued since the 1980s with the aim of encouraging exports and substituting imports (RBI Annual Report 1990, pp. 145 and 137).

This foreign-trade policy has clearly influenced the relative profitability of producing for the domestic market as opposed to the world market. Restrictions on direct investment by foreigners and the licensing of imports have moreover determined the quantity of technology available. Moreover, the indigenization program has even tried to influence directly the choice of technologies.

Measured in terms of the success criterion of a gradually declining foreign-trade deficit, neither selective protectionism nor India's selective integration in the world market have proven successful. To be sure, a significantly more differentiated structure of both traded commodities and foreign-trade partners has been achieved. And it is surely not least as a result of the barriers to world-market competition that India's economy has been able to develop a relatively broad industrial base. However, the heavy budgetary burdens stemming from export-promotion measures and a by no means relaxed balance-of-trade situation do indicate that India's foreign-trade policy has not yet succeeded in translating measures aimed at protecting domestic industry into measures aimed at developing this industry.

India's protectionism is both an attempt to implement a mercantilistic development strategy and an element of the redistributive regime of its monetary economy. It has given rise to a detailed *licensing policy* aimed at heading off certain effects resulting from the insulation of the domestic market, such as the tendency toward concentration

(World Bank 1987, p. 39). Aside from this supplementary function as regards protection, licensing is also a means of achieving the over-riding priority of enabling government to take the "commanding heights" of the economy. In the course of time, this general licensing procedure for industrial products has become an instrument of further structural-policy programs such as encouraging small industries, re-serving certain economic sectors for the public sector, regional plan-ning, and control of application.

The licensing procedure, to which every product is subject when it exceeds a given investment sum and which is implemented by the central government, has a direct influence on any of the more impor-tant business decisions (Wiemann 1988, pp. 49-51). It decides on:

-   whether any investment may be made in a given industry, region, or market segment, or whether the investment might be inconsis-tent with current reservation, decentralization, or cartel policies;

-   whether the capacity and product diversification planned are con-sonant with the estimated development of demand;

-   whether the technology is available domestically or whether co-operation with foreign firms is required for the desired technol-ogy transfer.

In this way, the Indian economic administration obtains a veto on virtually every level of production planning pursued by private-sector enterprises. It is apparent that the only reason why Indian firms do not respond to such far-reaching interference by in large measure re-fusing to produce is that their earnings are quite good in markets in-sulated by licensing. This practice results in a market structure that makes it possible to maintain high prices through quantitative supply restrictions, that thus supplements, or even replaces, profit realization with unearned income. In individual segments, this gives rise to the phenomenon, abnormal in monetary economies, of sellers' markets, a "forced non-availability" (Wadhva 1990, p. 454) of certain goods. Structural excess demand will always arise when, due to distribution or inflation factors, a high level of purchasing power encounters a supply limited by capacity licenses and prices being controlled.

What is meant by the latter is *administration of prices and the distribution of industrial goods* like fertilizer, steel, paper, pharmaceuticals. Administered prices apply for some sixty industrial goods, some 40 % of which are included in the wholesale price index. The objective is roughly as complex as that of the pricing policy for agricultural produce. On the one hand, it operates along the lines of social and development-economy needs: prices, for instance, are set below the market level so as to supply the government, poor segments of the population, or consumer industries less expensively with certain goods. This is associated with the obligation of - for the most part - public-sector enterprises to sell a certain percentage of their products at concessionary terms. On the other hand, there are also economic reasons for this price policy on the supply side: in part, prices are set far above the (world) market level so as to stimulate domestic production of such items as fertilizer. Furthermore, in analogy to agricultural price administration, the aim is to diminish the cost pressure on the inflation rate by fixing the prices for certain essential goods.

Ironically, such a system of administered prices places the enterprises concerned in precisely the situation that is pointed to in economics text books as the standard of perfect competition: they are price takers and adjusters of quantity (and presumably of quality as well). When the microeconomic goal is to stimulate production, the resulting stagnative tendencies are entirely consistent with high business profits. However, the problem of stagnant sellers' markets is exacerbated when the goal of price administration is to repress an inflation process. In such cases, profit earnings are also eroded, which normally gives rise to production curtailments. In such a state of repressed inflation, the value of aggregate goods supply is likely to increase more slowly than nominal incomes (see chapter 5.2, below).

The production constraint is, to be sure, in part forestalled by the last measure to be discussed here, namely by an employment policy applied at the microeconomic level. Under the conditions prevailing in India, employment policy constitutes, in the broadest sense, an element of the *regulation of industrial relations*. To protect jobs in the formal sector, firms can, given certain stipulations, be prevented from exiting from the market, even though they are no longer commercially viable. The RBI rates a company as "sick" when it meets all of the three following conditions:

(a) It has made losses in the previous year, and must expect further losses in the current and following year;

(b) displays a debt-equity ratio of 1:1; and

(c) has been in operation for at least seven years (World Bank 1987, pp. 51f.).

Other regulations in the field of industrial relations, like those on industrial safety, job security, and minimal wage rates, are intended to contribute to the training of a modern skilled workforce and to implement sociopolitical targets.

The individual regulations are so specifically attuned to given sectors of industry as to have a heterogenizing impact on the price of comparable manhours. Depending on whether a company is situated in the formal or the informal sector, whether it is large or small, organized as a private- or a public-sector enterprise, it will have to pay a different wage for the same labor. Moreover, by making it more difficult for insolvent enterprises to exit from the market, the above-mentioned employment policy can prevent the tightening up of production necessary for a given industry.

Other things being equal, the different prices for labor hamper any expansion of the enterprises and industries faced with comparatively higher wage costs. In the market segments protected by licensing, this need not necessarily find expression in below-average profit rates. Again, however, it is the international competitiveness of the products concerned that is impaired.

"Sickness", i.e. the prolonged disability of insolvent companies, has in the meantime taken on the dimensions of an enormous problem. The granting of tax exemption and the offer of debt refunding has surely led to "sickness" on the part of commercially sound enterprises as well, i.e. it has prompted abuses. This is indicated by the fact that the number of companies rated as "sick" is growing rapidly: it even more than doubled from 1983 to 1985. This is exacerbating a budget situation already strained, and on the other hand it is jeopardizing the solvency of the financial system. In 1985, namely, 17 % of all outstanding bank claims were held against companies in this category; i.e. the claims were overdue (Clad 1990a). Thus the same thing can be said here that was said of the related problem of government indebtedness: in such a situation, a restrictive monetary and fiscal policy is no longer a realistic option. The liquidity bottlenecks associated with such policies would spell the end of numerous companies and banks.

The discussion on the system of industrial and trade-policy regulations[107] thus lead into one of the main themes of this study. If this system is grasped as a possible response to the basic problem of development under the conditions of a monetary economy, it is evidently not by chance that the far-reaching interventions in production decisions were intensified at the end of the 1960s, when the danger of inflation was growing acute. India had to face the dilemma, virulent in all monetary economies, of eroding its monetary function through contrived expansion or of stabilizing it at the price of deep recession.

In the latter case, India's redistributive regime was at risk of losing the basis of its legitimacy, not only among the segments of the population affected, but also among the prominent elites. The rationale of industrial policy can therefore, independently of express objectives, be seen in the fact that it was intended to achieve expansion controlled in terms of development planning while at the same time maintaining monetary stability. A formation of prices geared to profit-taking and realized by enterprises in the marketplace was thus replaced with a revenue-securing insulation of markets realized by government with the means of economic policy.

This market insulation led to stagnative tendencies that correspond not to those due to a monetary anti-inflation policy but to dysfunctional interventions. What has been noted as their most clear-cut expression is the phenomenon of sellers' markets occurring in a number of segments. This is the way in which a repressed inflation appears in the goods market. It will be discussed in what follows.

5.2   Repressed Inflation

For agricultural economies like India, one particular problem of monetary development lies in the fact that a monetary economy deals with periodic scarcities of resources and goods in a specific manner. Even in a partially monetized economy, they find an outlet in high price rises, given a low level of agricultural development. In this way, the quantitative supply shortage, as it would appear in a barter economy (Sahlins 1972, pp. 33f.), is translated into scarcity of the value of produce relative to available income. In a barter economy, any surplus that might occur, possibly including even the food supply serving for subsistence, is therefore always reduced, while in a monetary economy the price rises indicate precisely that the producers are attempting to secure their surplus income (Spahn 1986, pp. 194f.).

In particular circumstances, causes exogenous to the economic process can thus again and again give rise to price-level increases that may trigger an inflation. In India, these conditions were given when, following a decade of excessive development financing, two successive drought years occurred and the balance-of-payments situation precluded any additional food imports. The reference to financing is important, because it was not the price rises for individual agricultural goods but the existing liquidity potential that constituted the actual economic problem. It is this alone that can lead a price-level burst into an inflation process, thus further increasing the current-account deficit. A shortage of individual basic foodstuffs, which in it-self can prove disastrous for certain population groups, will then take on the character of a general depreciation of nominal incomes that cannot even be evaded via a substitution of goods.

The process of inflation set off along these lines in the India of the late 1960s threatened to escalate when the loss of confidence in the rupee began to make itself felt in the development of a parallel econ-omy using foreign exchange.[108] India's economic policy responded to the situation chiefly by more and more deploying the sectoral policies just described, which included in particular measures aiming for di-rect price controls. Additional measures consisted of a forced development of the financial sector, the topic of the following section, and the use of a specific combination of selective and general credit policy. This combination reveals a great deal about the conceptual ba-sis of the anti-inflation policy practiced in India.

Selective and General Credit Policy

At the end of the 1960s, the RBI at first kept by and large to its gen-erally expansionary credit policy, i.e. monetization of government debt and refinancing of the banks (see Annex B), while seeking to curb the danger of inflation associated with this course by applying *selective restrictions*. Since then, its preferred instrument has been re-striction of lending, i.e. loans are granted against the stocks of agri-cultural goods to be financed as collateral.[109]

The Reserve Bank is here faced with the problem of being unable to discriminate between stocks serving to keep the supply of goods at a desired constant level and stocks kept because of speculative expecta-tions of sharply rising prices. The latter form, that is, for example, hoarding such goods as cereals and oilseed, regularly occurs after poor harvests and pours oil on the fires of existing upward price movements. In a socially and economically tense situation of this sort, the speculators obviously expect the central bank or the government to abstain from any restrictive monetary policy.

As justified as this supposition may be, or as understandable monetary passiveness is in the given situation, this combination of selective contraction and general expansion is equally unsuitable to eliminate the underlying problem. After all, stockpiling goods with speculative intent does stimulate the expectation of exorbitantly rising prices, and this expectation is, for its part, nurtured by the assumption that the central bank will be reluctant to initiate any far-reaching stabilization measures. The underlying cause is a high liquidity potential that permits rising prices to be pushed through across a broad front. True, in a given period the contrived scarcity of domestic credit supply will prove unable to achieve much: It is, rather, a release of precautionary stocks laid in by government that can remedy acute bottlenecks in the supply of goods and attenuate the price rises associated with them. But the consequence is that a policy of tight money, even in the intention of safeguarding food supplies, constitutes a more appropriate central-bank policy than, for instance, the passive supply of money propagated by structuralist circles.[110]

When, after 1973, the Reserve Bank was forced to switch to a generally restrictive policy, it went the other way and sought to alleviate the negative consequences for production by *expanding its selective lending policy*. This, for instance, entailed persistent net purchases of open-market securities, accompanied at the same time by expansion of the rediscount facilities for priority credit purposes. General credit policy sought in this way to reduce the money supply, while selective-credit measures had to be used to finance a larger supply of goods. An attempt was made in this way to maintain price-level stability in spite of a heavy burden from financing the deficit and to avoid crowding out private investment by allocating as precisely as possible the residual volume of credit to the uses for which it was desired.

Since this combination with any general restriction offers a selective option to circumvent it, the possibility of abuse is fairly obvious. And there are indications that the informal sector refinances itself to a considerable extent from formal-sector credits approved on social criteria, which relieves the former of the necessity of gaining direct access to the central bank (Gupta 1990, pp. 191f.). While any reference to possible abuse can be rejected with the argument that careful monitoring would be able to prevent any circumvention of restrictive measures and thus, in principle, presents no difficulty, delinking the central bank does represent a serious functional problem. It, or more precisely: the discount rate, loses its macroeconomic control function for the credit-market system. The more cogent objection is therefore that this instrument is unsuited to fight inflation, a measure repeatedly called for in India.

A glance at the make-up of the claims held by the Reserve Bank and the volume of domestic credit (see Annex B) provides indications that interventions were made in favor of a constant expansion of lending to the private sector.[111] In 1970/71 and 1976, the share of such credits grew sharply, as did the RBI's claims against the commercial and cooperative banks. Since, adjusted for price increases, the national product stagnated in relative terms for two consecutive two periods, this coincidence could point to a selectively generous credit policy on the part of the RBI, also entailing a generally expansionary impact. What might have been expected as more likely in a depression would have been a reduction of lending, in particular in 1976, when a price slump occurred.[112] But it is also possible that the RBI, as the "lender of last resort", saw itself constrained to make short-term loans in the crisis, i.e. that the expansion need not be attributed to its selective credit policy.

Empirically, it would thus appear that the general contraction accompanied by selective expansion did not succeed - certainly not least because of the failure to consolidate the government budget. This failure can be explained by subjecting the *conceptual foundations of this type of anti-inflation policy* to a critique. The following sentence gives drastic expression to the underlying notion of what inflation is and hence what defines anti-inflation policy: "*Inflation is sometimes described as the phenomenon of too much money chasing too few goods.*" (RBI Bulletin 1969, pp. 1905f.; see also RBI Report 1985, p. 11, §2.18). Seen in this way, anti-inflation policy implies establishing an equilibrium of goods and the volume of money by tightening the money supply and simultaneously increasing real production (Dhar 1988, p. 10). The sector-policy regulations also make a certain amount of sense within the scope covered by this understanding. They contribute to a "gentle" struggle against inflation to the extent that they seek to moderate prices directly, while they aim via other interventions both at preventing the threat of a restriction of production and creating latitude for sustained surplus income. Seen in this way, agricultural and industrial policy assume a function completely analogous to credit policy: "*(...) all anti-inflation policies must be selective or discriminatory or double-edged in the sense that they must curtail demand but not supplies.*" (RBI Bulletin 1979, p. 809).[113]

Two different arguments based on theoretical considerations can be opposed to the notion that the goal of an anti-inflation policy is to establish an equilibrium between goods and money: on the one hand, the supply of money in circulation is opposed not by goods but by liabilities - of government, foreigners, or commercial banks - with the central bank. On the other hand, this type of anti-inflation policy is forced to assume a not very plausible producer rationale: why should an average enterprise invest today when tomorrow it will be forced to sell its products at lower prices? Or why should the business sector as a whole expand real production when general credit policy at the same time gives reason for it to expect that the overall effective demand is shrinking?

Monetary policy aimed at stopping an inflation process seeks rather to prevent national incomes from continuing to rise by narrowing profits and lowering the employment rate accordingly. Its goal is to establish a balance between the stocks of claims and liabilities held in domestic currency - it having previously become more and more attractive to contract liabilities in the depreciating currency, and at the same time less and less attractive to hold claims.

In an economy like India, this objective does of course mean that precisely the sector at the core of economic-planning efforts is the direct point of leverage for enforcing this adjustment. Production restrictions in industry and layoffs among a protected skilled labor force stand diametrically opposed to the development-policy objectives of India's governments.

In addition, it is, in view of the existing dualism of formal and informal sector, uncertain whether or in what period of time the depression engendered in the formal sector by monetary policy will begin to show a moderating impact on rising prices in the informal sector.[114] In view of this problem complex, the search for alternative means of combatting inflation is only too understandable. But the search for functional equivalents to a money-supply policy is always linked to a theoretical notion of how the functional context of a monetary economy like India's is made up and what goals are to be achieved. In discussions on the Fourth Plan, scheduled to begin in 1966/67, the planning commission finally demanded emphatically a direct control over the distribution of prices and goods (Frankel 1978, pp. 255 and 267) in order to come to grips effectively with the inflation problem.

Repressed Inflation and Liberalization Policy

It will now be possible to sum up the preceding sections and go on to discuss the central thesis of this chapter: the chapter has considered the investment behavior of the Indian government, sectoral developments, and, finally, the RBI's credit policy against the background of anti-inflation policies that had become necessary; it in this way clearly focused on features accentuated differently in other presentations. Both the individual measures and the underlying notion of what anti-inflation policy is expected to achieve were interpreted as an attempt to strike a balance in terms of welfare economics between income growth and stability. If one accepts this ends-means approach of the traditional theory of economic policy,[115] the outcome of the programs and regulations described can only be traced back to inadequate implementation and/or illiberal leanings on the part of Indian development planning. Although neither the one nor the other is false, an attempt was made here to grasp this result systematically from the angle of development under the conditions of a monetary economy - and the supposed inadequacies in implementation as an infringement of certain constraints imposed by development under monetary conditions.

The upshot of this thesis is that India's economic policy has in this way succeeded not in removing the conditions for the emergence of an inflation process but merely in repressing inflation. It in this sense failed to meet its own goal of preventing a stagnant development of income and industry. Rather, the stagnation present since the mid-1960s can be understood as an enforced reverence made to the functional exigencies of a monetary economy. Seen this way, the *primacy of monetary stability* thus had its way behind the back of Indian economic planning. In order to substantiate this thesis, it is necessary to consider carefully what this type of anti-inflation policy achieved and what, seen in terms of its own intentions, it failed to achieve. This will be followed by a discussion of the liberalization policy of the 1980s as a reaction and an "attempted cure".

The agricultural-policy measures had their price-stabilizing impact in the sense that India has become largely self-sufficient, thus obviating the fear that, e.g., severe drought years might lead to an acute crisis accompanied by exorbitant price rises (Economic Survey 1990, p. 9). Nevertheless, the development of purchasing power of those employed in agriculture has on average continued to lag far behind the income development in other sectors. Seen in relation to countries with a comparable level of development, like for instance the People's Republic of China, India's agricultural production is clearly underdeveloped (World Development Report 1990, p. 184, Table 4).

The regulations in the industrial sector may have contributed to preventing deindustrialization and may also have fostered or maintained an extensively diversified structure. But the "sickness" of numerous enterprises and the low level of employment growth in this sector indicate that they have likewise been unable to prevent these tendencies of depression that would have been expected to develop from market processes.

This need not be attributed solely or chiefly to an inadequate implementation of policy measures. Rather, the *characteristic of a repressed inflation as opposed to an open inflation* is that it fails to provide any stimulating effect on the willingness to invest or to take on debts. Whereas in the case of open inflation a growing supply of money and credit fosters a rising tendency of prices, i.e. profit expectations and profit realization are mutually reinforced, monetary expansion here merely gives rise to an excessive supply of money and hits both enterprises and wage earners with income losses: the enterprises, because partial cost increases cannot be passed on; the wage earners, because the non-administered prices are all the more free to rise in view of the excess purchasing power.[116] The latter may be one factor explaining the persistent growth of the unregulated parallel economy in India. This dualism, actually a feature that must be surmounted by a monetary economy in the process of integration, will consequently have gained in depth.

As regards industrial and income growth, India's practice of combatting inflation can thus hardly be characterized as successful, even if restrained growth over a lengthy period of time may have been more acceptable socially than a drastic tight-money policy. India does at least appear to have succeeded in stabilizing monetary functions. And so it has become a commonplace in the literature on India's economic policy to attest to it sound and conservative monetary practices (Ahluwalia 1985, p. 108; Wiemann 1988, p. 87).

This proposition appears justified. It appears to be confirmed by a - compared to other developing countries - moderately rising price level, by an insignificant level of capital flight, except for one brief period,[117] and by a savings rate of over 20 % since the end of the 1970s, notably high for an LCD (International Monetary Fund 1990, p. 175). The structure of savings has clearly shifted in favor of its financial share and in a long-term direction. While at the end of the 1960s only roughly one third of household savings were held in a financial form, this figure had exceeded one half by the middle of the 1980s (RBI Report 1985, p. 45; Morris 1985, pp. 25ff.). Fixed deposits, and here in particular deposits with a term of over five years, make up the majority of these deposits. This shift toward financial and longer-term deposits was encouraged by comparatively high deposit rates and sizable tax exemptions (Shetty 1990a, p. 557).

Accordingly, the holding of money and the formation of financial wealth appears not only to have failed to come under acute threat, despite the high inflation potential, but also to have increased distinctly. The households could until then rely on the fact that government economic policy had both the will and the possibility to counter any unchecked price rises. This implicit safeguard maintained confidence in the domestic currency to such an extent that the above-mentioned saving incentives could take effect and provide a motive to restructure portfolios accordingly in the process of wealth formation. The repressed inflation appears to have succeeded in sustaining a sort of " wealth illusion". In the case of an open inflation, on the other hand, the risk is that people will immediately switch out of the domestic currency, as was feared in India from the end of the 1960s to the middle of the 1970s.

But, as will be discussed in more detail in the following section, a policy of this sort resembles drawing an uncovered bill on the future. The above-named indicators of the success of supposedly sound financial practices will have to be rated as far less positive when it is noted that they are due to the repression of an inflation:

-   The comparatively high saving rates of households is, in macroeconomic terms, also a reflex of high budget deficits, which in the 1980s made up a share of 6 - 9 % of national income, although the current-account deficit, making up a share of 1 - 2 %, will have to be deducted from this.

- Although this is impossible to verify in strict terms, there is reason to suspect that household savings in part represented passive cash holdings, the excess purchasing power of repressed inflation. These holding would thus constitute the counterpart to rationing in the goods markets.[118]

- One of the alarming indications is that the share of financial assets in the overall wealth accumulated by households has remained about constant since the middle of the 1980s (RBI, Report on Currency and Finance 1990, p. 4; Shetty 1990a, p. 555). This might indicate that the above-mentioned implicit safeguard, or insurance, element of a repressed inflation has lost some of its credibility and that the willingness to accumulate additional financial wealth has assumed a wait-and-see attitude. This appears only too justified in view of pressure on prices that is growing ever more difficult to control and is making itself felt disproportionately in the informal sector, as well as in India's loss of creditworthiness in the world financial markets, a topic of discussion in the international community.

- Finally, the real-estate boom associated with the economic upturn of the 1980s and an accelerated process of urbanization can be construed as an expression of repressed inflation, or of its untenable character. Not least as a result of rising prices, the housing problem has taken on such dimensions as to occasion the government to declare, at the end of the 1980s, relief of the problem as one of the priorities of national economic policy. This rise in property and housing prices might indicate a growing flight into tangible assets, which is taking place because of the excessive supply of money and the risk of depreciation of financial assets.[119] And the Indian government is supporting this type of accumulation of tangible assets. On the one hand, it sees in this development a partial solution of the problem of homelessness; on the other hand, it wishes to bind the liquidity of households and above all channel the immense volume of illegally acquired money back into official and legal forms of investment.[120] As correct as this approach may be given the circumstances, implying as it does to depreciate wealth accumulated by tax evasion through market forces, this policy displays a strong tendency to collide with a policy of repressed inflation. Rising housing prices, entailing sensitive cost-of-living increases, will lead to stepped-up wage demands or attempts on the part of firms to pass on the costs, thus initiating a process of inflation that will grow more and more difficult to bring to a halt.

Against this background, the *liberalization policy* inaugurated under Indira Gandhi and continued by Rajiv Gandhi and his successor V.P. Singh is accessible to an interpretation differing from those commonly given. The partial abolition of the licensing regulations, the dismantling of import barriers, and the release of prices hitherto administered can be seen as elements of an attempt to neutralize certain symptoms of repressed inflation. There is a great measure of consensus in the literature over the fact that the 1980s saw an average increase of profit incomes that had been eroded in the course of time. The "low profitability syndrome" associated with a repressed inflation was cured in some areas in that liberalization has broadened the latitude for pricing and production while an expansionary fiscal and monetary policy has provided for high effective demand.

The liberalization policy thus went on from the microeconomically applied monetary policy of the previous decades, but now by permitting partial price increases and in this way accepting shifts in the profit-price level (RBI Annual Report 1990, p. 74). Aside from price effects, this policy has not failed to generate quantity effects as well. But whether the intended "absorption" of purchasing power will prove able to solve the inflation problem, is a matter that can well be disputed. While this intention remains within the framework of the idea that adjustment occurs via the establishment of an equilibrium between goods and money,[121] it has in reality set off an accelerating process of adjustment inflation.

Owing to the expansionary character of this liberalization policy, government indebtedness has reached a dimension that has brought India to the brink verge of a *debt trap*.[122] The fiscally driven expansion was a necessary component of the economic upturn of the past decade to the extent that, in view of the given inflation potential, liberalization would most likely have come to nothing in the end. When government expresses a higher effective demand, the prospects of profit rise, and with them presumably the willingness on the part of business to invest. To be sure, the increasing government share of investment (see Annex C) reveals that the quantity effects stemming from private-sector activity chiefly reflect an improved utilization of capacities, thus making it impossible to speak of a sustained increase of the marginal efficiency of domestic capital.

The rise in government indebtedness, an almost unavoidable development for a redistributive regime of a monetary economy, can be illustrated with a limited number of data (Bhattacharya/Guha 1990):

Between 1970 and 1988, domestic indebtedness[123] rose fourteenfold in nominal terms, fourfold at constant prices, and by 59 % in the period between 1982-88 alone. Of the outstanding government debt, the RBI held some 40 %, the banks somewhat less than 18 %, the rest remaining with households. The monetized portion of the government debt rose twelvefold in this period, which, adjusted for prices, amounts to a factor of 3.5 (see Annex B).

The interest burden on this exploding debt has risen to corresponding levels. While in 1970/71 a good 1 % of tax revenues had to be expended to meet the net interest costs, i.e. interest expenditures minus interest revenues, the figure had risen to some 22 % in the fiscal year of 1988/89. As noted above, current expenditures are no longer covered by current revenues. The enormous interest payments, made in particular with the intent of motivating the households to invest in government bonds, contributed strongly to this fiscal imbalance (ibid.; Dasgupta 1990, pp. 325ff.). In view of this finding, it is fair to speak of a debt trap in that the burden of debt service is itself increasing the deficit and the day is not far when debt service will require further borrowing.[124]

The following section will discuss the disintegration of the financial system as a special problem entailed by the government debt, rising as repressed inflation continues. The final chapter will then deal with the question of what can be done in view of the increasing gravity of the situation.

5.3   Disintegration of the Financial System

India's economic policy declared encouragement of the financial system to be an integral element of development strategy, long before this found expression in official communiques of authoritative development institutions (World Bank 1989) and before interest in it awoke in connection with the transformation of a good number of planned economies into monetary economies. It therefore seems appropriate to discuss here in more detail the way in which economic policy was used to force the development of India's monetary and financial system. This will be followed by a consideration of the resulting deformations in the context of the problems addressed in the last two sections.

Development of the Financial Sector Following Independence

When independence came, India's monetary and financial system was comparatively well developed in institutional terms.[125] India had a central bank, a banking system developed under British colonial rule, and an indigenous financial system that had existed for centuries. The *Reserve Bank of India* was founded in 1935 as a corporate enterprise whose shareholders could be British or Indian citizens. It initially maintained this legal form after independence in 1947, although it was nationalized in 1949 by decree of parliament and under protest of the RBI's board of directors. This step was very much in accord with the British central-bank tradition, which is shared by the RBI. The RBI followed its model, the Bank of England, not only as regards its internal functional division into an "Issue Department" in charge of issuing bank notes and a "Banking Department" that, as it were, represents the commercial banks within the central bank and is in charge of lending. It also resembles the Bank of England in that it is not an autonomous central bank, and has - independently of nationalization - not been one since it was founded. Its dependence finds expression in various regulations (Aufricht 1961, pp. 343ff.):

- Its key economic criterion is that it is obliged to provide credit to the central government. To this extent, the RBI has only the option of restricting the total volume through lending to commercial and development banks or controlling the share of commercial lending by fixing the total volume.

- The governor and the vice-governor are appointed by the government for a five-year term, the rest of the board of directors is nominated by it.

- The government can dismiss the board of directors if it fails to meet its legal obligations, which of course include providing credit to the government. A decree of this sort must subsequently be presented to parliament for approval, just as government debts are in need of previous parliamentary approval.

- Having consulted the governor, the government can issue instructions which the Reserve Bank is obliged to carry out in the end, although it is permitted to publish a dissenting opinion.

- Purchases and sales of foreign currency by the Reserve Bank are undertaken at exchange rates largely determined by the government.

The RBI's legal status is, however, not identical with the latitudes it actually possesses. In the triumvirate consisting of finance ministry, planning commission, and central bank, the RBI has a watchdog function with regard to price-level stability. As discussed in 5.2.1, it seeks to observe this function chiefly with the aid of a specific combination of credit-policy measures. It in this way deals with only one element of the cluster of macroeconomic targets, although it is strictly obliged to bear other targets in mind as well.[126] Moreover, it has been from the very start the institution in charge of financial-sector development.

The *financial system*, at present subordinate to the central bank, had a dual structure when India became independent. It consisted on the one hand of the colonial banks that were based almost exclusively in the (coastal) towns and were specialized in financing trade. The indigenous financial system, on the other hand, basically consisted of money-lenders, indigenous bankers, and a variety of indigenous institutions doing business chiefly in the rural hinterland. It above all financed consumption spending, in particular expenses incurred in marrying off daughters, and, to a lesser extent, the seasonal demand for credit stemming from an agriculture still operating at a low level of monetization.

In other words, the two basic bank types making up today's financial system in India already existed in the formal sector, i.e. national commercial and cooperative banks. It was above all the commercial banks that experienced an upswing during the First and Second World Wars, since war financing provided for high levels of liquidity and business activity. But the consolidation-oriented macropolicy of the first post-independence years led, among other things, to a number of these banks becoming illiquid or even insolvent. The Reserve Bank was instructed to thin out the existing network of formal institutions by merging smaller and financially weak banks with larger banks (Khan 1980, p. 226).

The Reserve Bank also made attempts in the first years to integrate the indigenous financial system into the formal sector, i.e. to subject it to legal supervision and to grant it access to central-bank money in return. These attempts failed, however, because the informal financial sector had no lack of outside sources of refinancing, and was thus able to avoid legal regimentation (Wilson 1952, p. 230). The focus of

promotion activity that the RBI began to develop on top of its stabilization task thus increasingly shifted toward the formal sector of the
financial system.

The existing institutions were seen as inadequate to finance industrialization in general and the development plans in particular, as regards both required levels and the desired duration of commitments
(da Costa 1985, p. 69). The commercial banks, patterned on the English system, satisfied only the short- and medium-term credit wishes
of their industrial clientele, but were not in a position to provide
funds for long-term capital formation. India's development partners
thus envisaged a type of financing patterned on the German universal
banks, because they saw in them a mode of division of labor and collaboration between banks and industry that seemed beneficial to be-
lated development (ibid., p. 67; Gerschenkron 1962, pp. 16ff.).

And so in the course of time a number of so-called "Term Lending
Institutions" were created that represent a specific feature of India's
monetary and financial system. In what follows, they will be termed
development banks, although they are actually intended to integrate
functions of commercial and development banks (Basu 1977,
pp. 197 - 210) and are referred to in the terminology of the IMF as
"other financial institutions" (International Monetary fund 1990,
pp. 410f., R. 12f. and 32f.).

The focus of their business activity is to provide long-term loans
made at concessionary terms, although they otherwise apply commercial standards. They display features of a traditional development
bank owing on the one hand to their comprehensive services and financing of innovative projects and on the other hand to the way in
which they are refinanced:

> "The development banks, emerging as a result of state spon-
> sorship, derive most of their funds from the government, the
> central bank of the country and the public or private financial
> institutions. They have (...) no direct link with the ultimate

sources of savings. They are, in effect, merely distributive
agencies." (Khan 1980, p. 128)

The problems associated with this setup were addressed in the theoretical part of this study (chapter 3) and need not be repeated here. In
the course of time, various types and forms of business organization
were developed; only the most important of them will be mentioned
here.

As early as 1948, the "Industrial Finance Corporation of India"
(IFCI) was created; it soon led to the first establishment of a "State
Financial Corporation". There are now such state financial corporations in each federal state. Their task is to take charge of financing
small and mid-size industry.

Since, however, the IFCI appeared too cautious and conventional, the
"Industrial Credit and Investment Corporation" (ICICI) was founded
in 1955 with foreign support from, among others, the World Bank.
Neither the government nor the central bank contributed to its capital
stock; instead, it was given the legal form of a private-sector limited-
liability company. As such, it has developed numerous innovative instruments for financing industry (Khan 1980, pp. 134f.).

The last to be founded was the predecessor of India's most important
industrial-development bank. 1958 saw the birth of the "Refinance
Corporation for Industry", whose founding members included the Reserve Bank, the leading life-insurance corporation, and a number of
commercial banks. In 1964 it was incorporated into the newly
founded "Industrial Development Bank of India" (IDBI). As the
original name denotes, it was intended to refinance banks and, later,
the state finance corporations for long-term credits to mid-size industry. The capital for this purpose derived chiefly from the counterpart fund formed on the basis of a food-assistance agreement (the "PL
480 Agreement") between the governments of India and the U.S. The
establishment of this institution, which in part involved shifting the
refinancing of credits from the central bank to a new type of devel-

opment bank, proved to be of far-reaching consequences, as will be illustrated in the next section.

In the farming sector, an agricultural development bank was founded along similar lines. The "Reserve Bank of India Act" of 1935 had already provided for an extension of central-bank activities into this sector. Within the framework of refinancing policy, the RBI was not only expected to discount commercial bills with a maximum life of three months, but was also allowed, for purposes of covering seasonal agricultural financial needs, to discount such bills with a life of up to fifteen months (Aufricht 1961, p. 348). The granting of a credit contingent of this sort to "State Cooperative Banks", i.e. the central cooperative banks of the states, is in line with the traditional business activity of a central bank, even though longer-term claims do restrict its latitude.

The Reserve Bank extended its engagement in this connection by setting up two "National Agricultural Credit Funds" in 1955. One of these funds was used to provide long-term loans to the agricultural development bank, to state governments and mortgage banks so as to permit them in turn to hold capital stock in cooperative banks, credit cooperatives, etc. From the other fund, the stabilization fund, medium-term loans were granted to the SCBs in cases in which they were faced with liquidity problems when, for instance as a consequence of drought and similar natural calamities, they were able to recover only part of their loan claims (RBI Functions 1983, pp. 168f.).

In addition, in 1955 the Reserve Bank became the major shareholder of the "State Bank of India", which had emerged from the nationalization of the until then largest commercial bank, the "Imperial Bank of India". As a state bank, it was now expected to promote the expansion of the cooperative banks in rural regions and grant concessionary credits to priority sectors (Madan 1965, pp. 193f.).

The "All-India Rural Credit Survey Committee", whose report (RBI Committee 1969) represents a milestone in thinking on the development of rural financial systems, regarded even this as inadequate. The call for a national agricultural bank to finance long-term lending finally, in 1963, led to the establishment of the "Agricultural Refinance Corporation". Having been renamed in the interim, it in 1982 became today's "National Bank for Agricultural and Rural Development" (NABARD), the counterpart of IDBI for the agricultural sector. It took over from the Reserve Bank the entire task of refinancing rural banks and credit cooperatives. Aside from that, it supports the establishment of other institutions, provides services to the agricultural development projects financed by it, and invests in the equity of organizations providing services in rural regions.[127]

This phase of "institution building", in the course of which in particular certain refinancing contingents formerly maintained by the RBI were made independent, finally provided for the establishment of a deposit insurance and a credit guarantee program for small industry as well as the foundation of an investment fund, the "Unit Trust of India" (1964). This constituted the preliminary end of an epoch marked by the consolidation and the construction of various institutions geared to the needs of a developing country.

The parallel process of state-led industrialization had, however, also produced financial effects: as expected, the banks focused their lending on larger corporations that served government demand or were government-run and thus had a good credit rating. The financing of development plans at the same time became more and more precarious, for one thing because of the sheer level of public spending in relation to tax revenues, for another because of the growing, in part politically motivated, reticence of foreign and supranational donors.[128] Thus the RBI's promotional policy was more and more driven by motives of priority lending and the mobilization of savings. The development of the financial sector was to be used to achieve a massive increase in the volume of deposits, and the share of the credit volume remaining to the commercial sector was intended to be directed to those areas that, from the angle of development economics, appeared worthy of support.

The end of 1967 saw the proclamation of a *policy of social control of the banking system* (da Costa 1985, Chapter 9; Frankel 1978, pp. 397f.). Representatives of the sectors rated as having high priority were placed in the management bodies of the private banks. At least two board members were required to represent the agricultural sector and small industry.[129] On the national level, a "National Credit Council", which is still in existence, was set up to target and coordinate the sectoral allocation of the credit volume on the French model of indicative planning.

But the legal and organizational provisions were no more able to move the banks to grant credit as desired than were the previous means of "moral suasion". The so-called "Dehejia Committee" noted in the report it submitted in 1969 that industry borrowing was continuing to grow very much faster than the value of production, which found expression in excessive stockpiling (Khan 1980, p. 237). These observations might of course also have been an effect of the structural adjustment begun in 1966 that must on the whole have motivated enterprises to hold greater precautionary cash reserves and, on top of that, could have led to unplanned stockpiling. The banks most likely saw themselves forced in this situation to grant additional credit to avoid having to write off their claims because of illiquidity on the part of their borrowers.

Irrespective of this market constellation and a behavior on the part of the banks that can be explained in terms of it, - in the governments view - it was a blocked development of the financial sector which was to be sped up through government decree, i.e. through *nationalization*. The development-planning objective is clearly expressed in the preamble to the law nationalizing, in 1969, the fourteen largest commercial banks, and with them some 80 % of all bank assets: "(...) *its purpose was to control the heights of the economy and to meet progressively, and serve better, the needs of development of the economy in conformity with national policies and objectives"* (quoted after da Costa 1985, p. 97). The apparent aim was now to have a dependent financial system help realize the ideal program of "growth cum stability" as well as the various social-, regional-, and development-policy objectives. The higher level of government intervention was also manifested in the institution of a department in the finance ministry that in certain respects took on the role of a supervisory body or a corporate meeting in regard to the nationalized banks.[130] The Reserve Bank thus lost its exclusive competence in the regulation of banks and in lending, a process that was to continue in the sphere of industrial financing.

An *appraisal of India's financial system* after two decades of forced development reveals, in a nutshell, the following picture:

Measured in terms of its own objectives of bolstering the presence of commercial and cooperative banks in rural areas, the development achieved must be rated unreservedly as positive. The following table documents the quantitatively impressive expansion of the commercial banks.

Spatial Expansion of Commercial Banks since Nationalization

	June 1969	June 1984
Number of branches	8,262 (= 100 %)	45,332 (= 100 %)
Rural	1,833 (= 22 %)	25,372 (= 56 %)
Small towns	3,342 (= 40 %)	9,262 (= 20 %)
Cities	1,584 (= 19 %)	5,769 (= 13 %)
Metropolises	1,503 (= 18 %)	4,929 (= 11 %)

(Source RBI Report 1985, p. 63, and author's calculations)

Certain credit regulations were moreover designed to support a regionally and sectorally balanced spread of bank activities. They consist chiefly of targets aimed at ensuring that at least 40 % of all loans disbursed are granted to priority sectors and achieving a credit-deposit ratio of 60 % for rural branches of banks. Consequently, the industry share of the loans disbursed fell from 68 % (June 1972) to

37 % (March 1984) (RBI Report 1985, p. 68). This crowding out of industrial enterprises from loans provided by banks forms part of a conscious strategy of capital-market development.[131]

The structure of saving has shifted distinctly toward financial savings and long-term forms of investment, which, as was explained above, is encouraged through tax breaks and relatively high interest rates. The Indian government's budget financing absorbs a sizable share of this saving.

Finally, India has a highly differentiated financial infrastructure (see the schematic in Annex B). Apart from the diversity of financial institutions designed to match the specific financing needs of the sectors, there also exist various investment possibilities for households such as insurance, home building and loan associations, and investments funds. This strategy, supported by institutional investors and a highly liquid industry, has seen the development of a capital market of considerable breadth and depth.

At first glance, it would thus appear that essential goals of government promotion policy had been achieved, i.e. encouragement of the sectors and regions neglected by commercial lenders, mobilization of savings in financial form and over the long term, and the development of a system of institutions serving a great variety of financing and investment needs. Yet the dual structure of India's financial system continues. The informal financing sector, not covered by government supervision, has moved into the market niches opened up by regulation (RBI Report 1985, pp. 91-94). It offers on the one hand high-interest investment opportunities for assets stemming in large part from tax evasion and on the other hand relatively costly credits for trade and industry which are too small for the capital market and are rationed by ordinary commercial banks. These are some of the problems associated with the forced development of India's financial system.

Financial-Sector Development and Repressed Inflation

The expansion of the banking network promoted by the government runs along lines corresponding exactly to the developments in the agricultural and industrial sectors. Although even earlier there had been no lack of either declarations of political intent or legal groundwork for far-reaching government intervention, these options were not implemented and intensified until crisis management had grown imperative.

Already in the first Five-Year-Plan, the Reserve Bank of India had been instructed to promote the financial sector and exercise selective credit controls:

> "Central banking in a planned economy can hardly be confined to the regulation of overall supply of credit (...). It would have to take on a direct and active role, firstly in creating and helping to create the machinery needed for financing developmental activities all over the country and secondly ensuring that the finance available flows in the directions intended." (Quoted after RBI Bulletin 1984, p. 645)

The problems of the late 1960s suggested following a supply-side approach to financial-sector development (Mujumdar 1990):

Both the type and the extent of government development financing had proven unsustainable, and those responsible for economic policy at that juncture were convinced that the challenge they faced was to reestablish an "equilibrium of goods and money" that had broken down. An increased number of bank branches was now to increase the supply of financial services and/or, indirectly, the supply of savings. As was discussed above, on the credit-supply side this approach is based on the idea that the returns on the projects to be financed are determined by microeconomic and real economic factors, so that all that was required to realize the existing opportunities was to clear away the barriers to credit. On the side of the supply of savings, this involves the assumption, implausible in terms of the theory of income, that what is required to finance an investment is an advance of income, i.e. savings, and not an advance of money for production, which gives rise to incomes in the first place.

In what follows, the impacts of an approach to development of this sort will be analyzed empirically. It appears that pursuit of this approach has, in the macroeconomic environment as it was, led to a disintegration of the financial system. In a second step, an attempt will be made to document the disintegration phenomena, in order then, in a last step, to outline the most recent moves toward liberalization and reform. They can be understood as a contribution to resolving the complex of problems that have arisen, even though, in view of the level of indebtedness on the part of government, banks and business, the prospects of success will have to be seen as rather pessimistic. This pessimism sets the tone of the transition to the last chapter, which discusses a more radical proposal for resolving the problem.

The following phenomena may be regarded as *effects of supply-side financial-sector development*:

The profitability of the national banking sector is estimated to have fallen to the very low level of 0.15 % average return on assets (Clad 1990a; RBI Report 1985, pp. 84ff.). The reasons for this must be sought above all in priority lending and - closely associated with it - the administered structure of interest rates, in investment regulations on low-interest government bonds, and in the high overhead costs of an extensive branch network (RBI Bulletin 1986, p. 261). As might be expected, this has had very negative effects on the capital base and reserve formation of the banks.

The regulations on priority lending not only imply foregoing higher-interest forms of investment, which appeared justified to India's economic planners on grounds of welfare economics, but they have also raised the rate of credit losses. In 1986, for example, some 16 % of all claims were due to reserves ("arrears") for uncollectible credits

(Clad 1990a). In the industrial sector, the greater part of these arrears stems from small businesses, although their share among the "sick industries" appears somewhat smaller when the volumes involved are taken into consideration. The number of ailing, at least temporarily illiquid, enterprises has in the meantime reached a figure of over 200,000 (Economic Survey 1990, p. 60).

In the agricultural sector, the ratio of loans repaid as stipulated to loans disbursed by the cooperative banks is not much above 50 % (RBI Report 1985, p. 72). A debt-relief program for rural debtors, passed in May of 1990, provides for cancelling, under certain conditions, all outstanding debts up to 100,000 iR. The banks receive full compensation for this debt relief from federal and state governments.[132] This spreading phenomenon of claims rated as uncollectible ("overdues") is as a rule attributed to improper declarations of bankruptcy on the part of borrowers and other shortcomings in implementation or supervision. Again, these reasons may be entirely relevant in specific cases. If however, the analysis of the causes is left at that, the problems underlying this approach to financial-sector development are bound to remain in the dark. These problems consist in the procedure - justified with welfare-economic arguments - of approving lower-interest credit for selected projects, in that such projects, seen from a real economic angle or from the point of view of social returns, represent profitable investments.

In fact, however, the projects that are in the end financed at the lower interest rates are the less profitable undertakings, which implies commercially low returns on investment and lending and higher probabilities of losses. That is to say, the problem, seen from the perspective of this study, does not consist in the fact that lending discriminates, e.g. between uses for consumption and investment. Rather, it consists in the method of attempting to effect this discrimination with the aid of loans provided to preferred debtors at interest rates below the market rate. Direct allowances in the form of material and technical support would represent a more adequate type of explicit or implicit subsidy. This would make it possible to identify social- and development-policy deficits, whereas otherwise unprofitable production projects are summarily financed, which, in economic terms, constitutes consumption.

The deficiencies of the financial sector named above have been registered by most observers, although, as was indicated, they have for the most part been traced back to improper use. On the other hand, the rise of a comparatively deep and broad capital market and sizable increase of the volume of saving, by an annual average of 18 % (EPW, March 17 1990), is as a rule booked on the credit side. Several considerations on the macroeconomic conditionality of a flourishing capital market and rising volumes of savings do, however, not suggest that these achievements call for any unreservedly positive evaluation.

Owing to the numerous direct and indirect credit regulations - aside from those motivated by considerations of development, social, and regional policy, there are also minimum-reserve and liquidity regulations - banks in India can contract only a low share of their claims at commercial terms. The - except for some fluctuation - persistent capital-market boom experienced at the end of the 1980s (e.g. IDBI 1989, p. 1) has seen the banks faced with growing problems in finding sound borrowers for the credit they are in a position to supply. They themselves are therefore becoming more and more active in the capital market.

In the literature, this is usually represented as a process of disintermediation (EPW, March 17 1990). It does, however, appear more problematical that this process indicates a sort of adverse selection between the financing of credit and equity, thus leaving the banks with borrowers who on average fail to meet commercial standards (Clad 1990).

But the danger inherent in this is registered only when the development of the capital market is seen as a result of regulation of the financial sector in the face of repressed inflation. Regulation in tendency induces major investors and enterprises to take advantage of this form of financing. The capital-market boom itself would not be possible without the high level of liquidity stemming above all from the monetization of budget deficits. In a macroeconomic situation like the one in which India found itself in the late 1980s, a capital-market boom of this sort is more a sign for alarm than a glimpse of light on the horizon.[133] The consequences of this for the latitudes open to monetary policy will be discussed below.

Nor is the increase of saving a pure success indicator within a context of expansionary fiscal and monetary policy. The successful mobilization of deposits seen in the last two decades is closely linked with high levels of government spending:

> "When Government makes a disbursement, say, in salaries to employees, or payments to traders for goods received, there is an outgo of currency from the treasuries, a reduction in Government's deposits and an increase in banks' deposits with the Reserve Bank, and an increase in public's deposits with the banks." (RBI Bulletin 1950, p. 610)

Government salary payments and purchases of goods are increasingly transacted via the banking sector, so that there is a good chance that rising government spending will engender as a reflex a rising volume of deposits. In addition, the buildup of financial savings is promoted with tax breaks and encouraged with comparatively high mandatory deposit interest rates. In a measure difficult to determine, this could reflect the phenomenon of repressed inflation, the real economic counterpart of which is the appearance, in certain phases, of sellers' markets. The increase of the savings rate can thus only in part serve as an indicator of a successful mobilization of resources. In India, it is, instead, an indication of persistent deficit financing of the budget and a gauge of the success of the Reserve Bank in limiting the destabilization effects associated with it.

This interpretation of the mobilization of savings is diametrically opposed to that advanced in connection with any supply-side approach. In the latter view, higher available savings make possible greater income growth (e.g. World Bank 1989, pp. 33 and 36). What would be surprising in this case is the more modest income growth experienced by India precisely in the years in which the highest formation of savings were recorded.

If the mobilization of savings and the development of the capital market are seen in the context of a repressed inflation, a more skeptical judgement would be called for than might appear at first glance. The two-tier system of liquidity supply has also changed under the impression of this type of anti-inflation policy. There are signs pointing in the direction of a *disintegration of the financial system*. It appears in tendency that the two- or threefold task of the RBI - namely to provide stability as the central bank, to encourage the financial system as a development institution, and to finance government expenditures as a kind of dependent state commercial bank - has led to this situation. The RBI as it were embodies institutionally the regime of repressed inflation: the RBI can be used to point out in exemplary form the development and the rationale of this regime and to demonstrate one of the symptoms revealing the deformations resulting from it.

This thesis will be substantiated in three steps: the first step will be to demonstrate how the commercial and cooperative banks are crowded out of refinancing with the Reserve Bank; the second topic for examination will be the position of the national development banks in bank refinancing and direct financing in the agricultural and industrial sectors; and the final step will be to discuss the dichotomous structure of the supply of liquidity that results on the one hand from the relationship between RBI and finance ministry and on the other hand from the relationship between the development banks and the banking sector in the narrower sense of the term.

The *crowding out of the commercial and cooperative banks* from global refinancing with the RBI becomes evident when the balance of the central bank, more precisely: its asset side, is subjected to scrutiny (cf. Annex B).

The first thing to be noted is a relative decrease of claims against banks on the asset side of the RBI. Claims held against foreigners, the government, the banks, and the - as per IMF classification - "other financial institutions", such as IDBI etc., have on the whole been falling steadily at exponential rates since the end of the 1970s. This is largely a result of the rising volume of claims held against government. One single noteworthy exception is the second half of the 1970s, when the influx of foreign currency represented the dominant factor.[134] The percentage rise in credit granted to the other financial institutions, i.e. to "term lending institutions", including NABARD, also appears to have been responsible for a certain amount of the money-supply expansion in the 1980s.

The share made up by commercial and cooperative banks in the claims held by the RBI are an exact mirror image of the government share. In 1966/67, the bank share reached a relative minimum in connection with the IMF adjustment program. This share again remained below this level in the middle of the 1980s and is now fluctuating between 1 - 2 %, while the government share, having reached a minimum at the end of the 1970s, has again risen to a level of some 80 %. The share of the banks is primarily the result of their refinancing of export credits,[135] which has thus taken over the position once held by refinancing activities serving global monetary-policy ends.

Secondly, the monetary component resulting from the refinancing of the banks is subject to wide fluctuations. On the other hand, the claims held on the development banks reveal constant growth. They have in the meantime reached a share of the RBI's assets amounting to 10 %. The fluctuations among the banks are a sign indicating that refinancing them forms the manageable residual factor of any control of the money supply. A residual control of this sort can hardly be assumed for the share of currency reserves, likewise subject to sharp fluctuations.

Finally, at least after 1973, it is possible to make out an anticyclical trend in the refinancing of banks that confirms this impression.[136] It can thus be stated by way of summary that the commercial and cooperative banks were crowded out of the RBI's lending that was motivated by monetary-policy considerations. Its place was evidently taken by deficit financing and, to a lesser extent, selective credit allocation although part of the increased importance assumed by the development banks has, via refinancing for specific purposes, benefitted the banks, as will be discussed below.

In this way, the commercial and cooperative banks have in tendency taken on the financial-intermediary character that has always been attributed to them in neoclassical theory (Shaw 1973). From the perspective of this study, however, the growing similarity between banks and investment funds or insurance companies implies a virtual dissolution of the two-tier system of liquidity supply. In formal terms, the money supply has been rendered exogenous as a consequence.

The declining significance of the RBI in bank refinancing corresponded to the *growing role played by the development banks*. Until the end of 1989, IDBI and NABARD refinanced 71 million iR of loans made to the banking sector, while for the RBI this item accounted for somewhat over 28 million (RBI Annual Report 1990, pp. 109 and 49). This must be seen in relation to the 1,760 million iR of outstanding financial assets of the banks (1989) and an increase of their lending amounting to 164 million iR (ibid., pp. 105f.).

That the "division of labor" between RBI and IDBI and NABARD more and more finds expression in the fact that the indirect credit approved by the development banks is assuming growing significance compared to their direct lending (RBI Report 1985, p. 73). The volume of direct credit approved by the IDBI makes up a third of all its lending, while its refinancing commitments in the narrower sense, i.e. credits made to banks and discounting of bills, account for 50 - 60 % (RBI Report on Currency and Finance 1990, p. 91, Statement 66). The ratio is similar with NABARD, whereby indirect lending - refinancing of state cooperative and rural development banks - has always been the focal point of its activities.

In the case of NABARD and IDBI, the functions of development bank, commercial bank, and central bank thus overlap. The problems this entails become evident when account is taken of the high share of outstanding credit claims they hold, e.g. against the cooperative banks in rural regions, and the great number of ailing enterprises in business and industry.

It is precisely the "sickness" phenomenon that makes it possible to illustrate the rationale of the two-tier system of liquidity supply, first anchored institutionally in the Peel Bank Act of 1844. A state central bank that abstains from direct lending to the private sector is in this way relieved of the rationale of a commercial bank, i.e. from the necessity of having, in view of certain liabilities, to deal with the uncertain prospects of collecting its claims. Uncollectible credits can thus jeopardize the existence of a commercial bank, but not that of a central bank.

In keeping with their function as development banks, the "term lending institutions" above all, in particular the IDBI, were forced to include claims against illiquid firms in their portfolios, if these firms were not in any case their main customers (Clad 1990a). The government supports them in such cases by providing special credit lines for the companies affected as well as other types of rehabilitation measures (Economic Survey 1990, pp. 60-62). If the IDBI, in its role as a commercial bank, could have no interest in cancelling its apparently uncollectible credits, it now, in its role as a development bank, receives subsidies for this purpose, and is thus at the same time obliged to comply. In this way, the one function supports the other, although the outcome means sustaining the "sickness" of enterprises.

Moreover, as a central bank, i.e. as a bank for refinancing industrial credits, it may then feel inhibited in restricting any refinancing that appears justified in terms of stabilization policy: this implies on the whole that the number of uncollectible banking-sector credits for which it would again in part be responsible would continue to mount. This it will seek to prevent in its capacity as a commercial and development bank, so that its central-bank function is impaired by these other two functions.

The institutional shift and autonomization of the refinancing formerly provided by the RBI has in tendency led to a *dichotomous structure of India's monetary system*. The RBI was obliged to delegate a good part of its bank refinancing activities to IDBI and NABARD. Instead of exercising the sole control over these development banks, it now shares this control with the "Banking Division" of the finance ministry, or has even been forced to cede a good part of it to this division. Its control extends in particular to budget planning, refinancing, and disbursements of credits approved by these institutions. On the other hand, the development banks themselves are in large measure responsible for credit approvals ("sanctions").

This has repeatedly given rise to discrepancies between disbursements and sanctions.[137] According to oral information provided by a high-ranking RBI officer, the development banks had in recent years to be reminded on various occasions that high credit approvals are not consonant with stability-policy goals. This indicates a conflict of interests between the disbursements determined by monetary-policy considerations and the approvals motivated by development-policy and institutional considerations. It must be assumed that this conflict is not one between control instances on the one hand and development banks on the other, but one between the RBI on the one side and the Banking Division and the financial institutions on the other side. This is indicated by the juncture at which the Banking Division was established, i.e. 1969, in connection with the nationalization of the banking system, and the growth- and development-policy perspective expressed in pertinent publications of the finance ministry.[138]

Nonetheless, it was the Reserve Bank itself that worked actively toward "delinking" the development banks established by it and originally directly dependent on it. Their endowment with an annual budget fixed in advance relieves the central bank's portfolio of long-term claims that can scarcely be instrumentalized for purposes of monetary policy. As much sense as this step makes when seen in isolation, it is nonetheless unsuited to opening up greater room for maneuver of the Reserve Bank when the banking system as a whole is simultaneously in the process of being "delinked". Instead of holding only short-term claims against the financial system that can be called in when it becomes necessary to restrict the money supply, the RBI has exchanged its direct control for a say in setting up the annual budgets of the development banks. Nor, moreover, does it have control over the direct claims it holds against banks in the narrower sense, in that these claims serve ends sacrosanct in terms of development policy.

The link between Reserve Bank and development banks has thus experienced an institutional slackening, although in financial terms it has gained in weight at the expense of the link between Reserve Bank and commercial banks.[139] To be sure, these volumes of refinancing must be seen in relation to the credit provided to the central government. The following figure illustrates the magnitudes.

The volume of credit disbursed via the so-called Long-Term Operations Fund corresponds roughly to 11 % of the supply of central-bank money in circulation (RBI Annual Report 1990, p. 107). Although this is not a negligible fund, its dimension takes on a completely different aspect when the volume of monetized budget deficits is taken into consideration. Moreover, these credits provided to the development banks are, as was already mentioned, refinancing funds that can scarcely be deployed for purposes of monetary policy. Thus Reserve Bank and government form one side of the dichotomized monetary system, whereby in this case the RBI can be more aptly termed a government bank than a central bank.

The other side is constituted by the financial institutions and the banks in the narrower sense. To be sure, the banks rely to a slight degree on refinancing by the development bank competent for them,

Outstanding RBI Claims against Development Banks, as Compared with Banks in the Narrower Sense and Deficits Financing (as of: June 1990, in millions of iR)

Reference

Reserve Bank of India

Long-term financing:

	National Industrial Credit (LTO) Fund			Nat. Housing Credit (LTO) Fund	From central-bank profits National Rural Credit (LTO) Fund	Stabilization Fund	Deficit financing[a]
	IDBI	Exim Bank	IRBI	NHB	NABARD	NABARD	Central Government
1985/86	25,899	2,600	100	-	20,050	6,200	- (61,900)
1986/87	28,753	3,450	250	-	23,550	6,300	132,810 (70,910)
1987/88	31,986	4,350	450	-	26,550	6,400	199,400 (65,590)
1988/89	35,283	5,300	700	500	29,850	6,500	264,430 (65,030)
1989/90	38,220	6,250	950	750	33,150	6,600	402,560 (138,130)

Short- and mid-term financing:

	IDBI IFCI ICICI SFCs	General Line of Credit NABARD	Refinancing[b] of Commercial and Cooperative Banks
1985/86	1,256	8,609	-
1986/87	825	9,497	-
1987/88	245	14,168	21,580
1988/89	424	22,777	39,370
1989/90	676	28,584	28,100

a Tab. 8.3 (in brackets: annual changes in holdings)
b Tab. 6.3
Source: RBI Annual Report 1990, p. 108, Tab. 9.3

but this component, crucial to the dynamics of income generation in a monetary economy, obtains credit chiefly from IDBI and NABARD.

The connection between this development and the anti-inflation policy practiced is obvious: the crowding out of the commercial and cooperative banks from refinancing with the RBI was a direct consequence of the fact that the RBI was attempting to compensate for the persistent monetization of government deficits. These banks were at the same time made into an instrument of development and structural policy, or more specifically: they were compelled to play a role in an anti-inflation policy aimed at striking an "equilibrium of goods and money". In order to pursue this complex objective, the RBI created an elaborate system of development banks. It is no longer able to control this system directly and effectively in the short run.

This has at least two highly problematical consequences: in the first place, stability-oriented central-bank policy is rendered virtually impossible in this way; instead, monetary policy is handed over to government budget planning and - to a lesser, but not negligible extent - the development banks, which can be controlled only indirectly. In the second place, the dichotomization of the financial system and the dissolution of the two-tier system of liquidity supply increases considerably the risk of sudden crises of confidence in India's banking sector and India's currency.

Attempts at Liberalization and Reform

Against this background, it will now be possible to view briefly the most recent attempts at liberalization and reform, which proceed from the recommendations made by the Chakravarty Committee, named after its chairman (RBI Report 1985). The measures taken and the reforms inaugurated can be summed up under the following headings:[140]

-    Liberalization and rationalization of interest rates: in connection with a comprehensive strategy aimed at activating India's money

market, the interest rates on short-term "call money", interbank
deposits, and bill discounts were deregulated. This is intended to
transform the former market for treasury notes into a genuine interbank market for short-term liquidity transfers. The volatility of
the money-market interest rates has, however, grown considerably in connection with this activation (RBI Annual Report 1990,
p. 68). In an additional important step, the maximum interest rate
for commercial credits (1988: 16.5 %) was replaced with a
minimum interest rate (Oct. 1988: 16 %) beyond which the banks
are free to exact a surcharge in keeping with the creditworthiness
of the borrower in question. This replacement of "ceiling rates"
with "floor rates" also extends to other types of credit, thus
achieving a more homogeneous structure of the array of interest-
rate regulations (Economic Survey 1990, pp. 101f.). These measures, as well as a market-oriented setting of returns on government bonds (Battacharya/Guha 1990, p. 782), are closely linked
with the above-mentioned problem of the low level of profitability in the banking sector.

-   New financing instruments: an additional goal of money-market
    activation finds expression in the circumstance that various in-
    struments, such as "certificates of deposits", standardized bonds
    ("commercial papers"), short-term treasury bills ("refinancing
    treasury bills"), and several other items, have now been autho-
    rized. This was intended to facilitate the banks' liquidity manage-
    ment. Although this is not officially seen in the same context, the
    introduction of such instruments must indeed be viewed against
    the background of an anticipated increasingly tense liquidity situ-
    ation.[141]

-   Financial infrastructure institutions in the narrower sense: one
    striking feature of the most recent developments in India's finan-
    cial sector has been the establishment of various subsidiary insti-
    tutions. These include above all a bank dealing exclusively in
    money-market papers ("Discount and Finance House of India"),
    an credit-rating agency ("Credit Rating and Information Services
    of India"), and a supervisory body for the capital market

("Securities and Exchange Board of India"). The RBI states (RBI Annual Report 1990, pp. 150 and 152) that the establishment of such additional institutions is characteristic for the phase that has now been reached: it consists in the consolidation of the banking system on the one hand and new forms of regulation on the other hand. Viewed pessimistically, however, these institutions could be read as an early-warning system set up with an eye to impending times of crisis.

- Capital-market development: the rapid growth of India's capital market has made necessary various legal regulations, the above-mentioned establishment of subsidiary institutions, and the authorization of new financing instruments like convertible obligations (RBI Annual Report 1990, pp. 113ff.). Originally, the expansion of the capital market was a desired secondary effect of the regulation of the banking system, in particular of the selective credit-allocation policy that rationed loans to major borrowers. The state banking system was intended above all to serve the weaker borrowers and the capital market was expected to cover the demand for conventional financing. The capital market now, however, appears to be on the way to becoming a source of revenue from commission and investment transactions (ibid, p. 150) for the banks themselves, thus increasing their profitability. Thus the capital market generally serves the purpose of privatizing business financing, which the banking system has been less and less able to offer at competitive terms in view of the strains facing it from priority lending, overdue claims, and as a result of its being compelled to invest in low-interest government bonds.

What is revealed in the reform attempts as interpreted in this way is a strategy of a gradual overhaul of India's financial system. Yet indebtedness, domestic and foreign, continues to grow. The high budget deficits or their monetization by the RBI have, as has been indicated, contributed to this need for consolidation in that they have led to a dichotomization of the financial system. The integration of the banks into a redistributive regime, in the end one of the factors contributing to the high level of government indebtedness, has also restricted the commercial viability of banking.

This has in the meantime reached such dimensions that even the financial system itself is becoming a budgetary burden, as is demonstrated in exemplary form by the "Agricultural and Rural Debt Relief Scheme". Once again, this situation results from the tendency of the redistributive regime of India's monetary economy to regulate both sides of the market, credit supply and credit demand, and thus to have to create a balance via fiscal transfers. This, among other factors, has led into the vicious circle of indebtedness, compensatory measures, and, consequently, growing indebtedness. The following chapter will present an outline of the latitudes remaining to India's economic policy in view of this problematical situation.

6   Ways out of India's Monetary Crisis

Each of the two preceding chapters is devoted mainly to one of the two essential aspects of any monetization process, namely the political legitimacy and the economic stability involved in any such process. The 1980s appeared to be marked on the one hand by the political crisis of a poor democracy and on the other hand by the attempt to combat the symptoms of repressed inflation. The repression of an inflation process can be explained with reference to the problems of legitimacy facing India's governments in that macroeconomic or monetary stabilization can scarcely be made to conform with the objective of providing at the same time for dynamic economic development and social equalization. To this extent, the repressed inflation results from India's dilemma as a poor democracy. It has, however, for its part heightened the pressure of legitimacy in that its inhibitory effects on income generation have diminished the existing latitude for redistribution.

The path inaugurated with the reform policy of the 1980s and intended gradually to overcome the crisis will be reconsidered briefly
with reference to the discussion conducted above. In this chapter,
consideration will be confined to the question of whether the reforms
are contributing to socially acceptable macroeconomic stabilization or
whether, instead, they are encouraging gains in efficiency and con-
sistency in regulatory policy. This will be followed by an attempt to
appraise the contribution of an austere monetary and financial policy
package that the International Monetary Fund (IMF) has been calling
for as a precondition for any further assistance for India's balance of
payments.

Hastened by a domestically tense situation, a government coalition restricted in its capacity to act, and the consequences of the Gulf War,
India's foreign-trade and fiscal situation has deteriorated sharply since
the end of 1990.[142] The following considerations will, however, abstract from these events, the consequences of which are as yet (i.e. in
1991) hardly predictable. They address the existing options - continuation of the reform policies, implementation of an adjustment program - from a general, development-policy perspective. In the present
situation, this perspective appears rather optimistic in so far as India
will, in the coming years, presumably have to pursue a rigorous policy of stabilization that is apt to permit no more than a limited measure of development of productive capacities and increase of per
capita income.

Both the reform policy practiced by Indian government until now
with an eye to expansion and a conventional stabilization package
patterned on IMF adjustment programs must, for reasons to be discussed below, be assessed skeptically. In India's present situation, the
economic view would appear to indicate a currency reform that could
create the conditions necessary for other proposed solutions to succeed. As far as the question of acceptance is concerned, however, this
study can go no further than to present some substantiated conjectures
derived from the contrast with the proposals previously discussed.

6.1   Macroeconomic Stabilization via Sustained Reform Policy

Liberalization in the industrial sector and in foreign trade has been discussed on the one hand in terms of its legitimacy aspect - its contribution to the relief and the partial withdrawal of government - (chapter 4.1), and on the other hand in terms of its economic aspect, in terms of which is has served to increase profit income in dosed measures (chapter 5.2). Liberalization brought some relief in that it either replaced several specific types of regulation with more global forms of intervention or abolished them altogether. Some aspects that deserve to be named in this context are the rationalizations of import tariff structures, the release of a number of industrial sectors from the licensing regulations, and the lifting of the price administration for a number of industrial products. These steps at the same tome entail a supply-side stimulation of production activities in that they improve microeconomic conditions for profit-taking. Macroeconomically, however, this has set off a restrained process of adjustment inflation that is becoming more and more difficult to control. Additional measures, like prolonging the positive list for license-free imports and relaxing the cartel regulations, appear, on the other hand, chiefly aimed at making allowance for the economic aspect. If the desired results occur, the economic success will, however, also lend a legitimatory force to such reforms.

Something analogous can be noted for the policy pursued in the financial sector. The establishment of subsidiary institutions, like for example a capital-market supervisory body, or encouragement of the money market provide relief for the government by replacing interventions in individual decisions with regulation of market conditions, the actors' anonymous surroundings. Seen in economic terms, the various measures must, however, be qualified as having more of a defensive character: what they would be expected to achieve is not stimulation of financing activities per se but consolidation of the banking sector and improvement of liquidity management. Viewed in the macroeconomic context, this would appear more adequate to preparing for the imminent eruption of a crisis.

The policy of real and financial reform was accompanied by an enormous jump in government demand that appreciably increased overall economic investment activity and utilization of capacity in industry. This coincidence of microeconomic deregulation on the supply side and macroeconomic stimulation did not come about by chance in the sense that the slackness in budget policy was a relic from times begone, whereas liberalization already represented the encouraging reorientation of the future. Instead, it was a precondition for the temporary success of a comparatively higher growth in income. A selective admission of foreign competition, the partial liberalization of insulated markets through delicensing, or the increase of average financing costs stemming from liberalization of interest rates are all reasons that should actually have occasioned Indian producers and investors to make more cautious arrangements. Negative effects on the level of aggregate production would most likely have occurred had it not been for the pull stemming from the demand side in the face of underutilized capacities. The latter, together with administrative precautions, also kept price rises in check for a while. The 1980s can thus be seen as the reverse image of the era of the Green Revolution. The latter was presumably unable to develop the impetus expected for the simple reason that it took place in a period marked by crisis management.

The reference to the inner connection between deregulation and expansion, not by chance recalling the practice - as opposed to the doctrine - of "Reagonomics", makes it plain that the Indian economy was not to be stabilized in this way. What was, on the whole, interpreted here as an attempt to break up the regime of repressed inflation by striking the ominous goods-money equilibrium entailed an exploding government debt and a balance-of-payments situation of crisis proportions.

Politics at the same time lost its legitimatory basis and found expression in a programmatic swing toward Hinduist fundamentalism in connection with a business-friendly pragmatism. The one-sided promotion of the urban middle classes and the big rural farmers has led to a situation in which incomes and living conditions have begun to develop far more unequally, which has directly encouraged a rural exodus as well as communal and religious conflicts.

Consideration of this latter state of affairs provides even more support for the economic argument stating that the first step required is to reduce the potential of inflation, in order then to advance a selective opening up of foreign trade and a step-by-step deregulation of domestic production. What speaks in favor of this sequence, which here seems advisable with regard to India's industrial and foreign-trade policy, includes, as was mentioned above, experience made by other countries in connection with liberalization of financial markets:

> "(...) those economies that largely avoided the adverse consequences from large-scale financial liberalization - sharp increases in interest rates, bankruptcies of financial institutions, and loss of monetary control - were characterized by stable macroeconomic conditions, a strong and effective system of bank supervision, and a gradual removal of controls on interest rates." (Villanueva/Mirakhor 1990, p. 510)

While the two last-named conditions, i.e. the strengthening of supervision and the removal of regulations on interest rates, have been met in part, this is not at all the case with regard to macroeconomic stabilization. It must therefore be asked whether traditional stabilization of the type sought be IMF adjustment programs have prospects of success.

6.2   The Adjustment Program and its Mid-Term Prospects[143]

In the first half of 1991, it became obvious that India would be forced to take recourse to concessional assistance. The balance-of-payments position had deteriorated to an alarming extent, the RBI's foreign-exchange reserves had fallen to unprecedented low levels, and India's rating as a borrower in international markets had deteriorated considerably. In this situation of acute macroeconomic crisis, India's government turned to the IMF as to the lender of last resort.

A country needing to draw on IMF credit tranches beyond 25 % of its quota is requested to submit a program designed to restore a viable balance-of-payments position. The broad objectives of such a program should, in the IMF's view, be external and internal stabilization in the context of liberal exchange and trade arrangements. The standard package therefore implies trade liberalization and a one-time devaluation or even market determination of the exchange rate concomitant with a restrictive monetary and budget stance. A restrictive macropolicy is intended to counteract the inflationary effects growing out of exchange-rate liberalization and excessive internal absorption. Excessive absorption is normally due to public-sector budget deficits.

The formal request for IMF resources and the conditions to be met for obtaining them are laid down in a "letter of intent" which is not released officially (Bhattacharya 1992, pp. 14-15). It contains various "performance criteria" and "policy understandings" which amount to what has become known as the conditionality of IMF-assisted programs, namely that disbursement of credit is conditional on compliance with these criteria and understandings. In keeping with the objectives of the program, conditionality applies to external, monetary and fiscal indicators.

The government of India and the IMF agreed on a so-called Stand-by Arrangement on October 31, 1991. For a period of 20 months, India is entitled to draw credit equivalent to SDR 1,656 million, to be disbursed in several instalments. Standard performance criteria refer to external, monetary and fiscal objectives of the government's adjustment program: the external objectives are monitored through quarterly floors on net international reserves of the RBI and clauses on the avoidance of multiple exchange practices; the monetary objectives are monitored through quarterly ceilings on the RBI's net domestic assets, with a sub-ceiling on RBI credit to the central government; and the fiscal objectives are monitored by means of quarterly ceilings on the overall borrowing requirement of the central government as well as an indicative benchmark on total bank credit to the general public sector (IMF 1991, p. 24).[144]

Several "structural benchmarks" were attached to the adjustment program, i.e. with respect to industrial policy, trade liberalization, domestic pricing policies, public-enterprise reform, financial-sector reform, tax reform, and expenditure control. These benchmarks are supposed to have been formulated with an eye to World Bank involvement. A structural adjustment loan/credit from the World Bank was approved on December 5, 1991. It is the World Bank's first policy-based loan to India (World Bank 1991, p. 5) and amounts to US $ 250 million on loan and SDR 183.8 million on a credit basis.[145]

In what follows, I will discuss in broad terms the effects of this adjustment program as they relate to the analysis presented above, i.e. of impediments to development in general and of India's crisis in particular. Because this study has been concerned with questions of development under monetary conditions, the discussion here will concentrate on macroeconomic aspects of adjustment. The adjustment process will be complex and not confined to economic issues, but macroeconomic stabilization is certainly an essential ingredient.

The intention here is not to enter into a debate on the IMF approach and its theoretical foundations in general but to evaluate the adequacy of the Fund-assisted adjustment measures to cope with India's present crisis. This section is thus meant to prepare the ground for the last section in which it will be argued that reconstitution of India's monetary economy appears to be indispensable for sustainable adjustment.

Three key requirements for stabilization follow from the analysis of a dilemma between stagnation and erosion as well as from the concept of India as a redistributive regime:

(1) The lingering erosion of the rupee has to be stopped, which is practically synonymous with breaking the dynamic of public debt.

(2) A collapse of investment and an endemic collapse of enterprises or banks must be prevented, while the fiscal component of aggregate demand will have to be reduced at the same time.

(3) It will be necessary to provide safeguards for the vulnerable part of Indian society, both as a demand-stabilizing device and because otherwise popular resistance to unbearable hardships will jeopardize adjustment.

The ongoing IMF- and World Bank-assisted program will therefore be evaluated against the background of these criteria. This will first require a discussion of its main components, namely external monetary and fiscal policies. Qualitative estimates of their likely effects will be followed by a more general account of the program.

It is important to note that even prior to October 1991 India's government adopted measures broadly in accordance with standard prescriptions set out by the multilateral institutions.[146] They have been stepped up as a means of addressing the rapidly deteriorating situation in the aftermath of the Gulf War. Thus, these earlier attempts at stabilization and reform will have to be taken into account in so far as they represent forerunners of the 1991 program.

The following table shows macroeconomic data of the Indian economy and IMF staff projections for the fiscal year of 1991/92.

External Objectives of the Program

The external objectives of the Indian adjustment program aims at sustaining external payments due on imports and debt. A viable balance-of-payments position is therefore equivalent to a current-account surplus covering the amount of service on external debt.[147] Basically, three policies have been implemented to achieve improvements toward that end: first, depreciation of the rupee exchange rate; second, promotion of exports and liberalization of imports; and, finally, import compression measures in times of acute payments crisis. Exchange-rate policy and export-oriented trade liberalization have been pursued since the mid 1980s, and they are certainly highly essential components of a mid-term strategy.

The exchange-rate arrangement implemented by the Indian authorities in recent years has been crawling-peg policy, i.e. discretionary intervention to devalue successively. It is a declared government goal to find a substitute for discretionary price determination and move toward partial or full convertibility in the sense of an exchange rate determined by supply and demand.

The problem with this type of exchange-rate policy is, as indicated by failure to achieve a sustainable external balance, that exchange rates are not a price like that of any commodity: an exchange rate is the price of an asset determined by the willingness to hold this asset. Any depreciation or even uncertainty as to whether the authorities are committed to keeping the rate fairly stable will then lead to a self-fulfilling prophecy: any expected depreciation will create pressure for depreciation, but any actual devaluation will renew corresponding expectations.

That depreciation breeds (expectations of) further depreciation is indicated by the fact that a rupee devaluation even beyond the inflation differential to reference countries failed to materialize in a current-account surplus. The macroeconomic disadvantage, i.e. a bias toward overvaluation due to expected devaluation, appears to have been stronger than any competitiveness gains made via export promotion.

Given the volume of India's internal and external debt, it is a safe bet to hold foreign exchange instead of claims payable in rupees. A more reasonable policy would therefore be to aim not at a "free rupee" but at a stable nominal rate, possibly after a one-time devaluation (IMF 1991, p. 17).

This will also be essential for export-oriented trade liberalization to succeed. As long as the trade account is exposed to the vagaries of

India: Basic Data. 1987/88-1991/92[a]

	1987/88	1988/89	1989/90	1990/91	1991/92 Staff Proj.
			(Annual percentage change)		
National income and prices					
Real GDP at market prices	4.9	9.7	5.0	5.0	3-3[a/b]
Nominal GDP at market prices	13.9	18.8	12.1	16.0	14-15
Consumer prices (end-period)	9.8	8.6	6.6	13.6	...
Wholesale prices (end-period)	10.7	5.7	9.1	12.1	9.0
Industrial production index	7.3	8.7	8.6	8.4	...
External sector (on the basis of U.S. dollars)					
Exports, f.o.b.	21.4	12.8	18.8	9.1	5.7
Imports, c.i.f.	11.8	19.3	4.6	11.5	- 8.6
Non-oil	7.5	23.5	1.6	4.1	- 7.5
Oil	41.7	-3.0	24.6	52.1	-13.8
Export volume	14.4	11.3	17.5	4.0	4.2
Import volume	-2.3	8.2	4.4	3.9	- 5.7
Terms of trade	-7.2	-8.0	0.9	-2.2	4.6
REER (end of period) 2/	-3.1	-10.2	-7.3	-8.7	...
Central Government budget					
Revenue and foreign grants	8.6	16.3	7.8	14.6	29.2
Expenditure and net lending	8.4	16.1	18.9	14.5	8.3
Current expenditure	13.1	16.9	19.9	16.6	10.3
Capital expenditure and net lending	-2.2	14.0	16.3	8.6	2.1
Money and credit (end-period)					
Domestic credit	15.1	16.9	19.8	16.5	13.4
Government	18.0	14.3	21.4	19.7	10.6
Commercial sector	13.5	19.0	18.6	14.1	15.6
Total liquidity (M3)	16.0	17.8	19.4	14.9	13.0
			(In % of GDP)		
Gross investment	22.7	23.9	23.6	23.3	21.5
Public sector	10.4	9.9	10.7	10.5	9.5
Private sector	12.2	14.0	12.9	12.8	12.0
Gross domestic savings	20.3	21.1	21.7	19.9	18.8
Public sector	2.2	2.0	1.7	1.1	2.2
Private sector	18.1	19.1	19.9	18.8	16.6
Central Government budget					
Revenue and foreign grants	12.0	11.7	11.3	11.1	12.6
Expenditure and net lending	19.7	19.2	20.4	20.1	19.1
Deficit	7.7	7.5	9.1	9.0	6.5
Public sector deficit	10.3	10.0	12.5	12.5	10.0
External sector					
External current account deficit	2.4	3.2	3.0	3.4	2.7
Debt service ratio	29.4	29.8	27.7	27.8	26.5
External debt	21.4	21.0	23.5	24.0	30.6

[a] Date are for April-March fiscal years unless otherwise stated.
[b] Real Effective Exchange Rate

ad-hoc management, any export-oriented restructuring appears virtually impossible. An overvalued and unstable rupee that coincides with reduced protection for domestic producers is then likely to promote deindustrialization rather than modernization.

Monetary Objectives of the Program

The objective of monetary austerity is twofold, namely to lower inflation and to defend international reserves (IMF 1991, p. 15). To achieve this, the Indian authorities are combining indirect means such as additional cash reserve requirements and higher administered interest rates with direct means such as reduced facilities for refinance and directed credit.

The divergence between the approach of the Indian authorities and the standard monetary-policy package is noteworthy when the dichotomization of the Indian financial sector is taken into account. The standard prescriptions, stressing the need for allocative efficiency, recommend raising interest rates across the board instead of effecting selective increases (IMF 1991, p. 33). However, the analysis presented above (see chapter 5.3) suggests that a diminishing control capacity on the part of the RBI forces it to fall back on selective control.

But if the financial system is dichotomized, then it is also questionable whether performance criteria set at the RBI level (IMF 1991, p. 15) will prove effective in reducing bank liquidity. It would be equally important to consider credit policies of financial institutions, such as IDBI, that have assumed central-bank functions. Otherwise, targeted reduction in broad money growth will not be feasible.

Restrictive monetary policy, whether achieved by selective or general measures, will result in a higher level of interest rates. In net terms, this will lead to a reduction in the outstanding volume of debt, which is tantamount to insolvencies or illiquidities on the part of firms and, subsequently, banks. I will come back to this issue in the next section. However, the biggest Indian debtor, namely the government, is also affected by any such rise in average interest rates. This is all the more true as financial-sector liberalization since 1989 has implied a shift toward market financing of government debt. Thus, given the outstanding debt, the achievement of monetary objectives may impair another target of the program, namely fiscal consolidation.

Fiscal Objectives of the Program

The medium-term objective of fiscal consolidation is to reduce (net) government expenditure so as in turn to reduce the pressure on prices and external accounts. As the table above shows, the public-sector deficit amounts to 12.5 % of GDP (fiscal years of 1989/90 and 1990/91), as measured by the IMF. This indicates the amount by which the expansionary effect must be curtailed in order to neutralize government's impact on aggregate demand and prices.

The Indian government has announced a number of measures aimed at moving in the direction of a more balanced budget. Some of the more important of these measures are on the revenue side: an increase in corporate taxes and excise duty, partly to compensate for a reduction in import tariffs; privatization of public enterprises; and in general a major tax reform to be implemented in the first half of the 1990s. On the expenditure side, the government has proposed various reductions, the most substantial of which are: cuts in subsidies for exports and fertilizers, constraints on defense spending, fewer transfers to public enterprises, and general restraint in all expenditure items, including capital spending (IMF 1991, pp. 10-13). A politically sensitive part of the program aims at reducing the transfers made by the center to the state governments, while at the same time limiting their access to other sources of financing, in particular their borrowing from banks.

All these proposals require thorough structural reform of the Indian economy, given the huge share of the public sector in aggregate demand, investment and domestic credit, as shown in the figures above. It is too early to say which of these proposed measures will survive in the political process. And there is one item in particular that is conspicuously lacking in much public debate and in the IMF outline (Bhattacharya 1992, p. 96): the required service of internal debt. This, however, may create one of the major obstacles to fiscal consolidation, an obstacle stemming from fiscal and monetary austerity itself.

A brief glance at the figures indicates that the debt situation is rather precarious:[148] net interest payments on public debt, i.e. interest on borrowing minus receipts from lending, as a ratio to current revenue, has increased immensely. For the center, it rose from 7 % to more than 24 % in the decade from 1980 to 1990. The figures are 2.7 % and 10.0 % for the states respectively. The average gross interest rate (net of reserves and deposits at concessional rates) on the outstanding debt increased from 6.7 % in 1980/81 to 8.1 % in 1987/88. Moreover, the composition of public debt in terms of maturity and marginal interest rate has deteriorated seriously as a result of substantial "front-loading": e.g. a large amount of debt has been financed through zero bonds the interest of which accrues upon maturity. These payments are not included in published figures on government debt service.

These facts of public debt suffice, in my view, to justify some skepticism as to the sustainability of the adjustment and reform program envisaged. This is not to deny that important steps and, indeed, indispensable measures have been taken by the government in office. What has to be considered as a fundamental problem is, however, that essential preconditions for these steps to become economically effective, i.e. to contribute to stabilization, have been overlooked.

In sum, the empirical findings are:

- since the mid 1980s the exchange rate has depreciated by 60 % in nominal effective terms and 50 % in real effective terms;

- monetary policy was continuously tightened by raising interest rates, which was intended to reverse the capital outflow of non-resident Indian funds;

- a program of fiscal consolidation has been under discussion for several years, but serious moves toward launching have materialized only since the second half of 1991.

However, neither protracted devaluation nor tighter monetary and fiscal policy have led in the direction of a sustainable balance of payments position and an abatement of inflationary pressures. My conclusion from the empirical findings is that the huge internal debt accumulated by India's government is the crucial impediment to viable adjustment.

By way of contrast, and put in more general terms, both the IMF and ranking Indian government officials are adhering to a specific interpretation of the root causes of India's protracted crisis, and this interpretation is leading to rather different conclusions on the likely outcome of a standard adjustment program. It might be argued instead that their interpretation constitutes an impediment to first taking decisive steps, namely to eliminate the drag on the Indian economy stemming from a huge volume of debt.

The IMF maintains that the external difficulties have been caused by "excessive fiscal deficits" which have "pre-empted a large share of savings", plus "deep-seated structural rigidities leading to inefficient resource allocation" (IMF 1991, p. 32). Thus, increasing the savings rate directly by increasing deposit rates and fiscal austerity as well as structural adjustment will, it is thought, suffice to remove these "fundamental causes".

While it cannot be denied that all these factors have played a role, it is questionable whether it is appropriate to place them only in a framework of (excessive) consumption and allocative efficiency. This study suggests viewing these phenomena within the sphere of development under monetary conditions. This perspective makes it possible to see the fiscal deficit and structural rigidities as elements of a regime of repressed inflation. The result of "opening up" the economy is in that case likely to be less beneficial, since crucial prerequisites for successful consolidation are not existent. In particular, the burden of external and internal debt must be removed before stabilization can succeed. Only then will fiscal austerity be bearable and more profound reform of India's redistributive political economy become feasible.

6.3   Currency Reform as a Prerequisite of Macroeconomic Stabilization

When Finance Minister Sinha took office in 1990, he stated in his first speech before parliament that only comparatively radical measures could ward off the acute crisis: "The soft options stand exhausted."[149] What follows will propose such a radical option, namely a currency reform, and explain how it would serve to open up the room for maneuver that would make it possible to stabilize India's economy. This proposal is advanced from an exterior perspective and will to this extent have to be seen as parenthetical. It is not by chance that the grounds cited for inaugurating a currency reform at this juncture are above all of an economic nature: appraisals of whether a measure of this scope is feasible would require more intimate knowledge of the existing situation than is normally available to outsiders.

So why would a *currency reform in India* have been a decisive preparatory step for stabilization and adjustment? A currency reform going beyond altering the unit of account by merely striking out a few zeros[150] would depreciate the stock of claims held in the old currency via conversion to a new unit. This cut in wealth implies, conversely, that income flows should appreciate in relation to assets since they would remain roughly the same in nominal terms (Riese 1990, pp. 96f.; Tober 1989, pp. 35ff.). Put differently: the intention in depreciating to some extent available assets, is to create an incentive to acquire income and form new wealth. As opposed to traditional anti-inflation policy, a currency reform thus not only targets monetary stabilization, which finds expression in a heightened attractiveness of holding money and creating financial wealth. Its aim is at the same time to stimulate accumulation by providing greater constraints to earn income and by relieving the prototypic debtors of a monetary economy, the investors, of the liabilities they have contracted in the past, including the debt service on these liabilities.

The central problem of an adjustment program in today's India is to put the budget on a new footing, and consequently to free of debts this economy's biggest investor. A complete or partial annulment of merely the government debts would, however, aggravate the position of the banks and enterprises in relative terms, thus setting false signals for the future role of government in India's economy. The government would, in this case, again have to take on compensatory tasks in that the other actors, still highly indebted, would not be in a position to accomplish these tasks while pursuing their commercial interests.

A first argument in favor of a currency reform results from this consideration. Depending on the conversion rate decided upon, government debts could be depreciated to a large extent. That would relieve it of the burden of current interest and redemption payments, thus creating a necessary condition for a credible balanced or even surplus budget.

The redemption effected administratively by a currency reform would also be for the good of those nongovernment economic actors who, then and in the future, are expected to carry a larger share of income generation. This one act would do away with the problem of "sick industries" to the extent that they are defined by a "net worth" consumed by their outstanding debts (see chapter 5, above). If these debts were cancelled, the market conditions would at least be fulfilled that would make it possible to force them in future to abide by their budget constraint, without having to face an epidemic wave of bankruptcies from the very outset. Even the partial debt relief programs in the agricultural sector, often associated with political vote-buying, would be replaced with a general redemption of debts.[151] This would, it is true, on the one hand benefit major debtors as compared with small debtors. But on the other hand it would avoid creating entitlement rights that tend to induce corruption and thus serving to cement the power of individuals. Hence, thoughts on the future organization of India's system of economic policy likewise speak in favor of a currency reform.

In spite of all this, a measure so incisive may appear exaggerated at the present juncture. Typically, currency reforms are carried out or put an end to hyperinflation by restoring the acceptance of the currency issued by the monetary authority. In India, however, there are as yet signs neither of a hyperinflation nor of an acute loss of confidence in the rupee. Yet, even prior to the present critical developments, there were alarming signs in the shape of a boom in real estate and the capital market. These were symptoms of the efforts of Indian investors to look increasingly toward investment opportunities that could protect them against depreciation of their wealth resulting from the current inflation. In the mean time, the stock-market boom inspired by high liquidity has collapsed, drastic curtailments in imports, fiscal measures aimed at reducing the budget deficit, and internal and external unrest having led to a revision of investor expectations (EPW 1991). India's capital market has since then displayed sharp fluctuations.

In 1992, this seems not yet to have had any dramatic effects on the Indian rupee. And a currency reform at this juncture would have served the purpose of maintaining the fragile acceptance of the Indian currency. It would to this extent serve to avoid, not to eliminate a hyperinflation while at the same time holding open options for development and accumulation.[152] Hence three consideration of economic-policy in the narrower sense of the term speak in favor of a currency reform: the relief it would provide the government budget, the redemption from debts that would accrue to producers, and the elimination of the threat to the acceptance of the domestic currency. Yet good reasons are of course not the same thing as the conditions under which they will succeed. These must be sought on the one hand in the economic sphere and on the other hand in the sphere of legitimacy.

Not only domestic debt, but also foreign debt has become an urgent problem, as may be inferred from a debt-service ration of some 28 % (see Table, "India: Basic Data", above). With a foreign debt estimated for 1990 at 72 billion US $ (Country Analyses, 1990), India has entered the circle of the major debtor countries. Crisis broke out when its foreign-currency reserves were reduced to less than the value of what it imported in one month, because its foreign-exchange situation, in any case precarious, had deteriorated in connection with the Gulf War: the transfers sent home by Indians working abroad have diminished sharply, while expenditures in foreign exchange rose considerably as a result of increasing oil prices. The balance-of-trade deficit rose in 1990 from 6 billion US % (1989) to an estimated 8.2 billion US $.

At least three conditions would have to be fulfilled as *foreign backing for a currency reform*:

-    The creditors (creditor countries) would have to suspend India's debt service for a certain period of time and, to whatever extent possible, agree to cancel part of its overall debt. It would otherwise be highly implausible that the austerity required to service existing external debts could be sustained without risking a collapse of investment activity and/or unbearable hardship for large segments of the population, which would lead to desperate acts of resistance;

- India's most important trading partners, in particular those with currencies suitable as foreign-exchange reserves, would have to be prepared to forgo imposing one-sided import barriers and accept a selective protectionist insulation of the domestic Indian market for a set period of time;

- in view of the foreign-exchange situation, a one-time capital import would appear necessary to make it possible to defend the new exchange rate in the months following the currency reform.[153]

Without these major concessions, a currency reform would be likely to fail due to external adjustment pressures. But there should be interest in stabilizing India, not least in view of overriding, i.e. regional, considerations. The world-political constellation of which India, as a prominent nonaligned nation, is a prominent part has of course repeatedly led to situations in which was left to itself and its deceptively "quiet backwardness" (Rothermund 1991, p. 7).

Domestic backing for a currency reform would require far-reaching change in existing policies:

- Since all of the external measures aim at stabilizing the foreign-exchange situation, i.e. at achieving a balance-of-trade surplus such as that reached in a difficult situation in the middle of the 1970s, the prerequisites would have to be created through a social contract in the formal sector: moderate wage demands would enable the enterprises to practice moderate pricing-setting and dismissals policies, thus strengthening competitiveness of Indian products at reasonable exchange rates;

- repressed inflation could, potentially, be overcome by a currency reform, which would be in need of administrative support involving price deregulation aimed at creating production incentives and avoiding any claims to government compensation;

- the government would have to enforce its existing tax claims and seek to develop new sources of revenue, which should involve organizing the system of taxation in such a way as not to hamper either current production or investment activity.[154]

Such domestic backing obviously presents a precondition for success that would prove very difficult to meet. It might require a protracted decrease in real incomes or a temporary loss of real incomes on the part of those employed in the formal sector. The social consensus demanded here might be all the more likely to overtax the reasonable understanding of those affected, as the currency reform would be implemented prior to the complete breakdown of India's monetary economy. In a hyperinflation, fixed contracted incomes are as rule so sharply depreciated that those affected readily accept its being brought to an end, even if this means hardship for the majority: better a calamitous end than an endless calamity. But when the calamity is not yet fully manifest, the hardships entailed by a solution are experienced as being all the more oppressive.

Without in any way playing down the risk potential inherent in this, a comparison with the two ways out of the crisis discussed above clearly shows that they can hardly be preferred in view of the *problem of legitimacy*. The reform policy practiced until now has, as was mentioned above, chiefly favored the urban middle classes and big agricultural landowners. While the open preference shown to the middle classes was a major factor contributing to the electoral defeat of the Congress Party under Rajiv Gandhi, his successors' preferential treatment of the agricultural oligarchy has virtually led to a situation in which India's society is being worn out in communal, ethnic, and religious strife.

Stabilization on the pattern of an IMF program brings advantages above all to export-oriented enterprises and the owners of wealth. At the same time, it so burdens the government and domestically oriented industry as to make unavoidable extensive lay-offs, curtailments of welfare programs on the part of the government, and more or less far-reaching cuts in investment projects on the part of industry. These adjustment programs thus often encounter broad national protest. This protest is somewhat justified in economic terms to the extent that this type of adjustment entails neglecting development of the domestic market in favor of an orientation toward the world market, the ability to service the debt being the primary concern.

As a glance at the statement of financial assets demonstrates (RBI, Report on Currency and Finance 1990, pp. 16f.), the sectors profiting by a currency reform in India would be the net debtors of the economy, i.e. the government and the business sector. This administrative debt-relief measure would also cover a broad class of rural producers. The household sector and, to a lesser extent, the banks would be the aggrieved creditors.

To the extent that a sizable share of bank claims are in any case uncollectible, cancelling them by way of a currency reform would constitute no more than a formal act. Households enjoy a certain measure of protection to the extent that they own tangible assets making up on average roughly one half of household wealth. Directly following a currency reform, such assets would have a supreme value, since it is protected from monetary depreciation, and would begin to lose value only after the currency reform had begun to take effect since in this case the formation of financial wealth would grow in importance. A discriminating conversion rate that might, for instance, provide for a more favorable conversion of small savings would make it possible to organize the expropriation involved along lines consonant with objectives of distributive and social policy. To be sure, compensatory claims with the banks would have to be dropped and taken over by the government. In other words, any social cushioning of the hardships stemming from the currency reform would have to be balanced against the new government debts it would entail.

It can thus be stated by way of conclusion that a currency reform ahead of the necessary stabilization has weighty economic grounds on its side. It would not only lend credibility to the stabilization by improving the actual conditions for stabilization, it would also provide a more favorable framework for future development. From the very outset, an intervention as incisive as the one proposed here - i.e. one touching upon the property rights sacrosanct in a monetary economy - does not, in terms of legitimacy, appear any worse than the alternatives. Thus there are a number of reasons indicating that India's economic policy ought to consider this step before the erosion of the monetary system, with its drastic impacts on social and individual living conditions, advances any further.

Notes

1 A. Leijonhufvud (1966) inaugurated the rediscovery of the "monetary Keynes", who had fallen into oblivion in the face of IS-LM Keynesianism.

2 This may not be the worst place to illustrate the importance of a functionalist mode of argumentation or immanent criticism. Because decisions made in a monetary economy are taken with reference to the formation of value, in classical terms: the formation of exchange value, the term used here is accumulation, and not growth. It may be noted critically that what is involved in a monetary economy is not growth in the sense of the production of use values. But an economic theory insisting on this or presupposing it has no other choice than to abstract from the monetary character of the economy analyzed or to subject it to abstract negation.

3 For an approach of this sort and a complex discussion of the causal relationships between financial-sector policies and growth, see A. Gelb (1989).

4 Thus the title of a comprehensive study on the theory of financial development by M.J. Fry (1988). It provides a concise introduction to the theoretical discussion and then presents the models, empirical verifications, and development-policy implications associated with them. Fry's publication makes it possible to avoid recapitulating here the important contributions. A textbook survey less demanding in formal terms is presented by S. Ghatak (1981).

5 See R.J. McKinnon (1973, p. 7 and passim) and, in concise form, E. Shaw (1973, p. 80), who makes a policy of financial repression responsible for all deficits as regards allocation, growth, and distribution, in order to demonstrate its far-reaching effects: "The lagging economies have repressed real financial growth. Social losses have resulted. Income might have been higher with more thorough monetization. Savings-income ratios might have risen if savers had been offered feasible rates of return. Savings allocation might have been more efficient if interest rates had been used to discriminate ruthlessly among investment options. Employment could have been higher if capital had been substituted less often for labor. Possibly the distribution of income would have been less unequal if less reliance had been placed on the strategy of repression and interventionism."

6 Thus R.J. McKinnon entitles his third chapter "The Intervention syndrome", which treats a fragmented monetary economy as if it were a symptom of a disease. This disease, he notes self-critically even vis-à-vis his own two-gap model (1964), has never been analyzed by structuralism: "Repression is implicitly being taken for granted." (1973, p. 171).

7 "In many respects the state resembles a private sector in its behavior. One implication for us is that debts of the two sectors may be treated alike in analysis

of the lagging economy's markets: the distinction between outside debt and inside debt is dropped." (E. Shaw 1973, p. 51).

8   See **E. Shaw** (1973, p. 77): "The essence of financial liberalization and deepening is release of real rates of interest to disclose the scarcity of savings and to stimulate saving, to raise accessible rates of return on investment, and to discriminate more effectively between investments (...). An increase in interest rates gives the signal that capital is scarce, and the rational response of an economic system is to use capital more sparingly but labor and land more liberally."

9   See **R.J. McKinnon** (1964). This approach, which proceeds from a structural savings and foreign-exchange gap in developing economies, making a transfer of resources necessary, will be discussed in connection with the problem of constitution in chapter 2.

10 The following presentation chiefly relies on the contributions in **E.V.K. FitzGerald / R. Vos** (1989). The two best-known structuralist development economists working in this area are doubtless **S. van Wijnbergen** and **L. Taylor.** For particulars, see also **M.J. Fry** (1988, esp. Chapter 4).

11 The two aspects become clear in the defense presented by **E.V.K. FitzGerald / R. Vos** (1988, p. 28) against possible criticism of the structuralist planning euphoria: "There is no suggestion in structural economics that markets are in some sense 'bad' or that state planning is 'better', as some critics suggest. The central position is distinct: that markets work in structured ways quite different from that which neo-classical theory suggests and that state intervention of some kind is required for any market to function at all." The central role accorded to government for the functioning of markets conversely implies that "market failure" is seen as the permanent threat to a liberal system.

12 See on this, not closely restricted to the stabilization context, **E.V.K. FitzGerald / R. Vos** (1989, p. 14): "(...) care must be taken to ensure that basic needs requirements of the population are met independently of the effects of financial policies. In other words, investment should be financed, in the first place, by reduced consumption out of profits and not by increased profits at the expense of wages." This policy recommendation, indisputable in its intention, can, to be sure, only be implemented if enterprises - like classical capitalists - accumulate for accumulation's sake and refrain from so tightening up production processes that they earn the market interest rate. If government then seeks to control the "surplus", it must be prepared for potential investors to refuse their services.

13 The above-mentioned two-gaps topos suggests itself here, viz. a savings gap and a foreign-exchange gap. This study discusses this idea in more detail in 2.1.

14 **C. Bell** (1988, p. 764) begins his fundamental article on credit markets in development economics in this sense: "When output follows inputs with an appreciable lag, the agents organizing production will usually be involved in credit transactions, in the sense of exchanging future resources for present ones. The impulse toward such exchange will be all the stronger if output is also

uncertain; for then there are compelling reasons to smooth consumption in the face of fluctuating income." The real economic processes, uncertain or extending over time, can accordingly be stabilized individually through monetary transactions.

15   Both the derived character and the effects of money and credit potentially in-creasing instability find expression in **E.V.K. FitzGerald / R. Vos** (1989): "(...) the origins of financial flows are the systematic imbalances between the saving and the investment behaviour of economic agents (including financial intermediaries themselves) according to the logic of their respective institutional forms."

16   **E.V.K. FitzGerald / R. Vos** (1989, p. 26) summarize the structural position with reference to empirical data as follows: "(...) what data there is on aggregate private investment functions indicates that it is mainly a lagged function of aggregate demand (...). State investment (...) is a function of perceived development strategy rather than of considerations of probability (...). Finally, households and small producers invest in housing, farm improvements, or transport equipment as part of the expansion of their own productive income opportunities; and not as a portfolio choice (...)."

17   Of course this quantity equation, which describes an identity, becomes the basic equation of quantity theory when velocity of circulation v and transaction quantity T are, owing to certain hypotheses on their real economic or conventional determination, posited as constant. Any increase in the money supply then leads only to higher prices, the neutrality of the monetary sphere as opposed to the commodity sphere is ensured.

18   **M. Friedman's** image for an increase in the supply of money is a drop of money from a helicopter. This fully obscures market processes, the interaction of central bank and commercial banks, thus achieving the exogenization of the money supply. After all, his wish is to see this institutionalized when he recommends that central banks ought to follow a strict money-supply rule.

19   In the marginal case of a pledge to convert 100 % of bank notes into a reserve medium, these notes, would, it is true, no longer be able to be regarded as money in the strict sense of the word: they would then be a reserve medium. Such a constitution of money would correspond to the thought-experiment made by **H. Riese** (1989, p. 27f.), which imagines a monetary economy in which money no longer circulates as a currency but is merely held by the banks as a reserve with the central bank. The rest of the economy has only indirect reference to this stock of money in that it has a medium of exchange, i.e. transfers claims to money, not money proper.

20   This is the lever with which it can force through a contrived scarcity of pro-duction processes via a restrictive course by causing bankruptcies. On the whole, namely, it is not possible to return more currency $(1+i)M$ than what has been issued.

21 In **J.M. Keynes**, the liquidity premium is, to be sure, a category of monetary demand. Although this likewise makes possible a monetary explanation or monetary theory of interest, it does imply assigning a passive role to the creditor side, i.e. the money-supply side. This theoretical parti pris then biases numerous other propositions, in particular the suggestion of a policy of easy money as a means of eliminating underemployment - a recommendation that has gone a long way toward discrediting Keynesian theory. If, on the other hand, the liquidity premium is conceived as a category of money supply (**H. Riese** 1983), it is possible to avoid such - stated in plain terms - implausible inferences resulting from an overestimation of the money-demand side and a reduction of money to the role of a "lubricant". The rehabilitation of Keynesian economics was advanced considerably by this analytical study.

22 See the more detailed position elaborated by **G. Lachenmann** (1990, Chapter B, Part IV) from the angle of development sociology on the concept of the "rationality of action".

23 This asymmetry might be formulated pointedly as the feature that such a use of money is not subject to double accounting because no monetary variable can be estimated for the assets side of the balance.

24 The motives that in the Late Middle Ages occasioned the "feudal sovereign powers" to seek new sources of revenue, thus setting in motion the process which gave rise to the tax-based state, is described as follows by **A. v. Müller** (1986, p. 100f.): "One may, as the historians do, argue as to whether the motive for forming the modern state was that these sovereigns were seeking new finance options or whether they found enhancement of their rank, legal standing and power vis-à-vis their feudal competitors only in new organizations of their power and in new social alliances that simply cost more money. One thing in any case remains indisputable: the constitutive context of state and taxation." **H. Stürmer** (1986, p. 178) remarks on the critical nature of this issue for the early modern state: "The right of taxation was the core of all constitutional life and invariably in dispute - basically, the theater of an enduring struggle for over the apportionment of the burdens of state, often on the verge of open insurrection and civil war." The contributions in **R. Tilly** (1975, pp. 51, 97ff., 164, and passim) discuss the link between the rise of the nation state, taxation, and military expenditures.

25 Bureaucratization was thoroughly intended as an institutional expression of a Weberian rationalization process: it was to entail the establishment of rational principles of organization in the administration of the state, the separation of administration and politics and personal functions from official functions. Yet this appears to have taken place to a very limited extent. It was more akin to Parkinsonian bureaucratization, characterized merely by an inherently dynamic, merely quantitative growth of the state apparatus. See **H.D. Evers / T. Schiel** (1988, Chapter 8) on the variety of concepts of bureaucratization and empirical development, including those in Asian nations.

26 In the monetary theory of exchange rates, the balance of payments mirrors the domestic money market. Since the money market is grasped in terms of quantity theory, it is in the end the central bank's money supply in relation to the money supply of the reference country that determines the account of the balance of payments and the demand for foreign exchange. See **J.A. Frenkel / M.L. Mussa** (1985, pp. 716ff.).

27 Expressed in more formal terms, what was stated in the text implies that the determination of exchange rates must be interpreted along the lines of portfolio theory. The parameters determining the inclusion of a foreign currency in a portfolio are:
1) the interest to be realized for a claim in the currency, i;
2) the nonpecuniary return on such a claim, reflecting confidence in the predictability of changes in exchange rates and in the possibility of switching out of the currency in question, z;
3) the liquidity premium of forgoing claims in the currency in question, i.e. possession of this currency, l. A foreign-exchange market equilibrium is then characterized by the condition: $i+z=l$, the equilibrium between two currency areas by $i^a + z^a - l^a = i + z - l$, the index a standing for "abroad". The different strengths of currencies are expressed in the level of the liquidity premiums. The formulation of equilibrium given above implies that a weak currency will have to compensate for its low liquidity premium l by means of a high rate of interest i or an increase of z, e.g. by government guarantees. See **W. Schelkle** (1990, p. 296ff.) and **M. Lüken-Klassen / K. Betz** (1989, pp. 237ff.). See the exemplary discussion in **J.A. Frenkel / M. Mussa** (1985, pp. 725ff.), in the chapter entitled "Exchange rates as asset prices" on portfolio-theory interpretations of exchange rates in modern trade theory.

28 For the first stage - capable of short-term investment - Latin American countries are an example, which often caused major problems in connection with adjustment programs in that capital flows counteract the restrictive course of price stabilization. For the final stage, lack of contractibility, Italy may be cited as an example of an industrialized nation with a government debt so high that confidence in its currency, the lira, has been decisively weakened. It is able to attract long-term capital investment only by offering a high interest differential.

29 The setup of drawing rights with the International Monetary Fund (IMF) attempts to take this problem into account by permitting countries to draw a tranche only when such countries deposit domestic currency matching the foreign currency which is lent to them. This is nevertheless a fiction since the demand for the currency of the country drawing is of an institutional nature and not market-driven. Symptomatic of this is that only supranational institutions like the IMF, but never a commercial bank, demand deposits of Indian rupees or Argentine australs when lending to India or Argentina.

30 Cases are conceivable in which the direction of determination proceeds more from the demand for currency to domestic accumulation. What is meant here is a typical developing country that cannot expect any foreign demand for its

currency. It is thus forced to overcome this currency weakness by achieving export surpluses, which must go hand in hand with a change in its base of comparative advantage, a development of its productive capacities via domestic investment. But it is also possible to imagine countries, like Israel for instance, in which, owing to their special historical situation, there is a private demand for claims from abroad that goes some way toward supporting the generation of income. This means that such countries have already achieved the constellation of a mature industrial nation, which is a barrier to Israel's development.

31 In the liability-based economy, the debtor-creditor relationships that existed previously under extra-economic conditions are extended to economic conditions which had until then been regulated through loyalty ("reciprocity") or direct domination. It now is no longer status-dependent legal claims, but willingness to advance money, that controls access to resources used for production. The *scandalon* of a monetary economy is, in other words, that it totalizes a form of social relations that likely had their origins in religion, thus at the same time making production and reproduction possible in an a-social manner. See **K. Polanyi** (1979).

32 The reform of the agricultural tax in Japan during the era of the Meiji restoration is frequently cited as a tax reform that went far toward hastening this country's development as a monetary economy (**G. Ranis** 1959). See **R.W. Goldsmith** (1983, p. 22) on the development of civil law resulting from this tax reform.

33 **C.P. Kindleberger** (1984, p. 191) sums up the results of historical research as follows: "Initial views of the role of capital in the industrial revolution have been sharply revised by economic historians. Large amounts of capital were needed for chartered companies, like the East India, and for public works. (...) The needs of industry were miniscule." Developing countries today achieve investment rates of over 20 %, which is likely to be roughly twice as high as those achieved by today's industrialized nations in the 19th century.

34 The formation of financial and business conglomerates or cartels could be described in this way in modern financial terminology; what might be cited as examples are the zaibatsus in Japan or the collaboration between banks and industry in 19th century Germany. The internalization of market relationships in the firm makes it possible to come to grips with problems of supervision and control and the uncertainty for creditors associated with them (**M.C. Jensen / W.H. Meckling** 1976).

35 The presentation largely follows that of **M. Lüken-Klassen / B. Betz** (1989, pp. 221ff.). For the reasons named in the text, it is extended merely to include the two other actors and the development-policy context.

36 Even if they, like for instance traditional money-lenders, do not borrow outside capital with an eye to lending it, the principle of opportunity costs all the same requires them to treat any lending they make from their own savings as if it were based on a debt. This principle will prove below to be essential to understanding self-financed investments and interpreting the net worth of households.

37 It is, as is explained in the next section, true that opposing effects result from the fact that the probability that credit will be repaid increases in an inflation process, although this can also lead to losses as a result of maturity transformation and an anticipated response on the part of the central bank. The former stimulates lending on the part of banks and financial intermediaries, the two other factors are more apt to influence decision-making in the direction of stability-minded reticence.

38 In terms of the principle of opportunity costs, financing from retained profits resembles borrowing in that the enterprise concerned will always have to consider other uses to which they might be put as well. To this extent, the investor, as an owner of wealth, demands credit of himself and must demand repayment with interest. The enterprise behaves toward itself as if it were a bank.

39 To be sure, the proposition that the money supply recorded on the liabilities side of the central bank's balance sheet must, in economic terms, be interpreted as society's liability to itself implies that its net worth, corresponding to cash holdings and claims, must be understood as a liability held by the owners of wealth against themselves (**H. Riese** (1989, p. 7, ref. 19). This again follows from the logic of opportunity-cost thinking: people will treat their property as if it were assets to be turned to account and required them to earn interest income. Here, one must call to mind Weber's theory of developing capitalism: the members of Protestant sects accumulated wealth in the consciousness of in this way redeeming the liability stemming from their predestination.

40 **K. Bücher** (1920, p. 135) establishes this connection between state and economy in the early modern period: "The formation of a national economy is the fruit of the political centralization that begins toward the end of the Middle Ages with the rise of state-like territorial structures and was concluded in the 19th century with the creation of the centralized nation state."

41 The short-term credits given to enterprises by the portfolio holders, e.g. in the form of a current-account advance, have been omitted here in the name of simplicity. Such lending would correspond to relationship (5), although it would be less problematical for an enterprise in so far as it is also able to contract long-term liabilities. It can then, just as the portfolio holders, undertake a liquidity-preserving horizontal fine-tuning of its claims and liabilities, of its tangible assets of varying degrees of liquidity and its liabilities with different maturities.

42 The development-relevant integration of this sector or these economic units into the monetary economy would be indicated above all by long-term lending. A growing share of market production, seen by many authors as a relevant indicator, can, taken for itself, only imply that the productive households are forced to make money earnings due to a high level of indebtedness. This indebtedness may result from government tax claims or social obligations, need not, in other words, be connected with the production process.

43 That the neoclassical school nonetheless sees savings as the condition for investment results from the fact that it fails to discuss the problem of income generation as the outcome of a market process. For it, income has always existed in the valued form of initial stocks of resources. Income rises as a result of a "more efficient" employment of these resources, which increases the valuation of the initial stocks, seen by them as being located in place and time. An intertemporal reallocation, investment, requires a deferment of present consumption, i.e. temporally deferred consumption in the form of savings. Neoclassical growth theory logically discusses the effects of a stock of resources evolving exogenously, i.e. demographic growth and technological progress.

44 That investment and exports are the two categories of income formation can, in formal terms, be read from the macroeconomic saving and investment account: its asset side contains gross investment and net financial investment vis-à-vis foreign countries.

45 Even in a rigorous theory of the household such as that propagated by the neoclassical school, a higher rate of interest on savings need not necessarily lead to increased saving. Whereas the substitution effect of a higher interest rate may result in abstention from present consumption, the income effect runs in exactly the opposite direction. The net result is indeterminate.

46 Several monetary-Keynesian authors have in the meantime described this hierarchical interaction. See **H. Herr** (1986); **H.-P. Spahn** (1986, Chapter 6.4); **H.J. Stadermann** (1987, Chapter 26).

47 The following line of reasoning continues on from the excellent presentation of **M. Lüken-Klassen / K. Betz** (1989, pp. 231ff. and 244f.), although it condenses their step-by-step approach and slightly expands their model, namely by the dimension of government demand.

48 This equation goes back to the basic equations on the value of money in **J.M. Keynes** (1931, pp. 120f). See also **E. Shaw** (1973, pp. 23f.).

49 The argument stating that mark-up pricing presupposes imperfect market forms derives from neoclassical theory. There, the production constraint is scarce resources, not scarce advances of money. Perfect competition leads to full utilization of these resources at prices fixed by an omniscient coordinating authority, the Walrasian auctioneer. In this equilibrium, every owner of a resource, be it "capital" or "labor", receives precisely his marginal product. Enterprises are then price takers who receive no genuine profit. If, however, scarce advances of money constitute the budget constraint, then suppliers create finite markets. Instead of expanding production to the point where they become profitless price takers, they will be more apt to withdraw from the market. This is all the same consonant with perfect competition: Keynesian enterprises are, it is true, not prices takers (of goods), but they are "interest- and wage-rate takers", as is argued below.

50 The link between condition of macroeconomic realization and rationale of microeconomic decision-making consists in the fact that equation (7) can be interpreted as the macroeconomic expression of the production-price model (**P. Sraffa** 1960 and **H. Riese** 1983). The Sraffian production-price model defines a vector n of relative prices p from "production of commodities by means of commodities" as follows:

$$p = (1+r) A p + w \cdot l <=> p = w \cdot [I- (1+r) A]^{-1} \cdot l.$$

r is the uniform profit rate, A the nxn matrix of production coefficients, I the unit matrix, w the wage rate, and l the n-line vector of direct working inputs. This partial-analytic equation system used to determine the relative commodity prices can be employed to determine the price level when money wage rate w and profit rate r are given by the labor market and the capital market, respectively.

51 The decision-making process of producers, which need not be formulated rigorously for the purposes of this study, pose formal difficulties that are disregarded here. To give a brief indication of them: a production decision always implies theoretically an income aspect and a production aspect. It includes both a fixing of the level and the choice of a deployment ratio of (producible) means of production K and (non-produced) labor L. The theory of marginal productivity of course assumes that level and capital intensity, i.e. technology, can be determined simultaneously, which at the same time yields relative factor prices and - in connection with consumer preferences - relative commodity prices. On the other hand, capital-theoretic arguments have been advanced that a "reswitching" may take place and that inconsistent assumptions on returns to scale are required. The first argument, a recurrence of technology that cannot be ruled out on theoretical grounds, prohibits assuming a monotone-inverse relation between profit rate, alias interest rate, and employment of capital. The second argument points to the inconsistency in the circumstance that what is required for a clear-cut determination of level is decreasing returns to scale, whereas the assumption of perfect competition calls for constantly rising returns to scale. - The theoretical consequence of this critique is that any derivation of an equilibrium of relative commodity prices must have reference to a given level, i.e. must be separated from the determination of a balanced investment volume. The choice of capital intensity in the sense of a substitutional choice of technology is fully excluded from this consideration. It is in any case not of interest as long as its relation to the profit rate is neither clear-cut nor causal. This is why the text states that what is chosen, at a given interest rate, from the quantity of available technologies is the technology most adequate to maximizing profits. On this discussion and its significance for applied policy consultation, see **A. Nadal Egea** (1990).

52 **J.M. Keynes** (1931, pp. 125f.) For this process, i.e. that investments are made on the basis of optimistic expectations and that these result in windfall profits that confirm expectations, thus giving rise to new investments, Keynes borrowed from the Old Testament the image of the widow's jar. This jar was miraculously

replenished whenever it was emptied. In the same way, investments, made in such a constellation, will, simply by being undertaken, generate the windfall profits that stimulate them.

53 Empirically, it is, to be sure, not possible to rule out an increase in savings in connection with a restrictive monetary policy, although this cannot be explained in terms of a theory of income determination: saving is a function of income, income generation a function of investment; declining investment must in that case, ceteris paribus, reduce saving. Since, however, the propensity to save is a variable determined by human behavior, it can rise in a recession sparked by monetary policy, even though objectively the option of saving will, on average, fall as a result of the contraction of incomes.

54 One factor determining Germany's "economic miracle" was shaped by the elements just named: an undervaluation supported by amassing foreign exchange, accompanied by a stability-oriented monetary and budgetary policy and intended to fend off capital imports. Incidentally, in Bundesbank circles development assistance was first discussed when options were sought to effect strategic capital exports so as to avert any risk of revaluations. The foreign-exchange reserves had here already reached indecent levels (**O. Emminger** (1986, pp. 11ff.). On the role played by monetary policy in the German "Wirtschaftswunder", see **H. Riese** (1988).

55 **H.-P. Spahn** (1986, p 194n) makes note of this in his discussion of classical accumulation theory: "The difference from Ricardo's stagnation theory is that, in a monetary economy as opposed to a barter economy, scarcities of factors find expression not in a direct compression of the profit rate but in rises of the price level. By eliminating this production constraint, the monetary character of an economy at the same time generates a production constraint mediated via the interest rate; in this, it is not longer scarcity of resources but scarcity of money that is mirrored by the profit rate."

56 For the theory of the liquidity preference of interest, this cannot be explained directly: owing to their market position, enterprises and banks are able to safeguard their liquidity more easily in a process of inflation.

57 On inflation theory in development economics, see the overview published by **C. Kirkpatrick / F. Nixson** (1987).

58 As opposed to **H. Riese** (1986, p. 14 and passim), who speaks of the "conditional" validity of quantity theory, the present study prefers, more cautiously, to refer to a "transcendental" validity of the quantity equation. Riese's formulation in the end implies a growing money supply to be the condition of inflation and not merely the condition of its potential to arise.

59 This interaction of bursts in profit and income levels does of course recall the post-Keynesian spiral of "demand push" and "cost push". But the difference is that in this case a market process is indicated and a monetary phenomenon formulated.

60   **J. Robinson**'s (1938) theory of hyperinflation leads to the same result, though it argues not with the formation of wealth corresponding with income generation but with a direct erosion of the income cycle: hyperinflation can be identified when wage earners begin to reject payment in domestic currency. In this case, the price formation implied in equations (7) and (8) is no longer possible. The erosion process outlined here does, however, suggest itself more for farming-oriented economies without any widespread wage labor, since no such "power of definition" on the part of wage earners is likely in emerging monetary economies. Nonetheless, the two formulations are complementary. See also **H. Riese**   (1986, pp. 217-221) on Robinson's theory of hyperinflation.

61   In practicing a restrictive monetary policy, the central bank may come into possession of the tangible assets of enterprises as follows: when it calls in the claims it holds against portfolio owners (1), forcing them to call in their claims against enterprises (2), it then comes into possession of property rights of failing businesses and banks covering the volume of the claims to interest it holds against the economy. This demonstrates once again that the central bank is the creditor, not the debtor, of the rest of the economy.

62   Based on empirical theory, and from a structuralist angle, **H. Shapiro / L. Taylor**   (1990, p. 865) also argue against the night-watchman state, because market signals alone by no means favor the development process: "At issue is Gerschenkron's long-forgotten point about backwardness and inertia: more than a market signal is required to displace the previous 'equilibrium' in order to make nontraditional export markets and investment projects attractive. (...) (E)specially in poor countries, the state is (or was, in many parts of the world) the only entity with deep enough pockets to make beyond-market incentives sufficiently sweet."

63   Thus far, the only relevant attempt seems to have been undertaken by **H.-P. Spahn**   (1986, pp. 61ff. and 226ff.).

64   This problem has been identified in one form or another by development economists of differing provenance. **H. Shapiro / L. Taylor**   (1990, p. 867) make note of this in critical intent: "The (...) neoclassical suspicion that democracy is not compatible with economic growth unwittingly echoes some Marxist theories of the state." **H. Riese**   (1986, p. 286ff.) saw the underlying conflict in the fact that today's system of national currencies represents a concession to employment interests. This, he claims, forces investors to protect their interests in a system of "wage currencies", which generates the high level of instability displayed by the system. For adjustment now is no longer chiefly accomplished via real wage and employment, as it was under the gold standard, but in part via the exchange rate. It can, though, be doubted whether national currencies are merely a "yoke" (ibid., p. 287) for the owners of wealth. After all, switching to a different currency can also be a means of bending national economic policy to "the yoke of wealth interests".

65 Value is the product of price and quantity. Changes in value can therefore be traced back only to two analytically separable, though not observable, changes that may even run contrary to one another. The Neoclassical economists have in part chosen a different methodological way out of this aporia: they treat genuine variables of value as physical variables, which paves their way to clear-cut propositions. One example of this is their theory of capital. The value of means of production is formalized as a stock of machines, physical wear and tear taking on the role of the time dimension. Intertemporal macroeconomics in a substantive sense is then impaired by all sorts of paradoxes and technical modelling restrictions, as was demonstrated by the legendary Cambridge controversy. (See ref. 51, above).

66 Redistributive regime is therefore not intended to designate any third economic system beside capitalism and socialism, monetary economy and planned economy. This is the intention of **Elsenhans**'s concept of the "bureaucratic development society" (**H. Elsenhans** 1981, Chapter V). To be able to grasp this as a mode of production of its own, he takes recourse to Marxist class analysis and creates the new category of a "state class". But subsequently he is forced to make use of demand-Keynesian instrumentarism to be able to explain why these societies stagnate despite the constraint to produce a surplus. He sees the reason for this in low mass purchasing power, which offers little incentive to invest. Democratization and an increase of mass consumption are recommended as strategies for overcoming any such stagnative mode of production. Why it is that government consumption is unable to achieve this is an unfathomable issue in the perspective of the Keynesianism championed by Elsenhans. The present study, however, sees the causal relation between consumption and income generation as dubious. Accordingly, Elsenhans confuses the desired result of dynamic income generation with the means to achieve this end. - In view of the phenomenon noted, however, this study follows his lead. He too regards the redistributive function of state economic activities as the characteristic feature that is, in part, intended to replace the market mechanism. Accordingly, the centralization of power is to be seen against the background that monetary market control may conflict with the goal of social integration (ibid., pp. 129 and 138 passim).

67 This possible correspondence between wealth and employment interests is implied by the notion of a "second budget constraint". Thus, the chances of suppliers of labor and owners of resources of pushing through higher wages or higher prices increase when, in connection with an accumulation process, the available potential is utilized to the full.

68 The precautionary measures required under private law can be outlined with the principles stemming from Roman law: "*Pacta sunt servanda*" (creditor protection via adherence to contracts) and "*Ad impossibilia nemo tenetur*" (debtor protection via possible cancellation of straightjacket contracts).

69 One might, following **H. Riese** (1990), see the deformations in the fact that a monetary economy in this case takes on traits of a planned economy. This was

not done here because this would, in the name of comprehensibility, have required characterization of a planned economy. It might nevertheless be noted that redistributive regimes can be understood as "an alternative to plan and market", as a realization of the concept of perestroika. But as yet it is not possible to make out any macroeconomic control function in the perestroika model, neither of the money supply, of resource planning, nor of any third element. Unfortunately, it appears at the moment that "perestroika" is being used to make a conceptual virtue out of a political necessity.

70 This distinction has already been made with regard to Part II, since India intended, programmatically, to develop as a "mixed economy", although, for the understanding of this study, it nevertheless represents a monetary economy and is, nolens volens, developing as one.

71 In contrast, a national economy is defined, in classical terms, by a certain quality (productivity) of domestic labor, and in neoclassical terms by a specific endowment of resources. Currencies are consequently inessential - owing to institutional conventions - elements of external-trade relations that consist in the exchange of goods in accordance with the comparative advantage. The name given to the project of the "EC Domestic Market 92" follows this principle. Several member states seem in the meantime to have experienced justifiable doubts as to whether the real economic integration is actually creating a domestic market and not instead merely creating additional free-trade and free-movement advantages for the countries with strong currencies, without at the same time forcing these countries to do without their currency-related advantages. See **M. Lüken-Klassen / K. Betz** (1990) and **W. Schelkle** (1990) on this.

72 Thus the heading of the first chapter in **T. Kampffmeyer** (1987). There, the debt-cycle hypothesis is criticized empirically on the grounds that its assumptions on endurable debt-service rates are untenable, and rejected in theoretical terms because of the "politically and technologically conditioned unsolvability of the transformation problem" (ibid., p. 20).

73 On these problems for developing countries as well as on undervaluation as a development strategy, see also **H. Riese** (1986a) and **M. Lüken-Klassen / K. Betz** (1989, pp. 242 - 246).

74 Both structuralist and neoclassical liberal argumentations on financial-sector development can be found in **M.J. Fry** (1988, Chapter 17 and passim), the World Development Report (**World Bank** 1989) and in **T. Killick / M. Martin** (1990). - This eclecticism may be associated with the fact that development of the financial sector found heightened interest in connection with the debt crisis (**World Bank** 1989, pp. 82f.) after the neoclassical "counterrevolution" had already taken place in development theory. Experience made in Latin America has brought even dyed-in-the-wool neoliberals to the view that financial markets in developing countries tend toward excess reactions, which, from their position, indicates certain structural rigidities such as different speeds of price adjustment. On the other hand, structuralist development economics has recognized that

many structures can not at all be treated as given, but must also be seen as produced.

75 This structural effect was discussed in the postwar era as "dualism", although it was seen less as a phenomenon of evolution marginalizing a larger share of the population than as a strategically deployable feature of an industrializing agroeconomy (**A. Lewis** 1954). The subsistence sector, at a low level of monetization, was, as a reservoir of cheap labor and unutilized real saving, to support the modern sector. When this expectation failed to materialize, attempts were made to break up this dualism from the other side. The subsistence sector was now, via agricultural modernization ("Green Revolution") and linkage to the financial system, to be integrated into the monetary economy and modernized.

76 Economic sociologists and ethnologists reply to representatives of this integration strategy that it involves linking two incompatible rationalities, which would more harm than benefit informal economic processes. What predominates here, it is claimed, is a clientelistic mode of economic life based on reciprocity, while what holds valid for the formal sector are commercial principles that presuppose a delinkage of social and economic relations. This critique nonetheless shares the view presented in the text that financial-sector development should strive not to replace informal institutions but to promote their role by suitable means. Certainly, the latter can imply forgoing certain stimulating measures as long as the mode of operation of the informal financial system is not better understood. On the entire complex of issues addressed here, see **H. Trenk** (1991).

77 Some data from the "Länderbericht Indien 1988" of the German **Federal Office for Statistics** will be cited here by way of illustration: As far as religion is concerned, Hinduism is dominant, over 80 % of the Indian population being classified as belonging to this religion, not on the basis of any express affirmation, but on the basis of origin. The Moslem segment of the population, with its share of some 12 %, is, however, after Indonesia and Bangladesh, the third largest in any other country. The number of Christians, constituting a share of some 2.6 % (1981), still accounts for roughly 20 million persons. - The country's official language is Hindi, which is spoken by some 30 % of the population. Beside it, the constitution recognizes 14 other main and regional languages. The census conducted in 1961, however, found far more, namely 1652 languages and dialects. - The literacy rate for persons over 15 years of age was over 55 %, though the inter-gender differences are striking. The crass educational differences are, however, only one aspect of the fundamental differences in ways of life: India includes all levels of culture, from life in the metropolis of the 20th century to life in the "primitive" tribe subsisting on hunting and gathering.

78 Fiscal years begin on April 1 and end on March 31. Any dates given for development plans must be read minus (1951) or plus (1955) these three months.

79 The **Reserve Bank** (*RBI Bulletin* 1954, p. 729) thus writes: "(...) the antiinflationary measures that had been taken in the post-devaluation period might

have led to a gradual working off of the excess demand in the system and enabled the country to devote greater attention to problems of development. But with the outbreak of the Korean War (...), there was an upsurge of inflation in India, as elsewhere. (...) economic policy had to be geared to fighting this relentlessly."

80 For a brief presentation, see **S.V. Misra / V.K. Puri** (1984, pp. 332 - 335); see also **P.C. Mahalanobis**, "Draft Plan Frame" in: Government of India Planning Commission, Second Five-Year Plan: The Framework, New Delhi 1955, pp. 5 - 49.

81 This industrial-policy measure, initiated in the previous phase, is addressed because it forms part of the problem complex of "late development" identified here.

82 The information is from **E.P. da Costa** 1985. The "International Financial Statistics" began only in 1960 to supply a unified series on the real growth of the gross domestic product, the rate of change of central-bank money, and the current-account balance. The actual GDP growth rates are, incidentally, some 1 - 2 % above the values indicated by da Costa, which may mean that they are deflated with different price indexes. The difference in the growth rates between the Second Plan (da Costa: over 20 %) and the Third Plan (IFS: roughly 15 %) will therefore tend to be greater than it may appear here.

83 Money-supply aggregate M2 (M1 plus fixed deposits) showed below-average growth when compared with M1 (bank reserves and notes in circulation plus deposits on current account) and central-bank money (notes in circulation plus bank reserves). See Annex A.

84 A very good presentation of these years is given by **K.S. Krishnaswamy / K. Krishnaymurti / P.S. Sharma** (1987, pp. 20 - 25).

85 **B. Dasgupta** (1977, p. 43), for instance, writes: "The (...) strategy was, at the time of its formulation, independent of the new high-yielding varieties of seeds and would have been put into operation even if the former were not available. In fact, the draft outline of the Fourth Plan (1965) did not mention the high-yielding varieties specifically." What was responsible for the omission was in fact a negative attitude of the planning commission, which rejected the "Green Revolution" as American interference (**F.R. Frankel** 1978, pp. 281f.).

86 Between 1975-81, the government bought an average of 11 % of all grain produced, which implies a weighty position in the market. See **D. Rothermund** (1985, p. 167).

87 On the effects of the "Green Revolution", see the detailed information in **B. Dasgupta** (1977) and **D. Rothermund** (1985, pp. 163 - 168) for a short survey of the German-language literature.

88 These data are based on the *Economic Survey*.

89   See the most recent data in **S. Chakrabarti / A. Rudra** (1990, p. 2208). In opposition to the opinion dominant in the literature, these authors interpret the industrial stagnation of the 1970s not as a fall in the trend growth rate but as a cyclical downturn from the (constant) trend. Statistically, the divergent result can be traced back to the fact that the authors view a more lengthy period (1961-85). - An often-cited study on the phenomenon of industrial stagnation is **I.J. Ahluwalia** (1985).

90   See the recent study by **R. Nagaraj** (1990), who explains the industrial recovery of the 1980s using arguments stemming from the stagnation debate on the 1970s. The contributions to this debate are legion. A cross section of the positions represented is offered by the articles published in the *Economic and Political Weekly*.

91   The following passages from **A. Kohli**'s highly interesting presentation of the "Politics of Economic Liberalization in India" may be cited by way of explanation: "In India's political culture (...) the two packages of secularism and socialism and Hindu chauvinism and pro-business have tended to offer two alternative legitimacy formulae for mobilizing political support." (**Kohli** 1989, p. 308) "Whatever socialism has meant in practice - in India it has never meant anti-capitalism but rather state guided capitalism, involving planning, public sector emphasis, a state controlled economy, and a few anti-poverty programs like land reform - its electoral significance was always closely associated with a preference for secular over communal appeals.
In contrast, those who wanted to argue for business interests faced a dilemma: in a poor democracy like India, how do you mobilize the support of the majority, who are after all very poor? One solution to this puzzle was to cut the minority-majority pie at a different angle. If the poor were majority by the criterion of wealth, Hindus were the religious majority. Appeals to the majority religious community against minority communities, then, can be an alternate strategy for seeking electoral majorities by downplaying class issues at the expense of communal ones" (ibid., p. 309). **F.R. Frankel** (1976, in part. pp. 205ff.) also expresses herself in this vein with reference to earlier phases.

92   The cut-off point below which no license for investment is required is 500 million iR in so-called "backward areas" and 150 million iR elsewhere. These and other data on the liberalization measures taken as per **World Bank** (1987, pp. 48ff.).

93   Whether this ought to be termed a contribution to liberalization in that it leads to integration into the world market depends on one's theoretical preoccupation. A mercantilistic interpretation would thus be equally justified.

94   See **J. Nehru**, Speeches 1957-63, quoted after **A. Sen** (1982, p. 103). Critics like Sen see the evolution of a "creeping socialism" staged from above as a strategy to prevent the "grassroots revolution". If, it is asserted, Nehru spoke out for class struggle before the Second World War, he was, five months after coming to power, advocating a social-reforming and technocratic solution:

"Production became for him, then, the first priority. Now he wanted to minimize the inherent conflict between the owners of the means of production and the sellers of labour power in order to ensure continued production (...)". (**A. Sen**, ibid., p. 102).

95 On the principle of the "Gadgil formula" valid until today, although revised in part - and named after the then second chairman of the planning commission - the claim of a federal state to central-government budget funds is calculated as per the following criteria: 60 % of the funds as per population; 10 % on the basis of per capita income, if this figure had been above the national average over a three-year period; 10 % on the basis of actual tax revenues in relation to per capita income ("tax effort"); 10 % for persistent development efforts in the areas of irrigation and power generation; 10 % for special tasks like the need for flood control, urbanization, etc. (**F.R. Frankel** 1978, p. 312). In the most unfavorable case, a state thus receives only 60 of 100 % of central-government subsidies per capita; in the most favorable case, on the other hand, 110 %, i.e. 10 % more than the national average.

96 A highly controversial constitutional amendment was justified by government speakers as suited "to ensure that certain rights, particularly property rights of individuals, should not be allowed to stand in the way of the progress and well-being of society. The directive principles which embody social rights have to override those fundamental rights which are essentially private or individual rights." (Quoted after **F.R. Frankel** 1978, pp. 569f.).

97 The World Bank has prepared a confidential report that provoked headlines in India's financial papers. See **J. Clad** (1990a).

98 In India, the wages and salaries of the persons employed in the public sector have, however, not been raised since 1979. The resulting loss in real incomes was instead intended to be compensated for approximately by a system of cost-of-living allowances, although there is little agreement in the literature on whether this implies a quasi indexing or merely a more moderate erosion of real wages. See (German) **Federal Statistic Office** (1988, p. 100). Information on severe wage conflicts since the mid-1960s can be found in **F.R. Frankel** (1978, pp. 341f. and Chapter 12).

99 The annual report of the RBI Board of Directors for 1969 addresses precisely this dilemma of falling or stagnant revenues in the face of - inflation-related - rises in expenditures (*RBI Bulletin* 1969, pp. 1262f.) Yet it was still possible to lower the overall deficit by other cuts in the budget. Cost-of-living allowances for public-service employees and inflation-related food subsidies finally set in motion a self-sustaining inflationary process (**F.R. Frankel** 1978, pp. 512ff.).

100 This will be discussed further in connection with certain credit-policy measures taken by the RBI (section 5.1.3).

101 **I.M.D. Little** / **T. Scitovsky** / **M. Scott** (1970), **J.N. Bhagwati** / **A.O. Krueger** (1973) and **D. Lal** (1983) may be regarded as basic studies of this liberal orientation.

102 Although the literature sometimes contains propositions indicating wage indexes and thus a repeal of this mechanism, there is, in the strict sense, no such indexing. Even minimum-wage regulations , which might be most aptly termed as indexed in so far as they are designed to sustain a certain level of consumption, are for the most part not observed.

103 The yardstick for "too high" real wages is, in the line of argumentation advanced here, the required profit rate, while neoclassical theory sees it as a full employment utilizing the given stock of resources - a yardstick whose fictive, not to say: fully inappropriate, character becomes evident in development economics.

104 Here, too, a warning must be given against any belief in the panacea of increases in productivity: when the strategy pursued is to lower the price of wage goods, it can happen that prices fall more rapidly than quantitative productivity rises. To minimize the adverse production incentives resulting from this, attention must be paid from the very start to diversification options.

105 The production theory of a monetary economy must address the choice of technology as a discrete decision. In neoclassicism, the choice of technology is, on the other hand, formalized as a continuous substitution process between labor, capital, and, in given cases, land along the production function representing quantity of technology. The difference is in the end that here only labor is seen as a production factor and only labor and non-produced goods like land are regarded as resources.

106 The literature on the regulation of India's foreign trade is extensive, for which reason reference will be restricted here to the influential study by **J.N. Bhagwati / T.N. Srinivasan** (1975) and the more recent contributions in **R.E.B. Lucas / G.F. Papanek** (1988). They are representative for the contributions to the subject known outside India in as much as they criticize Indian protectionism from a liberal economic viewpoint.

107 Apart from the measures named, industrial-policy regulations include the *cartel legislation* (MRTP Act) (mentioned in 4.1) and the *taxation policy* likewise employed to foster certain industries and production activities. It does, however, constitute a conventional cost factor and should no longer be treated as a separate consideration in that what was said at the beginning of this section on cost-side explanations holds true for it.

108 While, as might be expected, the estimates on the absolute and relative level of black-market activities differ very strongly - they extend from shares of 10 - 50 % of the gross national product - there is widespread consensus on the "booming" of black-market activities: following the first two years of the Third Plan, i.e. beginning in 1963/64, they appear to have increased rapidly, then declined, in order then, following the first oil-price hike, to have increased very sharply again. Since then, a comparatively constant increase has been observed. It is not possible to reach a consensus on the measures taken during the state of

emergency, since the individual measuring criteria have produced completely conflicting results (**R. Datt** 1982).

109 This happens on the basis of the regulation on a certain "minimum margin", via credit ceilings, the establishment of minimum shares, or direct prohibitions (**S.B. Gupta** 1990, p. 389).

110 See the interesting study by **B. Chadha / R. Teja** (1990). The attempt to explain "how an expansionary monetary and financial policy can also lead to a famine when there is no national food shortage" (ibid., p. 46). They infer a warning from their case study on Bangladesh: "The view that famines are generally more a sectoral than a monetary problem in the past entailed fatal economic errors" (ibid., p. 47; author's trans.). This proposition is grounded in the simple realization that extreme price rises, possible due to previous expansions of money and credit, can produce famines among the poor that are as devastating as a quantitatively insufficient supply of food.

111 A directive to the banks (*RBI Bulletin* 1987, pp. 164ff.) published under the title "Credit Controls" is exemplary for the inconsistent procedures of the central bank. It objects to the sharp expansion of credit and demands: "It is essential that a re-emergence of inflationary pressures should be avoided and as such it is imperative that the growth of overall liquidity should be contained in 1987/88 to a level well below that in 1986/87". (Ibid., p. 164) It goes on to announce a selective interest-rate cut, hardly in line with the demand of tightening up liquidity: "With a view to reducing the cost of money and to impart flexibility to the interest rate policy, some changes are being made. The reduction in lending rates will provide relief to certain categories of borrowers for whom the interest rates have been raised sharply earlier." (ibid., p. 165)

112 High rates of interest in the money market indicate a higher bank liquidity preference, which would in any case lead to the expectation that the volume of overall credit granted, or at least that approved by the RBI, would be restricted.

113 Presumably, investments in this place will wrongly be presented as a supply category, because they create capacities for a future supply of goods. Yet it is precisely this double character of capital formation - of representing in the current period demand in the commodity market, while being for the future a supply of production capacities - that, stated in simple terms, is characteristic of the phenomenon of business cycles in monetary economies.

114 The relevant literature differs in its stance on the empirical question of whether and to what extend informal credit markets shackle the effectiveness of India's monetary policy (**K. Sundaram / V. Pandit** 1984).

115 The ends-means approach has been advocated above all by post-Keynesian scholasticism. It postulates that any economic-policy objective must be matched by a given set of policy instruments. Typically, the goal of full employment must be achieved through fiscal policy, currency stability through central-bank policy - an assignment whose origin in a technocracy supported by no market-related theoretical considerations is evident.

116 See **S.L. Shetty** (1990a, p. 555) on the "low-profitability syndrome"; see the (German) **Federal Office for Statistics** (1988, p. 100) on the erosion of the salaries of public-service employees.

117 See **B. Varman** (1989, Chapter 5); on the other hand, **M. Rishi / J.K. Boyce** (1990) estimate the measure of capital flight, in particular through underinvoicing of exports and overinvoicing of imports, as considerable.

118 This is, in a certain sense, indicated by the fact that toward the end of the 1980s a switch took place in favor of cash and short-term bank deposits among the financial assets held by households (**RBI**, Report on Currency and Finance 1990, p. 4, Statement 8; **EPW** 1990, pp. 1568f.). As soon as inflation fails to be brought under control by administrative means, inactive cash holdings are accordingly mobilized.

119 See **S.L. Shetty** (1990, p. 397) on the phenomenon of a housing boom in the face of stagnating productive investment in rural regions.

120 Data on the formation of tangible assets among households must be interpreted with caution as a result of the black-money component involved in financing them. **S.L. Shetty** (1990a), who in part confirms the flight into tangible assets (ibid., p. 557), can therefore at the same time point to a restrained formation of tangible assets among households (ibid., p. 555).

121 The liberalization policy of the 1980s had, incidentally, a precursor in the attempt of the Shastri Government (1965/66) to introduce a market-oriented price policy in the agricultural sector. This proved impossible in a highly inflationary environment because retailers were able to push through slightly rising prices via unregulated retail sales, and in this way the grain earmarked for stockpiling found its way around the government purchasing authorities (**F.R. Frankel** 1978, pp. 260f. and 437f.).

122 See **RBI** Annual Report (1990, p. 144) and the scenarios in **C. Rangarajan / A. Basu / N. Jadhav** (1989), who show that the continuation of borrowing would lead to a vicious circle of budget deficit, mounting inflation rate, greater budget deficit, etc.

123 See **C. Rangarajan / A. Basu / N. Jadhav** (1989, pp. 780ff.) on the differences between the various debt concepts; the concept used here refers in essence to the borrowing of the central government, which represents some 90 % of the public-sector debt held by national and international development banks. The Reserve Bank's deficit financing is here classified as its debt to the private sector.

124 A remark by **B.R. Bhattacharya / S. Guha** (ibid., p. 785) points in the same direction: "Government current expenditure -(comprising, W.S.) mainly defence, subsidy, interest payments and salary and wages - (...) continued to rise partly because of higher levels of prices and partly because of larger supply of goods and services."

125 **E.P. da Costa** (1985, pp. 65f.), for instance, writes: "(...) India on the eve of Independence does not easily fit into the stereotype of a developing country with a rudimentary institutional framework. There was savings and asset formation on a fairly substantial scale even in rural India. And there were financial intermediaries, even if they were only money-lenders servicing both consumer spending (funerals, marriages) (...) and productive enterprise like agriculture. (...) Industrial investment, in contrast to commercial investment, was not attractive to rural savers even with some sophistication, because of the risk factor as also the complexities of modern financial instruments." **S. Wilson** (1952, pp. 150 - 216) describes in detail the situation of India's financial system prior to and immediately following independence. The discussion here is based primarily on him.

126 **D. Khatkhate** (1990, p. 1856) describes the monetary-policy control in India as follows: "The monetary authorities have designed an array of policy instruments to regulate credit flows in planned direction. Though this implied close consultations between the Planning Commission, Finance Ministry and the Reserve Bank, it led to a monolithic decision-making process in regard to the monetary policy formulation and its implementation. As such, it could not have been different in nature, impact and scope from the fiscal policy of the government."

127 **F. Morris** (1985, pp. 16 - 21) provides a concise survey of the highly differentiated system of rural finance institutions; he summarizes: "India has followed the 'multi-agency' approach in providing rural finance. Under this approach, cooperative, commercial, regional banks and other field level institutions provide rural finance and are supported by Central and State Governments and national level institutions such as (...) (RBI, NABARD, The National Cooperative Development Corporation and IDBI). The field level institutions which provide credit to individual borrowers are: (a) primary agricultural cooperative societies providing both short-term and medium-term credit to their members; (b) primary cooperative land development banks or branches of State cooperative land development banks providing long-term credit to their members; (c) branches of commercial banks, and (d) branches of Regional Rural Banks (RRBs)." (Ibid., p. 16)

128 See **D.K. Mishra** (1985, pp. 38 - 44) on the rationale of financial-sector development as a solution to the fiscal problem in India.

129 **M.Y. Khan** (1980, p. 233) describes the normative foundations of the measures taken as follows: "The basic postulate of social control of Indian banking was that bank credit was an instrument for the attainment of socio-economic objectives of state policy. (...) It was a half-way house. It sought to remove the control of business houses over banks without removing private ownership of banks. This was sought to be achieved by reforming the management".

130 Initially, this department, today the "Banking Division", was part of the "Revenue Department" of the Finance Ministry. It task at the time of nation-

alization is described in an Indian financial paper as follows: "Its brief then was to act as the government's watchdog for implementation of the policies for which the banks were taken over." (*Economic Times of India*, 1990, p. 4).

131 Apart from these credit regulations, which are motivated by development policy, there are others that, in the strict sense, serve the ends of monetary policy: thus, for instance, a "cash reserve ratio" is required with the Reserve Bank that may be at most 15 %, and a certain percentage of deposits, in 1989 38 %, must be invested in government debt securities ("statutory liquidity ratio"). The latter regulation demonstrates the combination of monetary and budgetary policy objected to by **D. Khatkhate** (see ref. 126, above).

132 See **RBI** (Annual Report 1990, p. 151). This "Agricultural and Rural Debt Relief Scheme" was sharply criticized by the RBI before it came into effect: "(...) Reserve Bank of India governor R.N. Malhotra (...) fears it will have a disastrous effect on a credit system which already has Rs 150 billion in non-servicing loans on its books, four times the 1986 figures." (**J. Clad** 1990). The direct effects will, to be sure, prove disastrous only for the government budget. Indirectly, negative effects can then result for the banks, e.g. due to a future deterioration of the repayment habits of borrowers.

133 This was also signalized by the uncommented observation made by the **RBI** (Annual Report 1990, p. 110): "Despite a slow-down in industrial production, the buoyancy in the capital market continued much more vigorously during 1989/90 than in the previous year."

134 If in this case no counteractive monetary-policy measures are taken, i.e. if the expansionary money-supply effect is not sterilized, the success in foreign trade will obviously undermine its own basis.

135 See **RBI** (Annual Report 1990, p. 59): "Export credit refinance limits accounted for a major proportion (86.8 per cent) of total refinance limits." As regards the actual utilization of the refinance contingents, the share provided for the purposes of export credits appears to be even greater.

136 In the recession following 1975, deficit financing decreased, while credit provided to the banks rose. This reflects a failure to sterilize capital imports and a promotion of exports supported by credit policy. In 1980, on the other hand, credit to the banks was tightened up so as to counter the inflationary trend, in 1984 it expanded in the face of a severe drought.

137 In the past years, the discrepancy was often more than 30 %, i.e. the development banks approved roughly one third more loans then were actually disbursed. See. **RBI** (Report on Currency and Finance 1990, Tab. IX-8, p. 323) and **I.J. Ahluwalia** (1988, p. 162).)

138 See *Economic Survey* (1990, p. 99): "It is important not only to analyse the growth of total bank credit over the years but also to review the sectoral deployment of such credit. Priority sector advances (...) indicate very clearly that banks function as an important catalyst in the socio-economic growth process of

the country (...)." The tendency to downplay or disregard the problems concerning stability policy is revealed in the following quotation: "In the current financial year 1989/90 the basic thrust of the monetary policy continued to be on the controlled expansion of money and credit so that production activities in the economy would get adequate credit support while the liquidity growth in the system is moderated to contain inflationary pressures." (Ibid, p. 103) In fact, the expansion of the money supply was not controlled but excessive (**RBI** Annual Report 1990, p. 31).

139 "There has been a provision of substantial concessive financial support from the Reserve Bank of India to the financial institutions." (**RBI** Annual Report 1990, p. 105).

140 See **S.K. Verghese** (1990, p. 217). The attempt, likewise made for some years, to rationalize, and improve the reliability of, India's banking system by introducing electronic data processing will be mentioned here only in passing. On the other hand, the employee organizations concerned are offering massive resistance.

141 Thus the **RBI** in its Annual Report (1990, p. 59f.): "(...) banks were cautioned that they should not plan their credit on the basis of unchanged refinance from the Reserve Bank as overall monetary requirements could warrant changes in these facilities."

142 Within less than two years, India had two governments of a heterogeneous make-up that were forced to rely on weak and changing majorities. A budget for 1991/92 was no longer passed by the last minority government under Chandra Shekar, so that, at least until the summer of 1991, quarterly budget plans had to be made. Moreover, India is one of the ten countries identified by World Bank and IMF as being "most immediately impacted" (MII) by the Gulf War and was thus able to apply for immediate assistance in the form of concessionary credit. The 1.8 billion US $ disbursed to India in January of 1991 will, however, hardly suffice to compensate for the expected losses in exports and tourism, in transfers from Indians working in the Gulf States, higher costs for oil imports, etc. What is more, India's hitherto largest trading partner, the USSR, will in future doubtless be supplying less oil at soft terms and importing fewer Indian goods - at, it is true, a depreciated rupee exchange rate.

143 This is a revised version of Chapter 6.2 of the German edition. Developments later than 1990 are here taken into account, in particular the Stand-by Arrangement between the Government of India and the IMF as of October 31, 1991. It mainly relies on **IMF** (1991).

144 The theoretical bases of IMF adjustment programs in general and these monitoring conditions in particular are outlined in **IMF** (1987).

145 The loan has been provided by the International Bank for Reconstruction and Development (IBRD, the "World Bank" in a narrower sense), the credit by the International Development Agency (IDA). The latter is characterized by soft terms that apply only to least developed countries.

146 This culminated in the Indian government's Letter of Development Policy, dated November 11, 1991, which has been the subject of much dispute. This letter outlines a medium-term program of fiscal consolidation and reform of the industrial, trade, financial, and public sectors.

147 Interest payments on external debt are treated as capital-services imports, i.e. they constitute a negative item in the current account. Repayments reduce the stock of liabilities in the capital account, they constitute a capital export.

148 The calculations and figures are taken from **Battacharya / Guha** (1990, p. 783), the more recent ones from **Battacharya** (1992, pp. 96 - 98). They differ slightly from RBI estimates, mainly because of differences concerning interstate tax transfers.

149 See **K.K. Sharma** (1990). **Sinha** went on: "It is now imperative for us to start making necessary macro-economic adjustments." During the talks on the IMF stand-by agreement, the minority government under Chandra Shekar, since then resigned, has taken various measures and announced others aimed at increasing government revenues. These include increases in tariffs and income and corporate taxes.

150 Only this was the case in the heterodox adjustment programs of Argentina and Brazil, known as the Austral Plan (1985) and the Plan Cruzado (1986), respectively. One of the chief architects of the Brazilian plan, the later finance minister **L.B. Pereira**, described the most important elements: The basic measures of the Stabilization Plan consisted of:
(1) freezing all prices, wages and the exchange rate (...);
(2) de-indexing the economy;
(3) introducing a new currency, the Cruzado, in place of the Cruzeiro, *from which three zeros were removed*; and
(4) converting all term contracts (...) from Cruzeiro to Cruzados via formulas which would guarantee the recomposition of the average real price of the last six months."
(**L.B. Pereira** 1987, p. 1036) In such a formal sense, the chief economists of the World Bank also understood this currency conversion as a currency reform. The introduction of a new legal currency that does not alter the relationship between income flows and stocks of wealth is forced to rely on a supposed advance of confidence provided by a different name, a type of currency illusion. See **P. Knight / D. McCarthy / S. van Wijnbergen** (1986, p. 15).

151 "Buying votes" by granting subsidized credit or cancelling debts was practiced as early as in Indira Gandhi's first term of office (**F.R. Frankel** 1978, p. 522).

152 As demonstrated by the title of the article by **P. Knight** et al. (1986), the currency conversion mentioned in footnote 150 was accomplished to this end: "to avoid hyperinflation". The neostructuralist or heterodox adjustment programs have in the meantime failed, which is, at least in part, a result of the missed chance to effect a currency reform.

153 This could also be justified by the fact that India is one of the countries hardest hit by the Gulf Crisis. The IMF has already recognized this fact in granting some 2 billion US $ in short-term credits that are mentioned in ref. 142.

154 These requirements are met by one-time taxes on tangible assets, consumption taxes that in India yet make up the larger part of taxes, property taxes, and a payroll tax (**W. Lautenbach** 1949, pp. 530ff.).

ANNEX

Annex A: Development of economic indicators[1]

Chart 1

Rates of change of gross national product and consumer price index, 1960 - 1989

Charts 2.1 and 2.2

Rates of change of base money and M2, 1960 - 1989

Chart 3

Balances of trade and current account, 1973 - 1987

---

1 If not otherwise indicated, all data quoted from the yearbooks of "International Financial Statistics" (International Monetary Fund, var. issues)

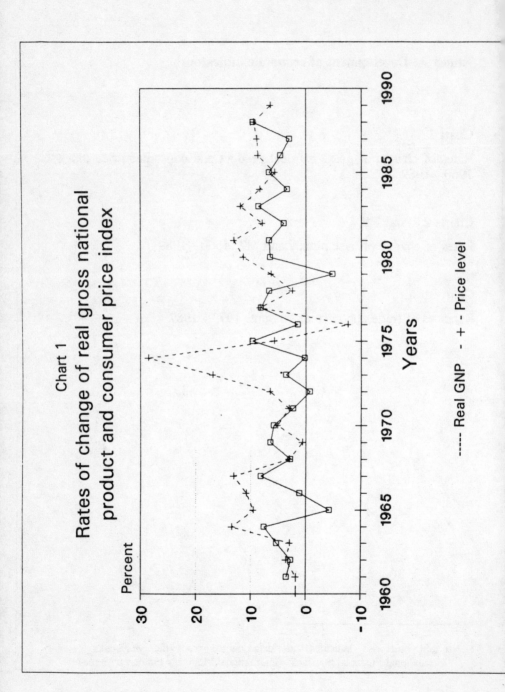

Chart 1
Rates of change of real gross national product and consumer price index

Percent

—— Real GNP   - + - Price level

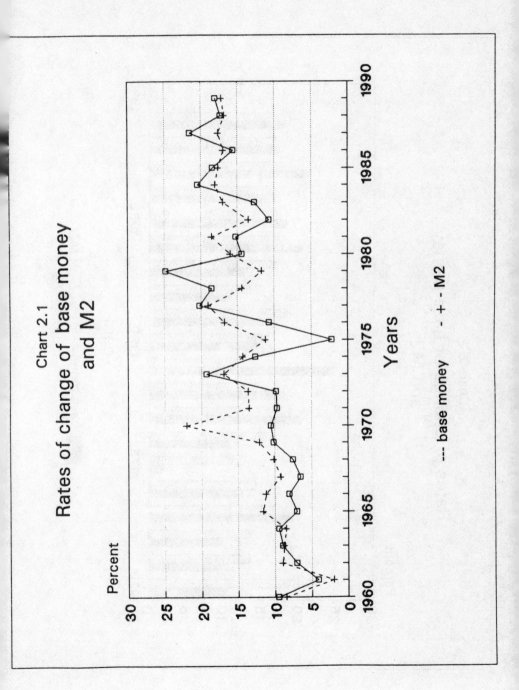

Chart 2.1
Rates of change of base money
and M2

--- base money   - + - M2

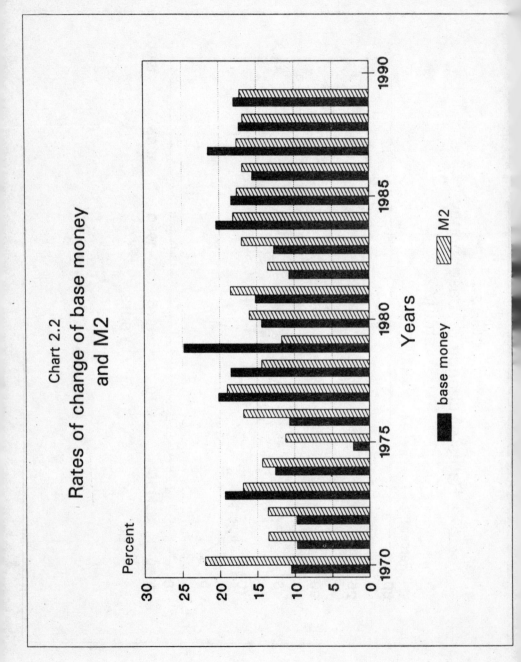

Chart 2.2
Rates of change of base money
and M2

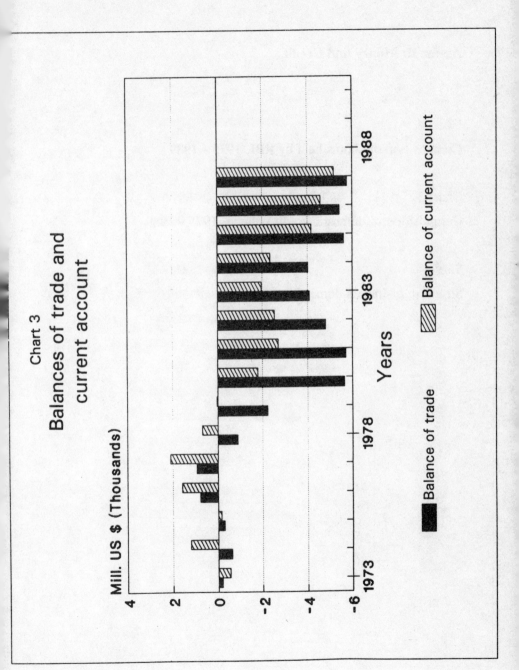

Chart 3
Balances of trade and
current account

Annex B: Money and Credit

Chart 4

Composition of claims held by RBI, 1975 - 1989

Chart 5

Composition of domestic credit volume, 1975 - 1989

Survey

Structure of India's domestic system

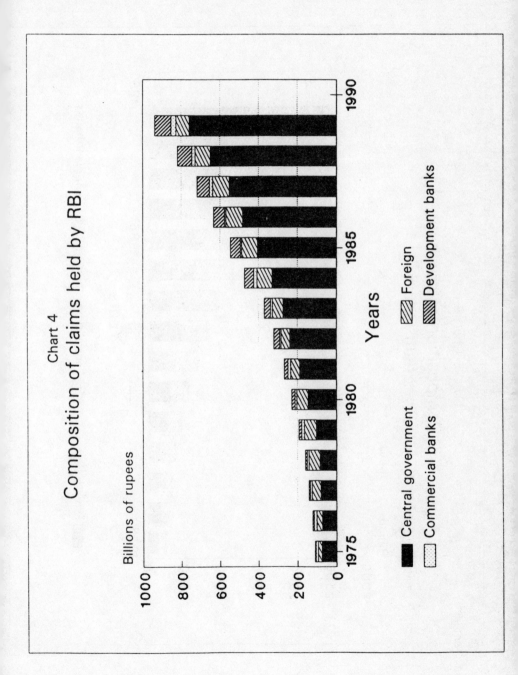

Chart 4

Composition of claims held by RBI

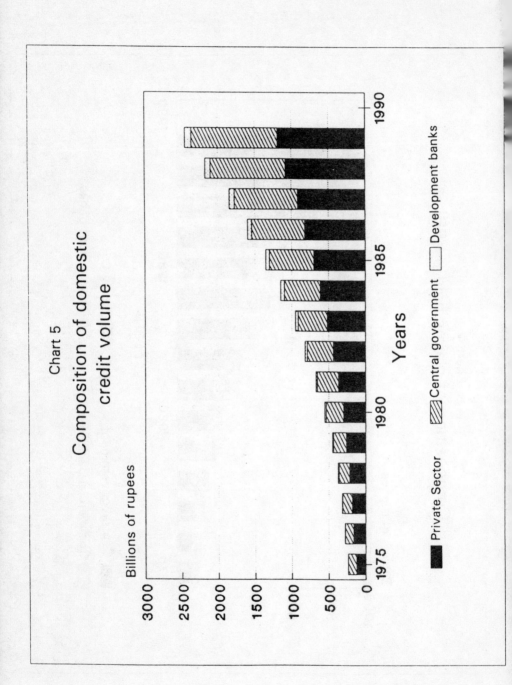

Chart 5
Composition of domestic credit volume

Structure of Domestic Financial System

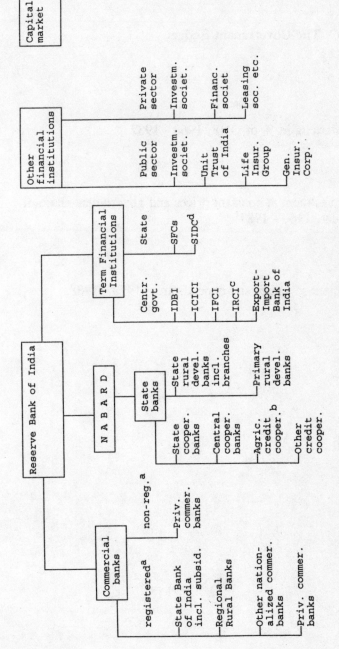

a: "Scheduled" or "non-scheduled"
b: "Primary Agricultural Credit Societies"
c: "Industrial Reconstruction Corporation of India"
d: State Industrial Development Corporation"

Source: in accordance with Morris, 1985, p. 2

Annex C: The Government Budget

Chart 6

Budget deficits in % of GNP, 1960 - 1987

Chart 7

Gross investment at constant prices and government share of investment, 1960 - 1987

Chart 8

Government revenues and expenditures, 1978 - 1988

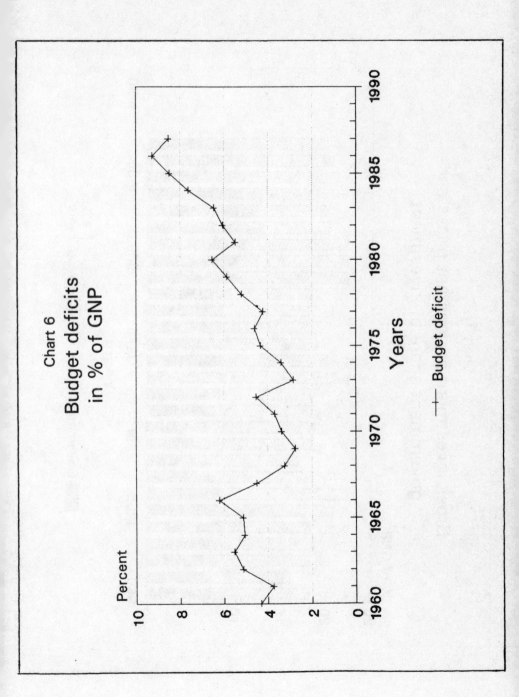

Chart 6
Budget deficits
in % of GNP

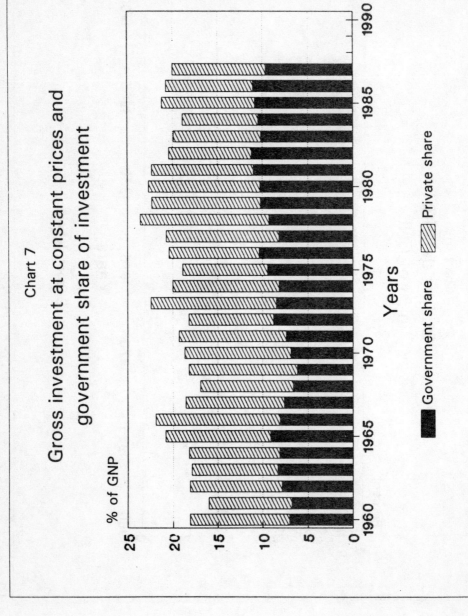

Chart 7

Gross investment at constant prices and government share of investment

Source: Nagaraj 1990

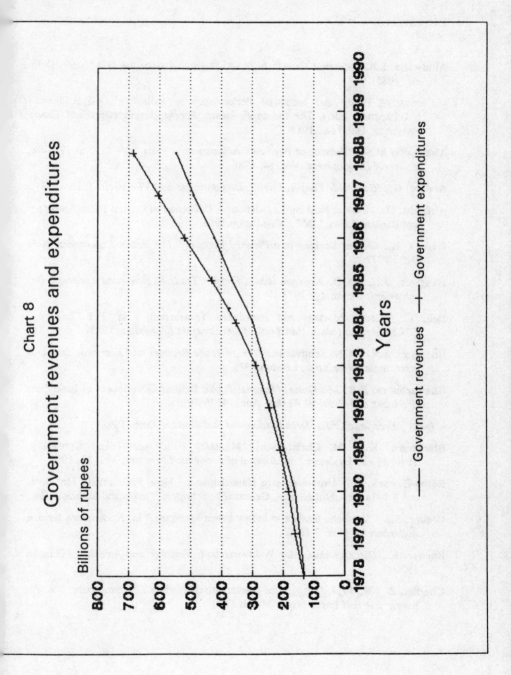

Chart 8

Government revenues and expenditures

Billions of rupees

—— Government revenues   —+— Government expenditures

Years

Literature

Ahluwalia, I.J., *Industrial Growth in India. Stagnation since the Mid-Sixties,* Delhi etc. 1985

-, "Industrial Policy and Industrial Performance in India," in: R.E.B.Lucas / G.F.Papanek (eds.), *The Indian Economy. Recent Developments and Future Prospects,* Delhi etc. 1988

Ahluwalia, M.S., "Balance-of-Payments Adjustment in India," 1970-71 to 1983-84, in: *World Development,* Vol. 14, 1986

Ardant, G., *Histoire de l'impôt, Livre I: De l'antiquité au XVIIe siècle,* Paris 1978

Aufricht, H., "Central Banking Legislation. A Collection of Central Bank, Monetary and Banking Laws," IMF, Washington 1961

Basu, C.R., *Central Banking in a Planned Economy. The Indian Experiment,* New Delhi 1977

Bhagwati, J.N. / A.O. Krueger (eds.), *Foreign Trade Regimes and Economic Development,* Cambridge 1973

Bell, C., "Credit Markets and Interlinked Transactions," in: H.B.Chenery / T.N.Srinivasan (eds.), *Handbook of Development Economics,* 1989

Bhagwati, J.N. / T.N. Srinivasan, *Foreign Trade Regimes and Economic Development: India,* New York, London 1975

Bhattacharya, B.B. / S. Guha, "Internal Public Debt of Government of India," in: *Economic and Political Weekly,* Apr. 14. 1990

-, *India's Economic Crisis, Debt Burden and Stabilisation,* Delhi 1992

Blackburn, K. / M. Christensen, "Monetary Policy and Policy Credibility: Theories and Evidence," in: *Journal of Economic Literature,* Vol. 27, 1989

Böhm-Bawerk, E., "Unsere passive Handelsbilanz," Neue Freie Presse Jan. 6, 8, and 9 1914, republished in: -, *Gesammelte Schriften,* Vienna and Leipzig 1924

Breuer, S., "Staatliche Banken in Indien haben Probleme," in: *Nachrichten für den Außenhandel,* Nov. 7 1990

Bücher, K., *Die Entstehung der Volkswirtschaft. Vorträge und Aufsätze,* Tübingen 1920

Chadha, B. / R. Teja, "Hunger im gesamtwirtschaftlichen Zusammenhang," in: *Finanzierung und Entwicklung,* March 1990

Chakrabarti, S. / A. Rudra, "Where is the Industrial Retardation," in: *Economic and Political Weekly*, Sept. 9 1990

Chandavarkar, A.V., "Die Entwicklungsfunktion von Zentralbanken," in: *Finanzierung und Entwicklung*, Dec. 1987

Chenery, H.B. / A.M. Strout, "Foreign Assistance and Economic Development," in: *American Economic Review*, Vol. 56, 1966

Chenery, H.B. / T.N. Srinivasan (eds.), *Handbook of Development Economics*, Amsterdam 1988

Clad, J., "Policy paralysis," in: *Far Eastern Economic Review*, March 1 1990

-, "Report criticizes Indian credit system," in: *Far Eastern Economic Review*, Nov. 11.1990a

Coats, W.L. / D.R. Khatkhate, "Monetary Policy in Less Developed Countries: Main Issues," in: *The Developing Economies*, Vol. 22, 1984

Collyns, C., "Alternatives to the Central Bank in the Developing World," *IMF Occasional Paper No. 20*, Washington 1983

da Costa, E.P., *Reserve Bank of India, Fifty Years (1935-85)*, Bombay 1985

Crick, W.F. (ed.), *Commonwealth Banking Systems*, Oxford 1965

Das-Gupta, A., "Personal Taxation and Private Financial Saving in India," in: *Economic and Political Weekly*, Feb. 10 1990

Dasgupta, B., *Agrarian Change and the New Technology in India. UNRISD Studies on the "Green Revolution"*, No. 16, Geneva 1977

Datt, R., "The Parallel Economy in India," in: *Indian Economic Journal*, Vol. 30, 1982

Dhar, P.N., "The Indian Economy: Past Performance and Present Issue," in: R.E.B. Lucas / G. Papanek, *The Indian Economy. Recent Developments and Future Prospects*, Delhi etc. 1988

Dickson, P.G.M., *The Financial Revolution in England. A Study in the Development of Public Credit 1688 - 1756*, London etc. 1967

Dornbusch, R. / A. Reynoso, "Financial Factors in Economic Development," in: *AER Papers & Proceedings*, Vol. 79, 1989

Economic and Political Weekly, "Qualitative Changes," March 17 1990

-, "Unbridled Speculation," Jan. 5/12 1991

Economic Times of India, "On shaky foundations," August 16 1990, Bombay

Elsenhans, H., *Abhängiger Kapitalismus oder bürokratische Entwicklungsgesellschaft. Versuch über den Staat in der Dritten Welt*, Frankfurt/Main. and New York 1981

Emminger, O., *D-Mark, Dollar, Währungskrisen*, Stuttgart 1986

Evers, H.-D. / T. Schiel, *Strategische Gruppen. Vergleichende Studien zu Staat, Bürokratie und Klassenbildung in der Dritten Welt*, Berlin 1988

Fischer, B., "Höchstzinspolitik, Inflation und wirtschaftliches Wachstum in Entwicklungsländern", in: *Weltwirtschaftliches Archiv*, Vol. 116, 1980

-, *Liberalisierung der Finanzmärkte und wirtschaftliches Wachstum in Entwicklungsländern*, Kieler Studien Nr. 172, Tübingen 1982

FitzGerald, E.V.K., "The Analytics of Stabilization Policy in the Small Semi-Industrialized Economy," in: E.V.K.FitzGerald / R.Vos, *Financing Economic Development ...*, loc. cit.

Fitzgerald, E.V.K. / R. Voss (eds.), *Financing Economic Development. A Structural Approach to Monetary Policy*, Aldershot etc. 1989

-, "Introduction," in: ibid.

-, "The Foundation of Development Finance : Economic Structure, Accumulation Balances and Income Distribution", in: ibid

Frankel, F.R., *India's Political Economy. 1947 - 1977*, Princeton 1978

Frenkel, J.A. / M.L. Mussa, "Asset Markets, Exchange Rates and the Balance of Payments", in: R.W.Jones / P.B. Kenen (eds.), *Handbook of International Economics*, Amsterdam 1985

Friedman, M., *Money and Economic Development. The Horowitz Lectures of 1972*, New York etc. 1973

Fry, M.J., *Money, Interest, and Banking in Economic Development*, Baltimore, London 1988

Gelb, A., "Financial Policies, Growth and Efficiency", PPR Working Paper, World Bank, Washington D.C. 1989

Gemmell, N., *Surveys in Development Economics*, Oxford, New York 1987

Gerschenkron, A., *Economic Backwardness in Historical Perspective*, Cambridge 1962

Ghatak, S., *Monetary Economics in Developing Countries*, London und Basingstoke 1981

Goldsmith, R.W., *Financial Structure and Development*, New Haven 1969

-, *The Financial Development of Japan 1868 - 1977*, New Haven 1983

-, *The Financial Development of India 1860 - 1977*, New Haven 1983a

Gupta, S.B., *Monetary Economics. Institutions, Theory and Policy*, New Delhi 1990

Heering, W., Geld, *Liquiditätsprämie und Kapitalgüternachfrage*, Regensburg 1991

Hemmer, H.-R., "40 Jahre Entwicklungstheorie und -politik. Ein Rückblick aus wirtschaftswissenschaftlicher Sicht," in: *Zeitschrift für Wirtschafts- und Sozialwissenschaften,* 110/1990

Herr, H., *Geld, Kredit und ökonomische Dynamik in marktvermittelten Ökonomien - die Vision einer Geldwirtschaft,* Berlin/Munich 1986

Industrial Development Bank of India (IDBI), *Report on Development Banking 1988-89,* Bombay 1989

International Monetary Fund, *Theoretic Aspects of the Design of Fund-Supported Adjustement Programs,* Occasional Paper No. 55, Washington D.C. 1987

-, *International Financial Statistics,* Yearbook 1990, Washington 1990

-, *India - Staff Report for the 1991 Article IV Consultation and Request for Stand-By Arrangement,* Washington D.C., Oct. 9 1991

Issing, O., "Notenbanken II: Verfassung, Ziele, Organisation und Instrumente", in: HdWW, Vol. 5, 1980

Janssen, K., "Monetary Policy and Financial Development," in: E.V.K. FitzGerald / R.Vos (eds.), *Financing Economic Development ...,* loc. cit.

Jensen, M.C. / W.H. Meckling, "Theory of the Firm: Managerial Behaviour, Agency Costs, and Ownership Structure", in: *Journal of Financial Economics 1976*

Jones, C. / M. Roemer, "Editor's Introduction: Modeling and Measuring Parallel Markets in Developing Countries," in: *World Development,* Vol. 17, 1989

Jones, R.W. / P.B. Kenen (eds.), *Handbook of International Economics,* Amsterdam 1985

Joslin, D., *A Century of Banking in Latin America,* New York 1963

Kaldor, N., "Social and Economic Aspects of 'Intermediate Regimes'," in: -, *Selected Essays on the Economic Growth of the Socialist and the Mixed Economy,* Cambridge 1972

Kampffmeyer, T., *Die Verschuldungskrise der Entwicklungsländer. Probleme und Ansatzpunkte für eine Lösung auf dem Vergleichswege,* Berlin: German Development Institute 1987

Keynes, J.M., *The Collected Writings; Vol. II: A Treatise on Money, Vol. I, The Pure Theory of Money,* London, Basingstoke 1971 (1930).

-, *The General Theory of Employment, Interest and Money,* New York 1936

Khan, M.Y., *Indian Financial System. Theory and Practice,* New Delhi 1980

Khatkhate, D.R., "Analytic Basis of the Working of Monetary Policies in Less Developed Countries," in: *IMF Staff Papers,* Vol. 19, 1972

-, "Assessing the Impact of Interest Rates in the Less Developed Countries," in: *World Development*, Vol. 16, 1988

Killick, T. / M. Martin, "Financial Policies in the Adaptive Economy," *ODI Working Paper No. 35,* London 1990

Kindleberger, C.P., *A Financial History of Western Europe,* London etc. 1984

Kirkpatrick, C. / F. Nixson, "Inflation and stabilization policy in LDCs," in: N.Gemmell, *Surveys...,* loc. cit.

Kitamura, H., *Zur Theorie des internationalen Handels. Ein kritischer Beitrag,* Weinfelden 1941

Knight, P. / D. McCarthy / S. van Wijnbergen, "Vermeidung der Hyperinflation," in: *Finanzierung und Entwicklung,* Vol. 23, Dec. 1986

Kohli, A., "Politics of Economic Liberalization in India," in: *World Development,* Vol. 17, 1989

Krishnaswamy, K.S. / K. Krishnamurty, K. / P.S. Sharma, *Improving Domestic Resource Mobilization through Financial Development,* India, Manila 1987

Krueger, A.O., "Importsubstitution versus Exportförderung. Warum eine Außenorientierung besser funktioniert," in: *Finanzierung und Entwicklung,* Vol. 22, 1985

-, "Economists' Changing Perceptions of Government," in: *Weltwirtschaftliches Archiv,* Vol. 127, 1990

Kumar, B., *Monetary Policy in India,* New Delhi 1983

Lachenmann, G., *Ökologische Krise und sozialer Wandel in afrikanischen Ländern. Handlungsrationalität der Bevölkerung und Anpassungsstrategie in der Entwicklungspolitik. Mit einer empirischen Studie über Mali,* Saarbrücken/Fort Lauderdale 1990

Lal, D., The *Poverty of 'Development Economics',* London 1983

Laum, B., *Heiliges Geld. Eine historische Untersuchung über den sakralen Ursprung des Geldes,* Tübingen 1924

Lautenbach, W., "Die Zinspolitik nach der Währungssanierung," in: *Finanzarchiv,* Vol. 11, 1949

Länderanalysen der Frankfurter Allgemeine Zeitung GmbH, Indien, Frankfurt/Main, Dec. 1990

Leijonhufvud, A., *Über Keynes und den Keynesianismus,* Köln 1973 (english. 1966)

Leite, S.P. / V. Sundararajan, "Issues in Interest Rate Management and Liberalization," in: *IMF Staff Papers,* Vol. 37, 1990

Lewis, W.A., "Economic Development with Unlimited Supplies of Labour," in: *The Manchester School of Economic and Social Studies,* Vol. 22, 1954

Little, I.M.D. / **T. Scitovsky** / **M. Scott**, *Industry and Trade in Some Developing Countries*, London 1970

Lucas, R.E.B. / **G.F. Papanek (eds.)**, *The Indian Economy. Recent Developments and Future Prospects*, Delhi etc. 1988

Lutz, F.A., "Das Grundproblem der Geldverfassung," in: *Geld und Währung*, Tübingen 1962

Lüken-Klaßen, M., *Währungskonkurrenz und Protektion. Peripherisierung und ihre Überwindung aus geldwirtschaftlicher Sicht*, Ph.D., published manuscript, Marburg 1993

Lüken-Klaßen, M. / **K. Betz**, "Weltmarkt und Abhängigkeit," in: H.Riese / H.-P. Spahn, (eds.), *Internationale Geldwirtschaft*, Regensburg 1989

-, "Binnenmarkt und Währungsunion," in: H.-P. Spahn (ed.), *Wirtschaftspolitische Strategien*, Regensburg 1990

Madan, B.K., "India," in: W.F. Crick (ed.), *Commonwealth ...*, loc. cit.

Mayer, T., "Die Struktur des Monetarismus," in: *Beihefte zu Kredit und Kapital*, Die Monetarismus-Kontroverse, Vol. 4, Berlin 1978

McKinnon, R.J., "Foreign Exchange Constraints in Economic Development and Efficient Aid Allocation," in: *Economic Journal*, Vol. 74, 1964

-, *Money and Capital in Economic Development*, Washington 1973

-, "Financial Liberalization in Retrospect: Interest Rate Policies in LDCs," in: G. Ranis / T.P. Schultz (eds.), *The State of Development Economics*, Oxford 1988

Ministry of Finance (ed), *Economic Survey 1989-90*, Government of India, New Delhi 1990

Mishra, D.K., *Public Debt and Economic Development in India*, Lucknow 1985

Misra, S.V. / **V.K. Puri**, *Indian Economy*, Bombay 1983

Mongia, J.N. (ed.), *India's Economic Policies*, New Delhi 1984

Morris, F., "India's Financial System. An Overview of Its Principal Structural Features," World Bank Staff Working Papers No. 739, Washington 1985

Mujumdar,N.A., "Agenda for Financial Reform," in: *Economic and Political Weekly*, Dec. 1-8 1990

von Müller, A., "Zwischen Verschuldung und Steuerrebellion. Die mittelalterliche Stadt an den Beispielen Florenz und Köln. in: U. Schultz (ed.)," *Mit dem Zehnten fing es an. Eine Kulturgeschichte der Steuer*, Munich 1986

Myrdal, G., *Asian Drama. An Inquiry Into the Poverty of Nations*, New York 1968

Nadal Egea, A., "Choice of Technique Revisited: A Critical Review of the Theoretical Underpinnings," in: *World Development*, Vol. 18, 1990

Nagaraj, R., "Industrial Growth. Further Evidence and towards an Explanation of Issues," in: *Economic and Political Weekly,* Oct. 13 1990

Neue Züricher Zeitung, "Indiens Haushalt im Zeichen der politischen Krise", March 14 1991

Newlyn, W.T. / D.C. Rowan, *Money and Banking in British Colonial Africa: A Study of the Monetary and Banking System of Eight British African Territories,* Oxford 1954

Obst-Hintner, "Geld-, Bank- und Börsenwesen", N. Kloten / J.H. von Stein (eds.), Stuttgart 1980

Park, Y.C., "Foreign Debt, Balance of Payments, and Growth Prospects: The Case of the Republic of Korea, 1965 - 88", in: *World Development,* vol.14, 1986

Patrick, H.T., "Financial Development and Economic Growth in Underdeveloped Countries," in: *Economic Development and Cultural Change,* Vol. 14, 1966

Pereira, L.B., "Inertial Inflation and the Cruzado Plan," in: *World Development,* Vol. 15, 1987

Polanyi, K., *Ökonomie und Gesellschaft,* Frankfurt a.M. 1979

Porter, R.C., "The Promotion of the 'Banking Habit' and Economic Development," in: *Journal of Development Studies,* July 1966

Preiser, E., *Bildung und Verteilung des Volkseinkommens,* Göttingen 1963

Rangarajan, C. / A. Basu / N. Jadhav, "Dynamics of Interaction between Government Deficit and Domestic Debt in India," Reserve Bank of India's Occasional Papers, Vol. 10, 1989, No. 3, Bombay

Rangnekar, D.K., "Industrial Policy," in: J.N. Mongia (ed.), *India's...,* loc. cit.

Ranis, G., "The Financing of Japanese Economic Development," in: *Economic History Review,* Vol. 11, 1959

Rao, V.K.R.V., *India's National Income, 1950 - 1980. An Analysis of Economic Growth and Change,* New Delhi etc. 1983

Reserve Bank of India, *Bulletin,* var. issues, Bombay

-, *All-India Rural Credit Survey Committee Report,* Bombay 1969

-, *Functions and Working,* Bombay 1983, (4th edition, first appeared in 1941)

-, *Report of the Committee to Review the Working of the Monetary System,* Bombay 1985

-, *Annual Report 1989/90,* Bombay 1990

-, *Report on Currency and Finance,* var. issues, Bombay

Riese, H., "Geldökonomie, Keynes und die Anderen. Kritik der monetären Grundlagen der Orthodoxie.", in: P. de Gijsel *et al.* (eds.), *Ökonomie und Gesellschaft,* Jahrbuch 1, Frankfurt/Main, New York 1983

-, *Theorie der Inflation,* Tübingen 1986

-, "Geldpolitik als Grundlage ökonomischer Entwicklung der Bundesrepublik Deutschland," paper deliverd at the annual congress of the Verein für Socialpolitik, Freiburg i. Br., Oct. 1988

-, "Geld, Kredit, Vermögen. Begriffliche Grundlagen und preistheoretische Implikationen der monetären keynesianischen Ökonomie.", in: H. Riese / H.-P. Spahn (eds.), *Internationale Geldwirtschaft...,* loc. cit.

-, "Schuldenkrise und ökonomische Theorie," 1989a, in: H. Riese / H.-P. Spahn (eds.), *Internationale Geldwirtschaft...,* loc. cit.

-, *Geld im Sozialismus,* Regensburg 1990

Riese, H. / H.-P. Spahn (eds.), *Internationale Geldwirtschaft,* Regensburg 1989

Rishi, M. / J.K. Boyce, "The Hidden Balance of Payments," in: *Economic and Political Weekly,* July 28 1990

Robinson, J., "The Economics of Hyperinflation," in: *Economic Journal,* Vol. 48, 1938

Rothermund, D., *Europa und Asien im Zeitalter des Merkantilismus,* Darmstadt 1978

-, *Indiens wirtschaftliche Entwicklung. Von der Kolonialherrschaft bis zur Gegenwart,* Paderborn etc. 1985

-, "Regional Disparities in India," unpublished MS, Heidelberg 1991

Sahlins, M., "The Original Affluent Society," in: -, *Stone Age Economics,* 1972

Sayers, R.S., *Central Banking after Bagehot,* Oxford 1957

Schelkle,W., "Peripherisierung in Binnen- und Weltmarkt," in: H.-P. Spahn, *Wirtschaftspolitische Strategien,* loc. cit.

Schultz, U. (ed.), *Mit dem Zehnten fing es an. Eine Kulturgeschichte der Steuer,* Munich 1986

Sen, A., *The State, Industrialization and Class Formations in India,* London etc. 1982

Sen, Am., "The Concept of Development," in: H.B.Chenery / T.N. Srinivasan (eds.), *Handbook...,* loc. cit.

Shapiro, H. / L. Taylor, "The State and Industrial Strategy," in: *World Development,* Vol. 18, 1990

Sharma,K.K., "India Increases Industrial Taxes before IMF Accord," in: *Financial Times*, Dec. 28 1990

Shaw, E., *Financial Deepening in Economic Development*, New York 1973

Shetty, S.L., "Saving Behaviour in India in the 1980s. Some Lessons," in: *Economic and Political Weekly*, March 17 1990

Spahn, H.-P., *Stagnation in der Geldwirtschaft - Dogmengeschichte, Theorie und Politik aus keynesianischer Sicht*, Frankfurt/Main and. New York 1986

- (ed.), Wirtschaftspolitische Strategien, Regensburg 1990

Sraffa, P., *Production of Commodities by Means of Commodities*, Cambridge 1960

Stadermann, H.-J., *Ökonomische Vernunft*, Tübingen 1987

Statistisches Bundesamt (Federal Office for Statistics), *Länderbericht Indien 1984*, Wiesbaden 1984

Stiglitz, J.E. / A. Weiss, "Credit Rationing in Markets with Imperfect Information," in: *American Economic Review*, Vol. 71, 1981

Stürmer, M., "Hungriger Fiskus - schwacher Staat. Das europäische Ancien Régime," in: U. Schultz (ed.), *Mit dem Zehnten...*, loc. cit.

Stützel, W., *Volkswirtschaftliche Saldenmechanik*, Tübingen 1983

Sundaram, K. / V. Pandit, "Informal Credit Markets, Black Money and Monetary Policy", in: *Economic and Political Weekly*, Apr. 21 1984

Taylor, L., *Macro Models for Developing Countries*, New York 1979

-, *Structuralist Macroeconomics: Applicable Models for the Third World*, New York 1983

Tilly, C. (ed.)., *The Formation of National States in Western Europe*, New Jersey 1975

Timmer, C.P., "The Agricultural Transformation," in: H.B.Chenery / T.N. Srinivasan (eds.), *Handbook ...*, loc. cit.

Tober, S., "Theoretische Aspekte einer Währungsreform mit historischem Appendix über die westdeutsche Währungsreform 1948," unpublished Thesis, Free University Berlin, Berlin 1989

Tobin, J., "Money and Economic Growth," in: *Econometrica*, Vol. 33, 1965

Trenk, M., *Der Schatten der Verschuldung. Komplexe Kreditbeziehungen des informellen Finanzsektors*, Saarbrücken and Fort Lauderdale 1991

Varman, B., *Capital Flight. A Critique of Concepts and Measures. Including a Case Study of India and the Philippines*, HWWA, Hamburg 1989

Verghese, S.K., "Financial Innovations and Lessons for India," in: *Economic and Political Weekly*, Feb. 3. 1990

Wadhva, C., "Economic Advisory Council's Report on the Economy," in: *Economic and Political Weekly March 3 1990*

Wadia, F.K., "Agricultural Price Policy," in: J.N. Mongia (ed.), *India's ...*, loc. cit.

Wiemann, J., *Indien. Selbstfesselung des Entwicklungspotentials*, Berlin, German Development Institute 1988

van Wijnbergen, S., "Stagflationary Effects of Monetary Stabilization Policies. A Quantitative Analysis of South Korea," in: *Journal of Development Economics*, 1982, No. 10

Wilson, S., "The Business of Banking in India," in: R.S. Sayers (ed.), *Banking in the British Commonwealth*, Oxford 1952

Wolff, P., *Stabilisierungspolitik und Strukturanpassung in der Türkei 1980-1985. Die Rolle von IWF und Weltbank in einem außengestützten Anpassungsprozeß*, Berlin, German Development Institute 1987

World Bank, *India: An Industrializing Economy in Transition*, 3 vols., Washington 1987

-, *World Development Report 1990*, New York 1990

-, *India : Structural Adjustment Loan and Credits*, Washington D.C., Nov. 13, 1991